Sports Law:
A Narrative

Dwight M. Kealy

Attorney at Law

College Professor of Business Law

New Mexico State University

Contents

Preface

Some sports fans love statistics, but most people prefer listening to a story more than a list of facts. My goal for this book is to create a college Sports Law textbook that reads like a story that can be enjoyed as an audiobook by a larger audience.

Instead of thinking about this book as a textbook, imagine that I am sitting next to you having a conversation on a cross-country road trip. You are sitting next to an attorney who passed the bar exams in California and New Mexico, practiced law, thinks about law, and teaches various law courses. I can help you pass your law-related undergraduate and graduate courses. I can help you pass the bar exam. But most people don't want to sit next to a stack of flashcards.

It seems more natural for us to share stories on our journey. If we hear that a coach at a public high school got fired for praying with his team, you may wonder if that violates the U.S. Constitution. If we hear that a state revoked a sports agent's license so that the agent can no longer work as a sports agent in that state, you may wonder if the state could do this. It may also make you wonder if the state could revoke the license of a real estate or insurance agent.

Some may read this book as an excuse to read about sports. Some may read it as an excuse to read about the law. Either is fine with me. Most of the people who read my chapter on agency law will never become sports agents, but they may serve on a board of directors for a company, charity, or homeowners' association. The same principles of agency law apply in all these contexts. I just think the law is more accessible—and fun—when we talk about it through sports.

Thank you to attorneys John Babington, Jeremy Evans, Daniel James, Samantha Rice, and my students at New Mexico State University for your feedback.

Sincerely,

Dwight M. Kealy
Las Cruces, New Mexico
March 2025

Chapter 1: Agency Law

Agency law is a fundamental area of legal study that explores the relationship between two parties: the principal and the agent. In this relationship, the agent is authorized to act on behalf of the principal in various transactions and legal matters. This chapter explores the formation of the agency relationship, the duties owed by agents and principals, and specific issues involving sports agents.

Principals and Agents

Although the focus of this book is sports, the study of agency law extends beyond the world of sports and sports agents. It even extends beyond other occupations where a worker is referred to as an agent such as a real estate agent or insurance agent. For example, corporate executive officers are agents of their corporations, employees are agents of their employers, and even babysitters serve as agents for the child's parents or legal guardians.

The two parties that form an agency relationship are called the principal and the agent. The principal is the athlete, boss, employer, corporation, parent, etc. They are the ones with control. The agent is the individual agreeing to act on behalf of the principal and to be subject to the principal's directions.

Agents have the power to bind the principal to contracts, and principals can be held responsible for acts the agent does within the course and scope of their agency relationship. This responsibility is rooted in the legal concept called *Respondeat Superior*. *Respondeat Superior* holds that a principal can be held vicariously liable for the actions of an agent when the agent's actions are within the scope of the agency relationship.

Liability under *Respondeat Superior* varies depending on if the agent is an employee or an independent contractor. An independent contractor is "a person who contracts with another to do something, but who is not controlled by the other." Independent contractors are often self-employed and use their own tools and expertise to complete a task for another. An employee, on the other hand, is someone who is paid to perform services under the control of an employer who can control what and how something will be done. Employers often provide the tools and tell employees not just what needs to be done, but also how it will be done.

The distinction between an employee and an independent contractor is crucial for liability purposes. Principals are typically liable for unintentional torts committed by employees when they occur within the course and scope of their employment. However, principals are generally not liable for unintentional torts committed by independent contractors. For example, if I own a roofing business and one of my employees accidentally crushes a car by dropping a pallet of tiles, I could be held vicariously liable for the damage to the car even though I did not personally cause the damage to the car. If, on the other hand, I hire an independent contractor to install a roof and the independent contractor crushes a car by dropping a pallet of tiles, I should not be held liable for the damage to the car done by the independent contractor.

Agency Formation

An agency relationship is established when a principal agrees to authorize an agent to act on the principal's behalf and the agent agrees to be subject to the principal's control. Unlike most contractual relationships, an agency relationship can be formed without financial consideration. Consideration is the bargained for exchanged where someone agrees to do something in exchange for receiving something. For example, if my neighbor is expecting an important package to be delivered that won't be delivered without someone signing for its receipt, I could agree to sign for the package even though I am not my neighbor's employee and even though there is no bargained for exchange for me to receive some benefit for signing for the package. I am signing the package simply as a favor for my neighbor. We do not have the legal consideration necessary to form a contract in this situation, but we can still form an agency relationship because my neighbor agreed to authorize me to sign for the package, and I agreed to act on my neighbor's behalf.

The principal must have contractual capacity, which is the capacity to conduct transactions and control one's business affairs. The agent, on the other hand, does not need to have contractual capacity. The agent needs only the minimum mental capacity sufficient to consent to the agency relationship.

For example, in most situations, one does not have contractual capacity until reaching the age of 18 years old. However, most 15-year-olds do have the minimum mental capacity sufficient to consent to an agency relationship. With this in mind, and assuming the following is within the scope of a particular parent/babysitter agency relationship, a 15-year-old babysitter could order pizza, have it delivered, and obligate the parents or guardians to pay for the costs associated with this pizza purchase contract. The parents/guardians would be the principals with contractual capacity. The babysitter would be the agent who can bind the principal to contracts made within the course and scope of the agency relationship.

Principals and agents can manifest their consent to enter an agency relationship either **expressly**, which means written or spoken in words, or **impliedly**, which means manifested by conduct. However, in most states the equal dignity rule requires that if the contract being executed must be in writing, then the agent's authority must also be in writing. An example of a contract that generally needs to be in writing to be enforceable is a contract concerning an interest in land. Therefore, although many agency relationships may form orally or be implied by conduct, an agency relationship established for the purchase of land would need to be in writing to be enforceable. We will discuss more contracts that require a writing to be enforceable when we cover the Statute of Frauds in Contract Law.

Agency by Ratification, Estoppel, and Operation of Law

In addition to forming an agency relationship by expressed or implied consent, agencies can also form by ratification, estoppel, and operation of law.

Ratification

Agency by ratification occurs when a principal affirms a contract proposed by someone who is not the principal's agent. As we mentioned, an agent can bind principals to contracts. This can be executive officers signing leases on behalf of their corporations or grocery store employees selling lettuce for their stores. Ratification is different. Ratification exists when someone who is not an agent seeks to bind a principal to a contract that the principal should be free to reject but may choose to accept.

For example, you are not my agent, and I am not your principal. I have not given you any expressed or implied authority to bind me to anything. But imagine that while listening to this audiobook, you may determine that this would be a great textbook for your alma mater. You make a few phone calls and sign a contract to sell thousands of copies of this book to your alma mater at a discounted price. You sign the contract as my agent, but again, you are not my agent. The contract even memorializes your specific agent fee payable to you or the charity of your choice. A month later, I receive a check with an order to send the books you agreed I would send at the price you said I would charge. Am I obligated to sell these books at this price? NO! You are not my agent, and you cannot bind me to any contract to sell my books any more than you could sign for me to sell my house or car. But, before getting too frustrated at your audacity and presumptuous fee, I should look at the check, and maybe count the zeroes. Although you are not my agent, I could ratify this contract, which is simply affirming a contract to which I would not otherwise be bound.

Agency by Estoppel

An agency relationship may also be established by the concept of estoppel. Estoppel is a fancy word in law for "stopped." Agency by Estoppel exists when a principal causes a third-party to believe that another person is the principal's agent, and the third-party acts to his or her detriment in reasonable reliance on that belief. If this happens, the principal can be "estopped" from not honoring the agreement made between the third-party and the person the principal led the third-party to believe was the principal's agent.

For example, let's imagine that you and I are golfing with my friend Sergio who happens to be a business broker—and a good golfer. I own a business, and you're interested in buying it. While golfing, Sergio tells you in front of me that I have agreed to allow Sergio to sell my business for me. I chuckle and add, "That's right."

In truth, I never agreed to have Sergio be my agent or really do anything other than beat me at golf, but I hear him tell you this, and I don't say anything to correct his false assertion. You then ride in the golf cart with Sergio as you coordinate with him to purchase my business from me. I then refuse to sell you my business, arguing that I am not bound by Sergio's sale because he was not my agent.

Could I be bound by Sergio's contract with you? The question is: Did I cause a third-party (you) to believe that another person (Sergio) was my agent? Then, did you reasonably rely on this representation to your detriment? If so, I could be bound by the contract under the theory of agency by estoppel.

Agency by Operation of Law

An agency can also be formed by Operation of Law. These are based on social policy. For example, courts expect that parents will pay for things like the necessary food and medical services of their children. This means that even if a parent has never expressly or impliedly agreed to pay for the child's food or medical bills, a court may determine that the child was acting as an agent of the parent when purchasing these things. This allows creditors to seek payment from the principal, that is the parent, for these necessary items.

Legal Purpose Requirement

An agency relationship can be established for any legal purpose. This is broad, but it has limits. It means that an agent providing a urine sample for an athlete to defeat a drug test would be outside the scope of an agency relationship. This is what former National Football League (NFL) agent Josh Luchs alleges he did for a player as a ball boy for the Oakland Raiders in the 1990s.

It would also be inappropriate to facilitate cheating on college entrance exams, bribe college coaches, and falsely designate children as athletes for sports they didn't even play to get children of wealthy parents into elite colleges. This is what William "Rick" Singer did in the college admission scandal often referred to by its FBI code name, "Operation Varsity Blues." For this, Singer was sentenced to serve 3.5 years in federal prison.

Although seemingly not as scandalous, in many states it is also illegal for an individual to act as an athlete agent without first registering as an athlete agent with the state. For example, in Florida, acting as an athlete agent without first registering as a Florida athlete agent is a third-degree felony, punishable by up to five years in jail and a $5,000 fine. Violating these agent licensing statutes gives the relationship an illegal purpose and can render an agency agreement void and unenforceable.

Duties of an Agent

As a way to introduce agency formation and the duties of an agent, let's talk about sports agent Rich Paul. Rich Paul is famous for being a top NBA sports agent, representing players like LeBron James. For non sports fans, Paul is also famous for being the husband of singer Adele. In 2021 former Dallas Mavericks center Nerlens Noel sued Paul claiming that Noel missed out on $58 million because of Paul's breach of his fiduciary duty, negligence and gross negligence, and breach of the duty of good faith and fair dealing.

Here is an excerpt from *Nerlens Noel, Plaintiff v. Richard Paul and Klutch Sports Group, LLC*, Defendants. **In the words of the Court:**

Nerlens Noel, Plaintiff v. Richard Paul and Klutch Sports Group, LLC, Defendants

United States District Court, N.D. Texas, Dallas Division
CIVIL ACTION NO. 3:21-CV-2485-B
Signed September 9, 2022

A. Factual Background

This is a dispute between a professional athlete and his former agent. Plaintiff Nerlens Noel (Noel) is a professional basketball player in the National Basketball Association (NBA). Defendant Paul is a sports agent who is the "founder, [chief executive officer (CEO)], and Board Member of Defendant [KSG]," a sports agency.

Noel began his NBA career as a member of the Philadelphia 76ers after being selected in the first round of the 2013 NBA draft. After three and a half years in Philadelphia, Noel was traded to the Dallas Mavericks during the middle of the 2016–17 NBA season. Noel had a successful finish to the season with the Mavericks and became a restricted free agent the following summer. When the NBA free agency period opened in July 2017, the Mavericks offered Noel a four-year contract worth $70 million. Noel's agent at the time of the offer was Happy Walters (Walters).

Around the time Noel received the Mavericks contract offer, Noel met Paul for the first time at a birthday party for a former teammate [Ben Simmons]. At the party, Noel claims that Paul "made a pitch to become Noel's agent." The pitch consisted of Paul telling Noel that he "was a [$]100 million man" and that, if Noel fired Walters and hired Paul, Paul would get Noel a deal at the league maximum salary. According to Noel, Paul also "advised Noel that he should cease negotiations with Dallas, accept [a] single year qualifying offer, and seek a max deal on the free agent market the following season."

Paul's pitch was successful. The month after the party, Noel terminated his relationship with Walters and executed a Standard Player Agent Contract (the SPAC) with Paul. "The SPAC is a standard form agreement used for all NBA player and agent contracts." It is drafted by the National Basketball Players Association (the NBPA), which is a union for NBA players. Shortly thereafter, Noel—on Paul's advice—accepted a one-year, $4.1 million contract to play for the Mavericks. In accordance with the SPAC, Paul "received a payment of 4% of the value of [Noel's] contract," compensation Paul would not have been entitled to had Noel accepted the long-term offer negotiated by Walters.

When the next season began, things took a turn for the worse. In "December 2017, Noel tore a ligament in his thumb...[,] had surgery to repair the ligament[,] and was forced to miss 42 games." After the season ended, Noel alleges that "Paul began to lose interest in [him] as a client." "[N]either Paul nor anyone at [KSG] presented any real proposals to Noel in terms of strategies or ideas on how Noel might secure a long-term contract or even a significant contract for the following season," Noel claims. As a result, Noel had "no real offers or deals" presented to him at the start of the 2018 free agency period, and he ultimately decided to join the Oklahoma City Thunder on a two-year, $3.75 million, league minimum deal with a player option for the second year that would allow him to test free agency again the following season.

Noel played limited minutes for the Thunder during the 2018–19 season, during which time he avers that "neither Paul nor [KSG] made any effort to try and secure contracts or deals on [his] behalf." When the season ended, Noel, on Paul's advice, declined his player option and once again became a free agent. *Id.* When free agency began that July, rumors had circulated in NBA circles that Noel was primed to sign a new, lucrative three-year deal with the Thunder. *Id.* Noel believes that the rumors were started by Paul, a KSG employee, or the Thunder. Unfortunately, however, these rumors never materialized, and, after receiving no offers from other teams, Noel signed a one-year league minimum deal to return to the Thunder for the 2019–20 season. Noel posits that the false rumors about the three-year offer from the Thunder caused other teams to shy away from pursuing him during free agency on the assumption that Noel's return to the Thunder was predetermined.

Sometime thereafter, Noel learned from a former coach that the 76ers had been interested in signing him, but that "Paul did not take and/or return any of the calls from the 76ers." Noel "also learned that Paul was not returning or taking calls from other team representatives who were interested in signing Noel for their respective teams." "Concerned about the lack of effort or results, Noel contemplated terminating his relationship with Paul sometime in January 2020," but decided not to after a KSG employee, Lucas Newton, "informed [him] that [KSG] had been talking to [the Thunder] on his behalf and that [they were] planning on offering Noel a three-year deal for between $7 and $10 million per year." However, on the first night of free agency the following November, "Noel did not hear from a single team." When Noel inquired about the Thunder's purportedly impending offer, Newton "advised [him] that the Oklahoma City deal was still in play and that they were just trying to move money around on the books to create cap space for the deal."

For reasons not pleaded, the Oklahoma City offer/deal never came to fruition. Noel later learned that, during the free agency period, two other teams had each been "trying to contact Paul, but that Paul was not taking or returning those calls." Noel ultimately signed a one-year, $5 million deal with the New York Knicks, which Noel claims was arranged only after the Knicks reached out to one of Noel's friends, who then connected the Knicks with Paul. After years of frustration, things "came to a tilt in December 2020 when [Noel] learned that Paul had a history of mismanaging and ignoring" clients who were not deemed "marquee," "costing them significant money." *Id.* For this reason, "Noel...terminated his relationship with Paul and [KSG] on or around December 19, 2020."

B. Procedural Background

Sometime before this suit was filed, a payment dispute arose between Paul and Noel that provoked Paul to file a grievance against Noel, initiating the arbitration process provided for in the SPAC. Noel answered Paul's grievance, initiated his own in response, and then, on August 23, 2021, filed the instant lawsuit in Texas state court against Paul and KSG. Noel brings claims for breach of fiduciary duty, negligence and gross negligence, and breach of the duty of good faith and fair dealing against Paul and KSG. He also brings a claim for breach of the SPAC against Paul. Additionally, Noel seeks a declaratory judgment stating that the arbitration procedure provided by the SPAC "is invalid, void, and unenforceable."

Now let's recap the case that we just read. Noel was offered a four-year $70 million contract with Dallas. He turned it down because sports agent Rich Paul told him he "was a $100 million man." Noel then fired his sports agent, joined Paul, and ended up receiving contracts of only $4.1 and $4.75 million. This was no doubt devastating for Noel, but should his agent be liable for this?

Before discussing the duties of agents, here are a couple of practical business takeaways from the case.

1)   Sometimes the only way to get a client who is a former first-round draft pick like Noel is to sit next to him in Los Angeles at a private birthday party for his friend and former teammate, your client, Ben Simmons, the number one overall draft pick in the 2016 draft. This illustrates an obvious barrier to entry for any client acquisition business seeking the largest accounts.

2)   Did you notice that this lawsuit against Rich Paul arose after Paul first filed a payment grievance against Noel? Later in this chapter we will see that another athlete (Sheffield) sues his

agent (Sloane) after the agent first sues the athlete to recover his fee. If you are going to sue individuals for money, you should be prepared to have them hire an attorney, investigate all the facts, and maybe counter-sue you for money. The American Bar Association reports that an estimated two-thirds of legal malpractice claims arise as counterclaims to suits for legal fees. With this in mind, many insurance companies that offer legal malpractice insurance insist on reviewing a law firm's retainer agreements, billing practices, and collections procedures. They do this because the insurance companies know that if their insureds need to sue to recover a fee, it is likely the insurance company will have to pay to defend their insureds against future counterclaims.

Duties of Agents to Principals

Agents serve as fiduciaries to their principals. A fiduciary relationship is one involving trust and confidence where a principal has the duty to act in the best interest of their principal. We will discuss five duties agents owe principles: care, notification, loyalty, obedience, and accounting.

The Duty of Care

The duty of care requires agents to make decisions in good faith and in a reasonably prudent manner. The requirement is only that the decisions are made in good faith, not that the decisions end up being successful.

The reasoning follows the **Business Judgment Rule** that applies to corporate directors and officers. The Business Judgment Rule creates a rebuttable presumption that when making a business decision, directors and officers have acted on an informed basis, in good faith, and with an honest belief that their decision was in the corporation's best interest. It may end up being a bad decision, but as long as the agents were reasonably informed and acted in good faith, they will not be found liable for breaching their duty of care.

The 1981 case of *Zinn v. Parrish* established the standard that sports agents owe principals a duty of acting in good faith, not successful outcomes (*Zinn v. Parrish*, 644 F.2d 360, 361 (7th Cir. 1981)). In the case, agent Zinn sued former NFL defensive back Lemar Parrish for payment according to the terms of their contract. Their contract stipulated that Zinn should assist in negotiating job contracts, furnish advice on business investments, secure professional tax advice, and obtain endorsement contracts and off-season employment. "Despite his efforts, Zinn was unable to obtain off-season employment for Parrish." As an alternative, Zinn recommended that Parrish return to school to finish his college degree to prepare for when he would no longer be able to play football.

Athlete Parrish disagreed with the amount owed agent Zinn and argued that by not finding off-season employment, Zinn had failed to perform according to the contract. Parrish also argued that their contract was void for being illegal because Zinn provided investment advice without registering under the Investment Advisers Act of 1940. Regarding the illegality of the contract, the court held that Zinn's isolated investment transactions were an "incident to the main purpose of his management contract to negotiate football contracts and did not constitute engaging in the business of advising others on investment securities." Therefore, their contract was not void for being illegal.

As to whether agent Zinn had breached the contract for failing to find off-season employment, the "court found that Zinn at all times acted in good faith, with a willingness 'to provide assistance within his ability.'" With this, Zinn had satisfied the duty of care to his principal.

Similarly, if Rich Paul acted in good faith and in a reasonably prudent manner, he would not be liable to Noel even if his advice resulted in Noel receiving a worse contract. In the end, the *Noel v. Paul* case was dismissed based on a procedural issue. Namely, the parties had agreed in their Standard Player Agent Contract, or SPAC, that "Any and all disputes between the Player and the Agent involving the meaning, interpretation, application, or enforcement of this Agreement or the obligations of the parties under this Agreement shall be resolved exclusively through the Arbitration procedure set forth in Section 5 of the NBPA Regulations Governing Player Agents." Therefore, the case was dismissed to be resolved through arbitration as required in their contract.

The Duty of Notification

An agent has a duty to notify the principal of all material information acquired from the agency relationship. The law presumes that the principal is aware of any notice made to the agent. For example, the insurance company Geico was founded in Texas, has its headquarters in Maryland, and has agents in every state. If Geico is your auto insurance carrier and you need to notify them that you were in an accident, you do not need to travel to their headquarters. You can contact any Geico agent. The law will assume that the principal, Geico, received the notification you made to its agent.

Not only is informing one's principal a duty, it is also a good business practice. One of the frustrations experienced by Noel in the *Noel v. Paul* dispute was that Noel learned that "two other teams" had each been "trying to contact Paul, but that Paul was not taking or returning those calls." With many sports agents also being attorneys, it may be helpful to share the American Bar Association's rule on communication to use as a model for all agents.

Model Rules of Professional Conduct, Rule 1.4: Communications

(a) A lawyer shall:

(1) promptly inform the client of any decision or circumstance with respect to which the client's informed consent is required by these Rules;

(2) reasonably consult with the client about the means by which the client's objectives are to be accomplished;

(3) keep the client reasonably informed about the status of the matter;

(4) promptly comply with reasonable requests for information; and

(5) consult with the client about any relevant limitation on the lawyer's conduct when the lawyer knows that the client expects assistance not permitted by the Rules of Professional Conduct or other law.

(b) A lawyer shall explain a matter to the extent reasonably necessary to permit the client to make informed decisions regarding the representation.

The Duty of Loyalty

The duty of loyalty requires agents to act solely for the benefit of their principal and not promote their own interests or the interest of a third-party. Again, this applies both to sports agents representing athletes, and other agents such as directors and officers representing their corporations. Common examples of breaches of the duty of loyalty are self-dealing and usurping a principal's opportunity.

A **Self-dealing** exists when an agent takes an action to benefit the agent at the expense of taking an action that would benefit the principal. For example, imagine that I am a sports agent for an athlete who likes to rent a Ferrari for the week whenever the athlete has a game in town. I have a choice of two Ferrari rental providers. One charges $1500 per week. The other charges $2000 per week. Otherwise, the two cars and providers are identical. I pay the invoice through the athlete's account. The athlete will never see the invoice and wouldn't notice the $500 difference anyway. I could save the athlete $500 per week by using the less expensive rental provider, but the more expensive Ferrari provider is owned by my old friend, or my niece's coach, or someone who sometimes sends me concert tickets. Choosing the more expensive rental provider without disclosing it to the athlete would be a breach of my duty of loyalty because I am taking an action to benefit myself and not the principal.

Usurping a principal's opportunity (also called **usurping a corporate opportunity**) exists when an agent takes advantage of a business opportunity that rightfully belongs to the principal. For example, imagine that I am an agent for a wealthy, retired athlete. As the agent, I often get calls pitching various investment opportunities for the athlete. I research these deals and sometimes recommend them to the athlete. As a result of my efforts, the athlete keeps getting richer and richer, and sadly, I am not. One day I get a call asking if the athlete would be interested in purchasing an apartment building. It's a great price in a great location. I want this opportunity for myself, but if I take this opportunity for myself without disclosing it to my principal, I could be breaching my duty of loyalty by usurping the principal's opportunity.

Courts will consider the following questions to determine if an agent has wrongfully taken a principal's opportunity:

1. Was the opportunity discovered while the person was acting in the capacity of an agent?
2. Was the opportunity closely related to the activities of the principal?
3. Has the principal expressed an interest in, or expectancy of, acquiring that type of opportunity?
4. Were the principal's funds or facilities used in discovering or developing the opportunity?

Even if these questions reveal that the opportunity belongs to the principal, there is a way for the agent to take advantage of the opportunity without breaching the agent's duty of loyalty. Again, it comes down to communication. There is no breach of the duty of loyalty if, after full disclosure, the principal is given the opportunity to pursue the opportunity first and declines the opportunity or is otherwise unable to take advantage of the opportunity.

The Duty of Obedience

The duty of obedience requires agents to avoid acts beyond the scope of their authorization (*Gearhart Indus., Inc. v. Smith Int'l, Inc.*, 741 F.2d

707 (5th Cir. 1984)).

Because a principal can be bound by the actions of an agent, it seems reasonable to require agents to follow the lawful, clearly stated instructions of the principal. If my principal, an athlete, tells me not to buy a Ferrari as a necessary expense to my representation of the principal, and as the agent I buy the Ferrari anyway, I may have just lost my job and bought myself a Ferrari. Ordinarily, the principal is bound by the contracts entered into by the agent. But in this case, I would have exceeded the scope of my authority—that is, breaching my duty of obedience—and the principal would not be bound by the contract to pay for the Ferrari.

The Duty of Accounting

Agents have a duty to account for all property or funds that the agent has received or paid out on behalf of the principal. The right for a principal to require an accounting is foundational to the relationship, and unless otherwise agreed, there is no discretion as to whether an accounting may be required (2A C.J.S. Agency § 311). To ensure an accurate accounting of the principal's funds, an agent must avoid commingling the principal's funds with other funds. Commingling is the mixing of funds belonging to one party with funds belonging to another party. This often occurs when agents improperly mix their own funds with a client's funds.

Here is an illustration of a common problem involving agents and unearned client money. Imagine that I agree with a principal that I will serve as the principal's agent doing hopefully something interesting and of value for a fee of $10,000 per month. The principal pays me a lump sum of $120,000 at the beginning of the year to cover the cost of these services. I put this amount in my own personal account. We've had this arrangement for the past 12 months, and I see no reason why it will not continue for the next 12 months.

So, it's January, I have $120,000 in my personal account, and there's a car that I would like to buy right now for $120,000. I take the $120,000 and buy the car. The problem occurs next month when, for whatever reason, the principal fires me, and I must return any fees that I have not earned. If I only provided services for one month, I only earned $10,000. The remaining $110,000 needs to be returned to the client.

As a solution, California's athlete registration act and many state bar associations require sports agents and attorneys to hold client funds in a client's own separate trust account. A trust account is a legal arrangement where funds are held by a third party (the agent/trustee) for the benefit of another party (here, the principal/beneficiary).

This is how the above scenario would work using a trust account. The principal gives me $120,000 to cover the next 12 monthly payments of $10,000. I put the $120,000 in a trust account for the benefit of the principal. At the end of the first month, I transfer the $10,000 that I have earned from the trust account into my own account. If the principal fires me next month, I will return the remaining $110,000 held in the principal's trust account.

The practice of using trust accounts is so important that when I wanted to be licensed to practice law in New Mexico after moving from the private practice of law in California to accept my dream job as a College Professor of Business Law at New Mexico State University—go Aggies—the state of New Mexico required me to take not only their bar exam (the Uniform Bar Exam), but also an additional day of classes covering four New Mexico specific topics. These topics were on substance abuse, divorce law, Indian Law, and trust accounts. I heard a California Bar Association official once claim that the bar association investigates any incidences where an attorney's trust account has a negative balance because this often reveals attorney incompetence issues such as substance abuse, gambling addiction, or other wellness issues.

Here is an excerpt about trust accounts from California's Miller-Ayala Athlete Agents Act:

> 18897.2. A trust fund shall be established when an athlete agent is the recipient of the athlete's salary. An athlete agent who receives any payment on behalf of the athlete shall immediately deposit the payment in a trust fund account maintained by the athlete agent in a state or federally chartered financial institution.

Duties of Principals to Agents

Principals also owe duties to their agents. We will discuss four duties principals owe agents: compensation, reimbursement and indemnification, cooperation, and safe working conditions.

Compensation

Principals owe a duty to compensate agents for services faithfully performed for the principal. If an agent completely performs according to the terms of a contract, the principal must pay the agent the contract price. If an agent acts in good faith but is unable to complete the contract, the agent may still be entitled to compensation under the theory of *quantum meruit*. *Quantum meruit*—Latin for the amount deserved—is a reasonable sum of money to be paid for services rendered when the amount due is not stipulated in a legally enforceable contract. However, agents are not entitled to compensation for their services when they have willfully disregarded their duties to the principal (2A C.J.S. Agency § 337). Agents are also not entitled to payment if their agency relationship serves an illegal purpose.

For example, in a case involving sports agent David Sloane and pitcher Justus Sheffield, Sloane argued that he had agreed to negotiate a contract for Sheffield in exchange for receiving five percent of Sheffield's signing bonus. Sheffield received a $1.6 million signing bonus for which Sheffield expected to be paid five percent. That would be $80,000. But Sheffield only paid Sloane $48,000. Sloane sued Sheffield to recover the full $80,000 to which he felt entitled.

Here we have another example of an agent suing for money that will backfire. What is someone likely to do when sued? That's right, call an attorney. Now there is an attorney studying everything agent Sloane did to see if there were any errors that would excuse Sheffield from paying the former agent Sloane $80,000. What they discovered was that although agent Sloane was a registered athlete agent in Florida and Alabama, he was not yet registered as an athlete agent in Tennessee when he entered his agreement with Sheffield. That violated Tennessee law. Therefore, their initial contract was unenforceable as an illegal contract, and principal Sheffield was not required to compensate Sloane for his services.

Reimbursement and Indemnification

Principals owe a duty to reimburse agents for any expenditures incurred as a direct consequence of the good faith execution of the agency relationship. The rule is based on the concept that a principal's request for an agent to spend money in furtherance of the agency relationship creates an implied promise that the principal will reimburse the agent (2A C.J.S. Agency § 361).

Principals also owe a duty to indemnify their agents for any damages resulting from acts made by their agents in the good faith execution of the agency relationship (2A C.J.S. Agency § 324). Indemnification is the promise to make another party whole for any liability, damage, or loss incurred by another. Whereas reimbursement involves repaying an agent for the good faith costs the agent spent, indemnification involves principals compensating agents for costs stemming from third-party claims.

For example, imagine that I am an employee at a large sports agency firm. And remember, employees are agents of their principal, their employer. If within the course and scope of my employment, I buy plane tickets to fly an athlete to interview with a team, my employer would have a duty to reimburse me for the cost of the tickets. If within the course and scope of my employment I hit a baseball that breaks a third-party's car window, my employer would owe a duty to indemnify me for any damages demanded of me in this car owner's claim.

Cooperation

In every agency relationship, there is an implied promise that the principal will cooperate with the agent and do nothing to thwart the effectiveness of the agency (2A C.J.S. Agency § 322).

Why would a principal do something to prevent the success of an agent? In the 2016 case *NRT New England, LLC v. Jones*, homebuyer Jones signed an exclusive representation agreement to buy a home with a licensed realtor named Andrea Woolston. The agreement established that Woolston would be the exclusive agent for finding, negotiating, and purchasing a property. The agreement also established that for her efforts, Woolston would receive a commission equal to 2.5 percent of the purchase price of any property purchased by Jones. The agreement stated that the buyer would not deal directly with any other broker, agent, or licensee during the term of the agreement.

In response, agent Woolston spent hundreds of hours researching properties and arranging visits on available properties until Jones sent Woolston an email informing Woolston that he had just purchased a house for $1,375,000 through another agent, named Mary Jane Burt, with whom he had also signed an exclusive representation agreement.

Buying a property through agent Mary Jane Burt clearly thwarted the effectiveness of the Jones and Woolston agency relationship. Woolston sued Jones for breach of contract, demanding 2.5 percent of the purchase price of the home Jones purchased according to the terms of their original agency relationship. Woolston won. The court awarded her the 2.5 percent of the $1,375,000 purchase price, which was $34,375, plus her attorney's fees and costs (*NRT New England, LLC v. Jones,* 162 Conn. App. 840, 134 A.3d 632 (2016)).

Safe Working Conditions

Principals also owe agents the common law duty of providing safe working conditions. Principals must inspect and warn agents about any unsafe conditions. As employers, principals must also comply with worker safety laws such as state workers' compensation insurance laws and federal regulations such as the Occupational Safety and Health Administration (OSHA) Act.

Sports Agents

If we are talking about agency law in sports, we should probably talk about sports agents. In 2022, Forbes magazine listed Scott Boras as the year's top sports agent. In that year Boras, a lawyer by training, negotiated contracts worth a total of $3.8 billion for his 106 major league baseball players. This included a $330 million deal for Bryce Harper with the Phillies, a $325 million deal for Corey Seager with the Rangers, and a $324 million deal for Gerrit Cole with the Yankees. For his role as the sports agent negotiating these contracts, Scott Boras earned $191 million in commissions.

Examples like Scott Boras can lead business-minded sports fans to wonder, "What would it take for me to become a sports agent?" The answer is pretty straight-forward: You become a sports agent the same way you become a real estate agent or an insurance agent. You follow the rules of the applicable governing body. For example, most states require real estate agents and insurance agents to be at least 18 years of age, not a felon, attend a certain number of hours of education, and pass a state administered examination. Once these requirements are satisfied, an individual can be an agent representing clients and earning commissions for selling houses or insurance policies. These agents can also lose their licenses if they fail to comply with the rules of the governing body.

The power to issue and revoke a license serves a consumer protection role by giving a governing body control over who should and should not be allowed to be an agent. To understand the rules of these governing bodies, we need to look at state law, uniform laws, and the rules established by sport unions.

State Law and Uniform Laws

States are free to make their own laws so long as these laws do not violate the U.S. Constitution or their own state constitution. This can result in varying punishments by state and even situations where an activity is legal in one state and illegal in another. For example, the death penalty is a legal punishment in some states and outlawed in others.

To provide consistency across the states, uniform laws are often proposed for adoption by all the states. States can then choose to accept, reject, or modify these proposed laws. The organization that proposes these laws is often the Uniform Law Commission. The Uniform Law Commission is a non-profit founded in 1892 to help bring clarity and stability to critical areas of law. Common examples of uniform laws are the Model Penal Code which sought to standardize criminal law throughout the United States, the Uniform Commercial Code which governs commercial transactions and was adopted by all states, and for our purposes, the Uniform Athlete Agents Act (UAA) of 2000, which was revised in 2019. This act governs the activities of athlete agents and has been enacted in 42 states. Even in states where the act has been adopted, the penalties and requirements may vary. This results in different athlete agent rules in different states. For example, California, which has not adopted the UAA, requires sports agents to register with the Secretary of State, pay a $30 filing fee, and purchase a $100,000 surety bond (*Ca. Bus. And Prof'l. Code § 18895*). In Florida, the initial application fee is $630.00 and failure to register is a third-degree felony with penalties of up to five years in jail and a $5,000 fine.

Sloane v. Tenn. Dep't of State

It is important to note that agents must register in every state that requires registration where they may be acting as an athlete agent. As mentioned, when sports agent David Sloan began representing pitcher Justus Sheffield in 2012, "Sloane was [already] a registered athlete agent in Florida and Alabama, but not yet registered in Tennessee" (*David Mark Sloane v. Tennessee Department of State, Business Services Division*, No. M2019-00126-COA-R3-CV). Sloane then applied and was approved as an athlete agent in Tennessee before representing Sheffield in the 2014 MLB draft where the Cleveland Indians drafted Sheffield in the first round and paid him a $1.6 million dollar signing bonus. For this, Sheffield paid Sloane $48,000, but Sloane argued that they had agreed that Sheffield would pay five percent of his signing bonus, which would be $80,000, not $48,000. When Sheffield refused to pay the full $80,000 Sloane sued Sheffield to recover his fee. "During the lawsuit, Sheffield discovered that Sloane was not registered as an athlete agent in Tennessee when he first initiated contact with him." Sheffield's new agent, Bo McKinnis, reported this to the state of Tennessee. In September 2016, the state of Tennessee fined Sloane $10,000.00 for initiating contact with Sheffield prior to Sloane's registration as an athlete agent in violation of Tennessee's code section 49-7-2114(b)(1); and $15,000.00 for acting as an athlete agent prior to Sloane's registration as an athlete agent in violation of Tennessee Code 49-7-2014(a) and 49-7-2114(b). The fines were later reduced to $10,000 plus $740 in investigatory costs.

Sport Union Regulations

Players unions are organizations that represent the collective interests of professional athletes in a specific sport. These unions negotiate with league officials and team owners on behalf of the players to secure fair wages, benefits, working conditions, and other rights. Like states, a sport's players union can also make rules that impact agents.

The NFL Player's Association requires an application fee of $2,500, a graduate degree from an accredited college or university or at least seven years of sufficient negotiating experience, a background investigation, a two-day seminar, successful completion of a multiple-choice, proctored examination, and a valid email address. Yes, it lists a valid email address on its list of requirements. Major League Baseball's Players' Association requires an application fee of $2,500, a background investigation, and a written examination. The NBA Player's Association requires an application fee of $2,000, a four-year degree or enough relevant experience, a background investigation, and passing a grueling examination that only 53% (93 out of 174) of test-takers passed in 2018.

So how in 2022 did Shyra Johnson become the youngest ever certified NBA agent? She followed the governing rules. She registered with the state of Florida as required by state law, graduated from Florida Atlantic University, and she passed the NBA Players Association Agent Certification exam at age 21. "The previous record-holder was Drew Rosenhaus, who was 22 years old when the University of Miami graduate, who counts Dolphin's receiver Tyreek Hill among his clients, was certified as a sports agent" (Weinberger, Z. (2022, March 29). *Move over Drew Rosenhaus. Shyra Johnson has become the youngest sports agent in history.* Palm Beach Post).

Of course, becoming a registered agent does not guarantee that one will make a living as an agent. In his 2018 article entitled,

Congratulations, You're a Certified N.B.A. Agent. Good Luck Finding a Client, New York Times reporter Kevin Draper reported that "sixty percent of certified agents did not represent any NBA players" in the previous season. "Twenty-four of the 30 players selected in the first round of the 2018 draft [were] represented by agencies that [had] negotiated hundreds of millions of dollars' worth of contracts. Another five [players were] represented by smaller agencies with a few NBA players. One player, the number six selection named Mo Bamba, represent[ed] himself. None [of the players selected in the first round were] represented by an agent [that had been] certified within the last two years (Draper, K. (2018, October 17). *Congratulations, you're a certified N.B.A. agent. Good luck finding a client.* The New York Times).

National Collegiate Athletic Association Regulations

In addition to state and union regulations, agents representing college athletes must abide by the rules established by the National Collegiate Athletic Association (NCAA). And these rules can change. For example, in 2019 the NCAA amended their rules to begin requiring that all prospective agents have at least a bachelor's degree. This may seem admirable from what is, after all, the National ***Collegiate*** Athletic Association. There was just one major problem with this rule: Rich Paul did not have a bachelor's degree. Rich Paul is or has been the agent for LeBron James, Lonzo Ball, Anthony Davis, Draymond Green, Chris Livingston, Scotty Pippen Jr., J.R. Smith, Tristan Thompson, Ben Simmons, and more. In 2023 Rich Paul was worth an estimated $120 million. But according to the NCAA's 2019 amended education requirements, he would not be allowed to become an agent because he did not have a bachelor's degree. If you are wondering how Rich Paul became a sports agent, it started with him selling vintage jerseys from the trunk of his car after completing high school. He then met fellow Ohio native LeBron James in 2002 and began working under James' then-agent Leon Rose. In 2012, Paul left Leon Rose to establish his own agency, Klutch Sports.

Rich Paul, Lebron James, and others blasted the NCAA for what was labelled, the "Rich Paul Rule." Within a week, the NCAA reversed course stating, "We have been made aware of several current agents who have appropriately represented former student-athletes in their professional quest and whom the National Basketball Players Association has granted waivers of its bachelor's degree requirement.

While specific individuals were not considered when developing our process, we respect the NBPA's determination of qualification and have amended our certification criteria" (Slagter, J. (2019, August 12). *NCAA dumps 'Rich Paul Rule' amid blowback on agent requirements.* MLive. With this, Rich Paul was able to continue representing NCAA athletes.

The Fourteenth Amendment

Imagine that like Rich Paul, you are a licensed NBA agent and even have some clients, but unlike Rich Paul, you are not a multi-millionaire. You have an expensive office, staff, and travel expenses that you believe are necessary to attract new talent—and you always need to attract new talent to replace the earnings you'll lose as your current clients retire or leave you for another agent. Now recall the "Rich Paul Rule" and imagine that the NCAA changed its rules so that you will no longer be eligible to be an agent for college athletes. With the NCAA's rule change, you will be unable to attract new clients out of college, and your business will die. Do you think you have any legal right to challenge the new NCAA rule?

Hold that thought and imagine that it was not the NCAA that changed the rules, but your state legislature. Imagine that the state changed its rules and now you no longer qualify to represent athletes. You will no longer be able to make a living in your field of work. Do you think you have any legal right to challenge this?

If the government is the one taking your license, you have some protections from the U.S. Constitution. The Fourteenth Amendment of the U.S. Constitution states, "No state shall…deprive any person of life, liberty, or property, without due process of law."

If the state takes away your license and ability to make a living, you could argue that they have deprived you of your property. It would not be fair for the government to take the tools from a carpenter if the carpenter cannot make a living without the tools. Similarly, if a state requires agents to be licensed, the agents cannot earn a living if a state revokes their licenses.

However, the Fourteenth amendment does not say that a state cannot take property. It says a state cannot take life, liberty, or property *"without due process of law."* Due process of law will require that the governmental entity involved hold an administrative hearing to give the sports agent an opportunity to be heard before the state can deprive an agent of the agent's license.

Now let's go back to the example of the NCAA's Rich Paul Rule. Would it violate the Fourteenth Amendment for the NCAA or a union to revoke an agent's license? The short answer is no. The Fourteenth amendment protects against deprivations of property by the state, and the NCAA and the player unions are not the state. A court determined that the NCAA is not a state actor in *NCAA v. Tarkanian*, 488 U.S. 179 (1988). Even the United States Olympic Committee, which was chartered by congress, is not a state actor (see *San Francisco Arts & Athletics, Inc. v. United States Olympic Comm.*, 483 U.S. 522 (1987). The Seattle Seahawks football team was found not to be a government actor even though their stadium was funded by tax dollars and the state would maintain a 10% ownership interest in the Seahawks if they were sold within 25 years after issuance of the stadium's construction bonds (*Stark v. Seattle Seahawks*, No. C06-1719JLR, 2007 WL 1821017, (W.D. Wash. June 22, 2007). It may still be possible to sue a non-governmental entity for terminating your license if the entity did not follow the contract you entered with the organization, but this would be a lawsuit based in contract law, not as a violation of your constitutional rights.

Who Can Have an Agent and What Do Agents Do?

What a sports agent will do for an athlete should be spelled out in a written Standard Representation Contract, or SRK. This is abbreviated as SRK because the letter K is commonly used by attorneys to abbreviate the word "contract." Common agent tasks include the agent negotiating job contracts, furnishing advice on business investments, securing professional tax advice, and obtaining endorsement contracts and off-season employment (*Zinn v. Parrish*, 644 F.2d 360, 361 (7th Cir. 1981)).

Who can have a sports agent has been complicated by recent changes in NCAA policies and state law. In 2021, the NCAA adopted a Name, Image, and Likeness Policy that, for the first time, allowed college athletes to maintain NCAA eligibility while also profiting from their name, image, and likeness. It also outlined that college athletes could use a "professional services provider for NIL activities" (Hosick, M. B. (2021, June 30). *NCAA adopts interim name, image and likeness policy*. NCAA Media Center).

Many states have also enacted NIL-related bills allowing college athletes to hire sports agents to represent the athletes on NIL issues. However, statutes regulating sports agents vary by state, and some states still "assume that sports agents are not permitted to represent student-athletes without sacrificing the athlete's eligibility" (LaRose, B., & Sawchak, M. W. (2021, August 2). Not So Alike: Current Impact of NIL Administration on the Regulation of Sports Agents. Robinson Bradshaw). This creates a potential hurdle for sports agents as they navigate compliance with state, federal, NCAA, union, and institutional rules. However, the trend appears for states to allow college athletes to benefit from their name, image, and likeness, and to allow professional agents to represent athletes in these endeavors.

A Practical Note to Athletes

In case there are any current or future professional athletes listening to this, I'll end this section about agents and agency law with the advice Oprah Winfrey once shared with tennis star Serena Williams:

"You sign every check. Never let anyone sign any checks."

Further Reading:

- https://www.uniformlaws.org/committees/community-home?CommunityKey=cef8ae71-2f7b-4404-9af5-309bb70e861e

Chapter 2: Contract Law

For those listening to this as an audiobook, I'll go ahead and apologize that the next few paragraphs may be a little tedious, but they lay out the roadmap we will follow throughout the chapter.

Contract Law Road Map

I like to use mathematics to help explain contract law. This is because contract law is like a mathematical equation where an enforceable contract is equal to A times B times C times D. To solve this, we just need to know the value, or in our case, the definition, of A and B and C and D.

$$\text{An Enforceable Contract} = A \times B \times C \times D$$

Here is the contract law equation that will be the roadmap that we will follow in this chapter: An Enforceable Contract is equal to A) an Offer, B) Acceptance, C) Consideration, and D) an Absence of Defenses. Expanding this we will see that an Offer is equal to 1) an objectively expressed intention to be bound, 2) containing sufficiently definite terms, 3) communicated to an identifiable offeree, and 4) inviting the offeree to accept the terms of the offer. Acceptance requires 1) unconditional assent that is 2) communicated. Consideration is the bargained for exchange given to support a current exchange of promises or performance. The defenses we will discuss are Illegality, Capacity, Fraud, Unconscionability, Undue Influence, Duress, the Statute of Frauds, Impossibility, Impracticability, and Frustration of Purpose (See Figure 1-1).

The only actual mathematics that will be helpful to recall is that zero times anything is zero. This means that if any one of our variables A, B, C, or D is a zero, then our answer will be zero, and we will not have an enforceable contract. Applying our definitions, this means that if there is no A) Offer, or B) Acceptance, or C) Consideration, or for D), if there are any applicable defenses, then we will not have an enforceable contract.

I'll also add a technical note for law students and lawyers reading this. Technically speaking, you have formed an enforceable contract when you have A, B, and C. That is, you have formed an enforceable contract when you have an offer, acceptance, and consideration. D, the defenses, are then available for the defendant to use to defeat the otherwise enforceable contract.

Figure 2-1
An Enforceable Contract = A x B x C x D

A. Offer
      1) An Objectively Expressed Intention to Be Bound,
      2) Containing Sufficiently Definite Terms,
      3) Communicated to an Identifiable Offeree,
      4) Inviting the Offeree to Accept the Terms of the Offer.
B. Acceptance
      1)   Unconditional Assent
      2)   Communication
C. Consideration
      1)   Quid pro quo
      2)   Current Exchange of Promises or Performance
      3)   Forbearance, Pre-existing Duty, and Substitutes
D. Absence of Defenses
      1) Illegality
      2) Capacity
      3) Fraud
      4) Unconscionability
      5) Undue Influence
      6) Duress
      7) Statute of Frauds
            a) Marriage
            b) Years
            c) Land
            d) Executors
            e) Guarantees
            f) Sale of Goods over $500.
      8) Impossibility, Impracticability, Frustration of Purpose

Preliminary Questions

Imagine that I am an athlete on my university's faculty baseball team, and you make shoes. We are thinking about an endorsement deal where you will pay me $1 million for the rights to put my name, image, or likeness on your shoes. You then decide, perhaps wisely, that this is a horrible idea. You do not make the shoes, and you do not pay me $1 million. Can I sue you for breach of contract?

You cannot successfully sue—or be sued—for breach of contract unless there was an enforceable contract. Therefore, the first question in contract law should be, "Was there an enforceable contract?"

To determine if there was an enforceable contract, we need to look at what law applies. In soccer a goal occurs when "the whole of the ball passes the goal line." In American football, the ball does not need to pass the goal line. The ball could touch the line, or be over it, or have a player in possession of the ball touch the pylon, or have the referee determine that a team was wrongfully denied a touchdown by the other team's "palpably unfair act." I include these details to remind us that rules matter. We wouldn't want to apply football rules to soccer, or vice versa. Similarly, the starting point to any legal analysis is to ensure that we are applying the correct law. In contract law, the Uniform Commercial Code (UCC) is the controlling law for the sale of goods. The Common Law is the controlling law for contracts for services and real estate.

The Common Law

The Common Law is a body of laws established over hundreds of years in the United States and, prior to the United States, in England. In the Common Law tradition, we look to the reasoning used in previous cases to resolve new disputes. The idea is that we expect similar cases to be resolved similarly. Judges look to past cases for resolving new cases, and we can look to these same past cases for guidance on how our own cases might be resolved.

The UCC

Unlike the Common Law, the UCC is a relatively new development. It was first published in 1952 to govern commercial transactions throughout the United States. The UCC has been adopted by every state, the District of Columbia, and the Territories of the United States. Among other things, it contains provisions designed to protect consumers and special rules for how merchants should resolve disputes with other merchants.

Once we know what rule to apply, we are ready to answer our question, "Was there an enforceable contract?"

The Parties to a Contract

Before answering if there is an enforceable contract, I need to introduce you to the parties of a contract. An offeror is the person who makes an offer. An offeree is the person who receives an offer. A promisor is the person who makes a promise. A promisee is the person who receives a promise. This follows more common examples such as the employer who provides employment to an employee.

An Enforceable Contract

An **enforceable contract** is formed when there is an exchange of promises that contains an offer, acceptance, and consideration. The parties to the contract must have the contractual capacity to enter the contract and the contract cannot be for an illegal purpose.

As a quick note for anyone studying for a bar exam, I will share that the definition that I used to pass the California and New Mexico Bar exams is this: an enforceable contract is formed when there is an offer, acceptance, consideration, and an absence of defenses. This is the format this chapter will follow. Other textbooks talk about "mutual assent" or "agreement" being required for contract formation. This is true, but "mutual assent" and "agreement" are then defined as an offer and acceptance, which my definition addresses. My definition may also appear to ignore contractual capacity and illegality, but I address these along with other possible defenses that can render a contract unenforceable.

Therefore, an enforceable contract is formed when there is an offer, acceptance, consideration, and an absence of defenses. With this as our definition, we need to ask:

- What is an offer?
- What is acceptance?
- What is consideration? and
- What are the possible defenses?

What is an Offer?

An offer is 1) an objectively expressed intention to be bound, 2) containing sufficiently definite terms, 3) communicated to an identifiable offeree, 4) inviting the offeree to accept the terms of the offer. If you don't have these four characteristics, you don't have an offer. And if you don't have an offer, then it can't be accepted. And if there isn't an offer that was accepted, then you don't have a contract. And if you don't have a contract, then no one could have breached the contract. And if no one could have breached the contract, then no one should be able to sue or be sued for breach of contract because there was no contract.

Let's walk through the four characteristics of an offer.

---

1) An Objectively Expressed Intention to Be Bound

Under the Objective Theory of Contracts, an offer must contain an objectively expressed intention to be bound. If we look at a situation objectively, we look at it based on the facts without regard to personal feelings or opinions. This contrasts with looking at a situation subjectively which looks to an individual's personal feelings or opinions.

For example, imagine that I purchase a new, high tech, hydrogen powered supercar for $1 million. I pick you up in the car and we drive around together. It is amazing, but when we get to our destination, it is so advanced that I can't figure out how to open the doors. Everything is automated and new, and frankly, frustrating. Exasperated, I yell, "I'm so frustrated with this car that I'd sell it to you now for $1000."

You then turn to me and say, "I accept." Uh oh. Did I just sell my $1 million hydrogen powered supercar car to you for $1000?

You demand that I give you the car. I refuse and then you sue me to have a court enforce our oral contract. We cannot know what is inside someone's mind, but looking at the situation objectively, it seems likely that a jury of my peers would realize that I did not intend to sell my car for $1000. I just yelled out a number in frustration. If I did not intend to be bound, then there was no offer for you to accept and we did not form an enforceable contract.

In the case of *Lucy v. Zehmer*, Zehmer owned a farm and Lucy wanted to buy this farm. For eight years Lucy pestered Zehmer to sell the farm, but Zehmer was never interested in selling. One night at a local restaurant/bar, Lucy changed tactics and said to Zehmer, "I bet you wouldn't take $50,000 for that place."

Zehmer replied, "Yes, I would too; you wouldn't give fifty." The night progressed with the men chatting, discussing the sale of the farm, drafting and signing a document for the sale of the farm, and whiskey. Yes, the court case makes it clear that there was whiskey.

Imagine the next morning a sheriff knocks on Zehmer's door with an eviction notice because, according to the document in hand, last night Zehmer sold the farm. Zehmer does not want to sell his farm, but now there is a piece of paper, perhaps wrinkled by last night's spilled whiskey, saying he sold the farm. He even signed it. Could this be an enforceable offer?

Zehmer argued that the contract should not be taken seriously because he was drunk and joking when he signed it. Or, in his own words, he "was high as a Georgia pine" and they "was just a bunch of two doggoned drunks bluffing to see who could talk the biggest and say the most." But using the objective theory of contracts, we don't ask the subjective feelings of the offeror. We look at the facts from the outside to see if a reasonable person would believe that an offer was being made.

And what do the facts of this case tell us? We learn that their contract was originally written in the singular for Mr. Zehmer to sign, but then crossed out and made plural so that Mrs. Zehmer could also sign it. And she did. The document also addressed what would be included in the sale and gave the buyer the right to inspect title to the property.

The court stated that "the record is convincing that Zehmer was not intoxicated to the extent of being unable to comprehend the nature and consequences of the instrument he executed, and hence that instrument is not to be invalidated on that ground" (*Lucy v. Zehmer*, 196 Va. 493, 500, 84 S.E.2d 516, 520 (1954)). The court added, "In the field of contracts, as generally elsewhere, we must look to the outward expression of a person as manifesting his intention rather than to his secret and unexpressed intention. The law imputes to a person an intention corresponding to the reasonable meaning of his words and acts"(Ibid citing *First Nat. Bank v. Roanoke Oil Co.,* 169 Va. 99, 114, 192 S.E. 764, 770).

In other words, Mr. and Mrs. Zehmer, we cannot know your internal, subjective thoughts. We will just look at the situation objectively, and looking at your situation objectively, it appears that you intended to sell the farm. So, you sold the farm.

An offer requires 1) an objectively expressed intention to be bound. We addressed the "objectively expressed" part. Now we will look at the intention to be bound. Sometimes you will see what looks like an enforceable contract that includes a statement that the contract is a "non-binding agreement." If it is non-binding, it is not an enforceable offer. Similarly, if you read a detailed endorsement offer to pay a specific athlete $1 million at a specific time for a specific service, but then read that this is merely an "offer to enter negotiations," you do not have an intention to be bound to the terms of the contract. Therefore, you do not have an enforceable offer for a $1 million endorsement contract. All you have is a piece of paper inviting the athlete to enter negotiations.

2) Containing Sufficiently Definite Terms

An offer must contain sufficiently definite terms. This requires the identity of the parties to the contract. Without the identity of the parties, a court would not know who owes a duty to perform a contract and for whom. On a practical note, if you are signing as an agent for a principal, make sure that it is clear that you are signing on behalf of the principal and not for yourself. For example, if you sign a $1 million lease for your employer's new facility, make sure it is clear, in writing, that you are signing your name not as an individual, but as an agent of your employer.

In addition to the identity of the parties, an offer must also contain sufficiently definite terms about the goods or services being offered. If land is being offered, there must be a description of the land and the price. The description should be akin to an address or APN that describes the exact borders of the land. It would be insufficient to have an offer to sell one acre of someone's ten-acre tract of land because we would not know if this is the acre in the northeast corner or the southwest corner, maybe by the pecans, street, or the acre surrounding and including the house. In the case of *Lucy v. Zehmer*, it was sufficient to describe the land simply as "Ferguson Farm" because this was the name of the specific 471.6 acre property that was the subject of the contract.

When a contract is for the sale of goods, the UCC is the controlling law. Generally speaking, the UCC is generous in what it will call a contract. For example, it will find a contract enforceable even without a contract price, stating that a contract is "not insufficient because it omits or incorrectly states a term agreed upon" (UCC § 2-201(1)). However, what the UCC does require is the quantity of goods to be sold. If a contract for the sale of goods includes a quantity, but no price, a court may enforce the contract using a market price for the goods to be sold. But if a contract for the sale of goods contains a price, but no quantity, the case will be dismissed for having insufficiently definite terms.

3) Communicated to an Identifiable Offeree

In order for an offer to be enforceable, the offer must be communicated to an identifiable offeree. How a contract must be communicated depends on whether the contract is a bilateral contract or a unilateral contract.

Bilateral Contracts vs. Unilateral Contracts

A bilateral contract contains a mutual exchange of promises. It is a promise for a promise. For example, image that you want to offer former NBA player Dwight Howard $50,000 to be the photographer at your office party. It would be good for company morale and at 6'11" with a wingspan of 7'5", you like that Howard could hold a camera nine feet in the air for an almost aerial view of your office party.

This is a bilateral contract because you are promising to pay him $50,000 in exchange for his promise to be the photographer at your office party. You need his promise because if he is not willing to do this, you need to know as soon as possible so that you can make other plans.

The same applies in commercial contracts. If you are not going to promise to provide me the goods or materials or services I require on a certain date for a certain price, I need to find someone else. If you do promise to provide something, I need you to follow through on your promise. If we form an enforceable bilateral contract and you do not follow through on your promises, I may be able to sue you for breach of contract.

Whereas a bilateral contract is a promise for a promise, a unilateral contract is a promise for an act. For example, think of reward contracts. Imagine that I offer $500 to the person who finds my lost dog. I don't want 1000 people yelling "I accept" and then suing me for breach of contract if I don't pay them each $500. ($500 x 1000 people is $500,000!) I don't want promises. I want my dog.

If you see or hear my offer, I have communicated my offer to you. But what if you find my lost dog, see my address on the collar, and bring my dog to my house having never seen or heard my announcement offering $500 to the person who finds my dog? If my offer was not communicated to you as the identifiable offeree—that is, if you did not see my announcement—then I did not make you an offer. If I did not make you an offer, you cannot accept it. I still hope you return my dog to me, but I would not be contractually obligated to pay you the reward.

An offer is only an offer if it is communicated to an identifiable offeree, and only that identifiable offeree has the power of acceptance. For example, Dwight Howard was the first overall draft pick in the 2004 NBA draft. He played in the NBA until the 2021-2022 season when he moved to the Taiwanese-based Leopards. He was an NBA champion, eight-time All-Star, eight-time All-NBA Team honoree, five-time All-Defensive Team member, and three-time Defensive Player of the Year. As mentioned, he is 6'11 with a wingspan of 7'5". Standing flat footed, he can reach up to 9'2" in the air. My name is also Dwight. No one has ever asked to measure my wingspan, but we can safely assume that it is under six feet. If someone offers to pay $50,000 for Dwight Howard to show up and shoot some baskets for a business or charity event, I can't yell, "I accept" to accept the contract. Dwight Howard was the offeree, not Dwight Kealy. An enforceable offer needs to be communicated to an identifiable offeree and only that identifiable offeree has the power to accept the offer.

4) Inviting the Offeree to Accept the Terms of the Offer

Our final element of an enforceable offer is that the offeror must invite the offeree to accept the terms of the offer. The parties are not just talking about the value of goods and services. The parties are not just talking about their schedules and capabilities. In order for an offer to be enforceable, there must be a point at which the offeror invites the offeree to accept the terms of the offer.

If this invitation was made to an identifiable offeree, and it contained sufficiently definite terms, and it contained an objectively expressed intention to be bound, it sounds like we have an enforceable offer.

Termination of Offers

Before we can talk about acceptance, we need to know if the offer is still available to be accepted, or if it has terminated for some reason. Offers may terminate based on the actions of the parties or by operation of law (Restatement (Second) of Contracts § 36).

Termination of Offers by the Actions of the Parties

The three ways offers can terminate by actions of the parties are revocation, rejection, and counteroffer.

Revocation

Revocation occurs when an offeror rescinds an offer. Revocation must occur prior to acceptance. For example, imagine that I have a student in my business law course who is a talented basketball player who is projected to be drafted in the first round of the next NBA draft. He sits in the front row. I can see his shoes under the desk. I imagine what it would be like to have a signed pair of Michael Jordan's shoes from when he was a student-athlete at the University of North Carolina. My eyes fill with dollar signs. I offer the student $1000 for a signed pair of his basketball shoes. He tells me he'll think about it.

Then I think about it. Maybe I look at my bank account. Maybe I look at my university's rules defining ethical (and unethical) conduct with students. Then I contact the student to inform him that I am no longer willing to pay $1000 for a signed pair of his sneakers. At that moment, I have revoked my offer. It is no longer available for acceptance. If after my revocation the athlete insists that he wants to sell me his shoes for $1000, he can make me a new offer to sell them to me, but then I would have the power to accept or reject his offer. My original offer to buy his shoes terminated when I revoked my offer, and it is no longer available for acceptance.

Revocation can be expressed or implied. An expressed revocation is a revocation expressed in words. For example, saying, "I withdraw my offer to sell my car to you for $10,000" would be an expressed revocation. An implied revocation exists when the offeror performs an act inconsistent with the existence of the offer, and the act is made known to the offeree. For example, if I sell my car to someone else in your presence or someone tells you they just purchased my car—and let's assume that I only have one car to sell—then we have an implied revocation. My conduct of selling the car to someone else is inconsistent with my ability to sell the car to you, and you are aware of this conduct. I have revoked my offer by conduct, and it is no longer available for you to accept.

Irrevocable Offers, Option Contracts

Contracts can be made irrevocable with an option contract. An option contract is a separate agreement between a buyer and seller that gives the buyer the right, but not the obligation, to buy a specific asset at a specified price on or before a specific expiration date.

For example, imagine that I am trying to sell my car for $10,000 and you think this is a great deal for a car that you will need unless you get that one job you've applied for in New York City. If you get the job in New York, you don't think you'll even need a car. If you don't get that job, you definitely will want to purchase my car. The problem is, you won't know if you got the job in New York for two more months, and you're worried that by that time, my car will already be sold. An option contract could be the solution.

To form an option contract, you could offer to pay me $500 to keep my original offer to sell my car to you for $10,000 available to you for a period of three months. This is essentially a new bilateral contract where you promise to pay me $500 in exchange for my promise not to revoke my offer to sell you my car for $10,000 for a period of three months.

Rejection

Rejection occurs when an offeree rejects an offer. Using the example above, imagine I offer a student basketball player $1000 for a signed pair of his shoes and he laughs at me, and says, "No way. I wouldn't sell you my shoes. These shoes are going to be priceless someday." The basketball player has rejected my offer. This terminates my offer. Now imagine that the player has a career-ending injury at practice that evening and realizes that $1000 for a pair of shoes is a pretty good deal. He calls me up and says, "I accept your offer to pay me $1000 for a signed pair of my shoes." The problem for him is this: there is no offer to accept. His rejection terminated my offer. It is no longer available for him to accept.

Counteroffer

A counteroffer is a rejection of the original offer and a new offer. As a rejection, the counteroffer terminates the original offer. It is no longer available for acceptance. As a new offer, the parties change roles. The offeree who received the original offer is now the offeror who is making a new offer. The original offeror is now the offeree with the power to accept or reject the new offer.

For example, imagine that I offer to sell you my car for $10,000. This is a fair price, but you offer a counteroffer of $5,000. I am insulted, frankly no longer want to sell you my car, and tell you that the new price for the car is $20,000. You laugh and say, "Ok, I'm just kidding, I'll pay the $10,000." I refuse to sell you my car for $10,000 and then you sue me for breach of contract.

Did we have an enforceable contract for you to purchase my car for $10,000? No. Ten thousand dollars was my original offer, but you killed that offer with your counteroffer of $5000. At the point of your counteroffer, the only offer on the table is your offer to pay $5,000 for my car. I could have accepted this, but I rejected it with my counteroffer of $20,000. At the point of my counteroffer, the only offer available for acceptance is my offer to sell you my car for $20,000. When you said, "Just kidding, I'll pay the $10,000," the joke is on you because there is no $10,000 offer available for you to accept. What you did was offer a new counteroffer of $10,000. This rejected my offer of $20,000 and replaced it with your new offer to pay $10,000. As the offeree, I now have the power to accept or reject your offer. You cannot sue me to enforce my original offer to sell you my car for $10,000 because you terminated my offer with your counteroffer to purchase my car for $5,000.

Termination of Offers by Operation of Law

Offers may also terminate by operation of law. This can be based on a lapse of time, destruction of the subject matter, death or incapacity of the offeror or offeree, or the supervening illegality of the proposed contract.

Lapse of time

Contracts can terminate based on the amount of time specified in a contract, or if no time limit is specified, a contract may terminate by operation of law after a reasonable amount of time. What a reasonable amount of time will be will vary depending on the contract. For example, the reasonable amount of time to accept an offer to purchase crates of raw tomatoes would be shorter than the reasonable amount of time to purchase cut timber or gravel. Contracts that specify a termination date, including option contracts, will terminate at the time specified in the contract and not after a "reasonable amount of time" imposed by law.

Destruction of the Specific Subject Matter of the Offer

Destruction of the specific subject matter of an offer terminates the offer. This is true even if the destruction is not communicated to the offeree. For example, if someone makes an offer for you to buy their house or horse, I am assuming that you are contemplating the purchase of a house that has not been destroyed or a horse that has not died. If the subject matter of the offer is destroyed, the offer is terminated.

Death or Incapacity of the Offeror or Offeree

Unless a contract is irrevocable, an offer terminates with the death or incapacity of the offeror or offeree. Just as I cannot accept a $50,000 appearance fee made to a specific NBA player, I also cannot accept an offer made to my grandfather that I find after his death. Offers are personal agreements between the parties and terminate with the death or incapacity of the offeror or offeree.

Supervening Illegality

When we discuss defenses, we will see that an illegal contract is void. It is unenforceable and has no legal effect. The same is true with supervening illegality. Supervening illegality occurs when a statute or court decision makes an offer that was originally legal now illegal.

For example, it was legal to buy and sell Cuban cigars in the USA until President Kennedy signed a law making it illegal in 1962. If you made an offer to purchase 1 million Cuban cigars—or any Cuban product—prior to Kennedy signing the law, you would not be forced to purchase a product that would now be illegal for you to purchase. Due to the supervening illegality, your offer to purchase 1 million Cuban cigars would terminate automatically.

On an historical note, not related to sports, President Kennedy's press secretary Pierre Salinger recalled JFK requesting "about 1,000 Petit Upmanns" on the night before Kennedy signed the Cuban trade embargo into law. These were Kennedy's favorite Cuban cigar. Salinger spent the next day searching greater Washington, D.C. cigar shops to procure as many Petit Upmanns as possible. The next day, Kennedy summoned Salinger to ask if Salinger had been successful. Salinger confirmed that he had accumulated about 1200 cigars. After hearing this, Kennedy signed the law banning the importation of Cuban products.

Acceptance

Now that we have an enforceable offer that has not been terminated by the actions of the parties or by operation of law, we need to see if the offer has been accepted. Acceptance occurs when the offeree communicates to the offeror unconditional assent to the terms of the offer. In a bilateral contract, this is when the exchange of promises is made. In a unilateral contract, acceptance occurs when the act required in the offer is performed. For example, if I offer $500 to the person who finds and returns my lost dog, acceptance occurs when an offeree finds and returns my dog.

In a bilateral contract, communication of acceptance must follow the rules stated in the offer or in a manner similar to how the offer was delivered if the offer did not stipulate exactly how acceptance may be communicated. For example, if the offer requires a response by the offeree in person at a designated location by tomorrow at midnight, the offeree must accept in person at the designated location by tomorrow at midnight. If the offer is delivered by email and is silent about how acceptance should be communicated, acceptance could be communicated by email or in a similar form of communication.

The communication of the acceptance may be "by written or spoken words or by other action or by failure to act" (Restatement (Second) of Contracts). Courts have applied this broad understanding of contract formation to enforce a contract where an individual simply clicks "I agree" or "I accept" to the terms of a contract on a website. This is true even when individuals do not read all of the conditions, and even if they would not have accepted the terms had they read and understood them (See In Fteja v. Facebook, Inc., 841 F.Supp.2d 829 (S.D.N.Y. 2012)). In 2023, a Canadian court even found that a thumbs up emoji was sufficient to communicate acceptance.

The Common Law uses the "**mirror image rule.**" The mirror image rule requires that the terms of acceptance must exactly match the offer without any changes or modifications. If the acceptance does not mirror the offer, the "acceptance" would be viewed as a counteroffer, which terminates the original offer and proposes a new one. For example, imagine that a team offers an athlete $5 million to play for one season, and the player responds by agreeing to play for $5 million plus an additional $1 million to serve as assistant coach. The acceptance is not a mirror image of the offer because there is a new term. It is a counteroffer which terminates the original offer.

Unlike the Common Law mirror image rule, the UCC, which governs the sale of goods, will allow some new or different terms in the acceptance unless acceptance is expressly made conditional on the new or different term.

The UCC is particularly generous in finding contracts between merchants. Any new or additional terms in the acceptance between merchants will not defeat a contract. Instead, the new or additional terms will be viewed as proposals to be added to the contract except in the following three situations:

> 1) the offer expressly limits acceptance to the terms of the offer,
> 2) the new terms materially alter the contract, or
> 3) notification of objection to the new terms has already been given or is given within a reasonable time (§ 2-207. Additional Terms in Acceptance or Confirmation).

What does this mean for merchants? It means that if you insist on your terms, then your offer should expressly limit acceptance to your terms.

If someone introduces new terms with their acceptance, you should quickly object to the new terms.

Consideration

To form an enforceable contract, we need a valid offer, acceptance, consideration, and an absence of defenses. At this point we have defined offer and acceptance. Now we need to discuss consideration.

Consideration is the bargained for exchange that serves as the glue to a contract. It is a *quid pro quo* exchange of promises between the offeror and offeree. (In Latin, *quid pro quo* means "something for something").

Consideration requires binding promises that induce a current exchange of performance from the promisee and promisor for something the parties are not already obligated to do. For example, I don't have to sell you my car, and you don't have to pay me $10,000. We have consideration for a contract when we exchange your promise to pay me $10,000—something you are not already required to do— for my car—something I am not already required to provide.

Consideration helps us distinguish between a contract and a gift. For example, imagine that I am a football coach, and you are a wide receiver on the team. We just won the championship game largely because of your three touchdowns. While cheering on the sidelines, I look you in the eye and promise, "I am going to pay you $10,000 for each of the three touchdown passes you just caught. That's a total of $30,000."

You respond, "I accept." Worried that I may forget, you even grab a clipboard, paper, and pen and document our contract. It clearly documents my promise to pay you $30,000 for the three touchdown passes that you just caught, and we both sign it.

The next day you ask for your $30,000 and I refuse to pay. You produce our signed contract. I still refuse to pay. You then sue me for breach of contract. It looks like I made an objectively expressed intention to be bound to you, an identifiable offeree, that contained sufficiently definite terms, and I invited you to accept the terms. Therefore, I made an offer. It is also clear that you communicated your unconditional acceptance to the terms of my offer. Therefore, we have an offer and acceptance. However, this will not be an enforceable contract because it fails for a lack of consideration. Why? Because my promise to pay you $30,000 did not induce any performance on your behalf. You had already caught the touchdowns. Therefore, there was no bargained for exchange which means there was no consideration and no enforceable contract.

Consideration also exists when there is forbearance. Forbearance is intentionally abstaining from doing something one has a legal right to do. For example, as a football coach, I may not want my players skiing or snowboarding during the season to avoid injuries commonly associated with these sports. To discourage these activities, I could enter into a contract promising to pay $10,000 to players who do not ski or snowboard for a specific 12-month period. At the end of the 12-month period, players could then demand payment according to the terms of the contract. At first glance it may look like there is no consideration because the players didn't do anything, but they did. They intentionally abstained from engaging in lawful conduct to conform to the terms of the contract. This is forbearance which is legally sufficient consideration.

More controversially, a number of female track athletes complained that their sponsor Nike stopped paying them when the athletes got pregnant. For its part, "Nike has said that it fulfilled its contractual obligations, which until late 2019 included the right to cut athlete pay for any reason" (Gregory, S. (2021, July 8). *Motherhood Could Have Cost Olympian Allyson Felix. She Wouldn't Let It.* TIME).

Instead of Nike being able to cut athlete pay for any reason, imagine that Nike had a provision where athletes would get a bonus for not getting pregnant. If the athletes had a contract provision where they would get paid for not getting pregnant—thereby restricting their lawful freedom to get pregnant—then not getting pregnant would be an example of forbearance which would be legally sufficient consideration. I am not recommending this because it could still be horrible for public relations and the athletes could argue that this is against public policy, but we're talking about forbearance, not effective marketing.

Pre-existing Duty Rule

Consideration is only valid when the performance is not already required by law or contract. For example, police officers cannot accept reward money offered to the public for information leading to the arrest of a suspected criminal because the police already have a preexisting duty to seek and provide information leading to the arrest of suspected criminals. Similarly, I once contracted with a moving company to move my household goods from one house to another. I prepaid the contract price in full. Before unloading at the second location, the movers demanded 50% more money to finish the job, arguing that the household goods were heavier than they had expected. With nearly everything I owned locked in their truck, at night, in a new neighborhood, I agreed to pay the extra amount knowing that this new contract to pay the additional amount would be unenforceable because the movers already had a pre-existing duty to move my goods for the previously agreed upon price.

Consideration Substitutes

There are a couple of situations where consideration is not necessary. For example, under the doctrine of **promissory estoppel**, a contract may be enforceable when a promisee reasonably, foreseeably, and detrimentally relied upon an offeror's promise even if the promise is otherwise unenforceable. For example, imagine parents promise to pay their child while the child is attending law school. In response, the child may choose a different law school, forego getting a job, and choose a different apartment. After this, imagine the parents shrug their shoulders and refuse to pay, joking that the child should study harder to learn that their promise was not enforceable because of its lack of consideration. It is true that this sounds like a gift that lacks consideration, but here we have a child who may have reasonably, foreseeably, and detrimentally relied upon the parents' promise. This satisfies the definition of promissory estoppel which can be a substitute for consideration.

Another situation where consideration is not necessary, is in modifications of contracts under the UCC. The UCC is the controlling law for the sale of goods, and at times it may emphasize the good faith fair dealings of the parties more than the strict contractual formalities of the Common Law. For example, consideration is not necessary to modify a contract under the UCC so long as the modification is made in good faith (UCC § 2-209). To illustrate this, imagine that you buy a bicycle from a store for $1000. You then take it home and discover that another location of the same store sells the bicycle for $750. You could return to the store the next day and suggest that there was a mistake. In response, the store could decide that it wants to charge the correct amount by modifying your bicycle buy/sell contract to $750. At the Common Law, we would say there is no consideration to support the $750 contract and you have a pre-existing duty to pay $1000. With the sale of goods, if the parties agree to the modification in good faith, the UCC will accept it.

Adequacy of Consideration

Courts generally do not evaluate the adequacy of consideration. Maybe someone wants to pay $10,000 for my car. Maybe someone wants to pay $100,000 for my car. Maybe someone wants to provide me with free meals at their restaurant for the rest of my life for my car. These could all satisfy the bargained for exchange required of legally sufficient consideration. However, a court may get involved to evaluate consideration if the disparity suggests that agreement to the contract was not voluntary. For example, if I sold a functioning automobile to you for one dollar, a court may inquire if this agreement was the result of conduct that could trigger defenses such as mental capacity, fraud, duress, undue influence, or unconscionability.

Defenses

Now that we have an offer, acceptance, and consideration, we need to look at possible defenses to contract formation. Defenses are arguments explaining why a party should be justified or excused for breaking a promise. For example, imagine someone entered into an enforceable contract to purchase a specific gold (or gold-looking) watch for $10,000. There is an enforceable offer, acceptance, and consideration, and the parties are obligated to perform according to the terms of the contract. One party will provide $10,000. The other will provide the watch. If either party does not perform according to the terms of their agreement, they risk getting sued for breach of contract. Except, in this illustration, the transaction took place in a dark alley where the offeror pulled out a knife and told the offeree, "You will not leave the alley alive unless you give me $10,000 for this watch." It seems like there should be a defense against making this an enforceable contract. The defenses we will discuss are Illegality, Capacity, Fraud, Unconscionability, Undue Influence, Duress, the Statute of Frauds, Impossibility, Impracticability, and Frustration of Purpose.

The Defense of Illegality

A contract with an illegal purpose is **void**. A void contract is one that has no legal force or effect. It is not legally binding or enforceable. It may be obvious that someone who performs their end of a contract to murder someone for $1 million is not going to be able to sue the offeror for $1 million upon completion of the act. Other acts may be less severe, but still illegal or against public policy, and therefore void.

Consider the dispute between sports agent David Sloane and pitcher Justus Sheffield. Sloane sued Sheffield for an $80,000 fee he was owed according to the terms of their contract. The problem for Sloane was that although he was a licensed sports agent in Florida and Alabama when they entered their contract, and he even would be licensed in Tennessee before Sheffield signed his $1.6 million dollar contract with the Cleveland Indians, Sloane was not a registered agent in Tennessee when they entered their contract in Tennessee. Tennessee requires sports agents to be licensed with the state before forming a contract with an athlete. Sloan was not. Therefore, the contract between Sloane and Sheffield was illegal. Therefore, it was void, and Sloan would not receive his fee.

Similarly, in *Zinn v. Parrish*, sports agent Zinn sued former NFL defensive back Lemar Parrish for payment according to the terms of their contract. Parrish responded by arguing that the contract should not be enforceable because Zinn acted illegally by providing investment advice without first registering under the Investment Advisers Act of 1940. In this case, the court held that Zinn's isolated investment transactions "did not constitute engaging in the business of advising others on investment securities" (*Zinn v. Parrish*, 644 F.2d 360 (7th Cir. 1981)). Therefore, their contract was not illegal and not void.

The Defense of Incapacity

In order to form an enforceable contract, both parties must have the capacity to enter into the contract at the time of contract formation. A party may lack capacity due to youth or mental incompetence. A contract entered into by a person who did not have the capacity to enter the contract is voidable by the person who did not have the capacity to enter into the contract at the time the contract was formed. Notice that the defense of incapacity does not say that all contracts formed with those who lack capacity are automatically void. It says that they are voidable. That means these contracts are able to be voided, but they are only able to be voided by the party who lacked capacity.

For example, most states recognize the age of eighteen years as the age of majority. Prior to the age of eighteen, individuals are considered minors and lack the capacity to enter contracts. Imagine a 35-year-old sports agent enters a contract with an up-and-coming 14-year-old tennis star. The agent agrees to pay the tennis star a guaranteed

$100,000 every year for the next 10 years in exchange for the tennis star giving the agent 5% of all endorsement deals that the athlete signs over the next 10 years. Then, at the age of 15, the tennis star suffers a career-ending injury. There will be no endorsement deals.

To get out of paying $100,000 per year, the sports agent may want to terminate the contract, arguing that the tennis player lacked capacity to enter their contract because the tennis player was 14 years old when their contract was formed. It is true that the 14-year-old lacked the capacity to enter contracts. However, the defense of incapacity says that a contract is voidable by the party that did not have capacity at the time the contract was formed. The 35-year-old sports agent did not lack capacity at the time the contract was formed. The then 14-year-old hopeful future tennis star lacked capacity. Therefore, the contract is only voidable by the former tennis player, not the 35-year-old sports agent. Unlike an illegal contract that is automatically void, this contract is only voidable at the option of the individual who lacked capacity. My guess in this situation is that the former future tennis star has no interest in terminating the agreement and can enjoy receiving $100,000 per year for 10 years in exchange for 5% of the zero endorsement deals that will probably materialize.

The Defense of Fraud

Fraud exists when one party makes a material misrepresentation of a past or present fact, knowing the statement is false, made with the intent to induce the other party to rely on the misrepresentation, and the other party justifiably relies on the misrepresentation causing them damages. In other words, one party to a contract lied with the intent to get the other party to rely on the lie. The other party did rely on the lie, and it caused them financial harm.

Noticed that the misrepresentation must be a material one. A material misrepresentation is one that goes to the basis of the bargain. A misrepresentation is material if you wouldn't have entered the contract had you know the truth. If you want to sell me your 1965 truck and tell me that it gets 40 miles per gallon, that is likely a lie, but it would not be material to me if I am just buying the truck to throw away the engine and make a trailer out of the truck bed. If I am just buying the truck for the truck bed, the truck's gas mileage is immaterial because it is irrelevant to why I am buying the truck.

There are two types of fraud: Fraud in the Execution and Fraud in the Inducement. **Fraud in the Execution** exists when a party to a contract is tricked into entering a contract. When this happens, the contract is void. For example, imagine that a sports agent goes around to different teams asking athletes to sign birthday cards for sick children and the athletes sign not realizing that they were signing an agency agreement. The agent made a material misrepresentation, knew it was false, intended to deceive the victim, and the victim justifiably relied on the misrepresentation causing damages. This is Fraud in the Execution because the athletes did not even know they were entering a contract. Therefore, this contract is void.

Fraud in the Inducement exists when a party knows it is entering a contract but does not understand the subject matter. When this happens, the contract is voidable at the election of the person who was defrauded. For example, imagine that you knew you were signing a contract to play for a team, but you thought it was with a team in Colorado and not a team in Florida. You were tricked. You can call the contract void or, if you decide that you like the Florida team, you could choose to keep the contract in force. The contract is voidable by the person who was defrauded.

The Defense of Unconscionability

The defense of unconscionability is available when there is unfair bargaining power between the parties resulting in a contract where consent is not voluntary, and the outcome contains oppressive and unfair terms that shocks the conscience of the court. To determine if a contract is unconscionable, the court will look at the time when the contract was formed to see if there was any unfair advantage taken by one party over another. If the contract was unfairly and oppressively biased toward the party with the superior bargaining power, "the court may refuse to enforce the contract, or it may enforce the remainder of the contract without the unconscionable clause, or it may so limit the application of any unconscionable clause as to avoid any unconscionable result" (UCC 2-302).

An example of where there may be unfair bargaining power is in a **contract of adhesion**. A contract of adhesion is a contract written *exclusively* by one party and presented to the other party on a take-it-or-leave-it basis. The defense of unconscionability gives the courts the opportunity to correct a contract when it appears that the party with superior influence was using the contract to take advantage of a weaker party.

For example, imagine that a national property manager presents a lease to an older widow that the widow must sign to keep a roof over her head. The lease was drafted by the property manager's attorneys.

The lease contains a clause that says that if the tenant ever misses a monthly lease payment, not only will she be evicted, but her personal property will serve as collateral for any debt owed to the property manager. The widow did not negotiate the terms of the lease. She just signed it. The widow then misses some payments, owes some money, and with contract in hand, the property manager seeks not only to evict the widow, but to also sell the widow's television, couch, blankets—ALL her personal property as collateral—to satisfy the debt she owes.

The lease is an enforceable contract and it said that personal property would be collateral, but we have unfair bargaining power and an outcome that may shock the conscience of the court. Therefore, the tenant could use the defense of unconscionability. In response, the court could refuse to enforce the contract, enforce the contract without the unconscionable term, or somehow limit the application of the unconscionable clause to avoid an unconscionable result.

The Defense of Undue Influence

The defense of undue influence arises in relationships where one party dominates another to the extent the other party lacks freewill. In these situations, the contract may lack voluntary consent and is voidable by the party that was unfairly influenced by the other party. Common examples involve the elderly who may fear that they will lose healthcare, housing, or other necessary assistance if they do not agree to give money or an inheritance to an individual caregiver who is in a more dominant bargaining position.

There is a presumption of undue influence when a contract enriches the dominant party in a fiduciary relationship. A fiduciary relationship is one involving trust and confidence where an agent has the duty to act in the best interest of their principal. This includes attorneys, financial advisors, and sports agents.

For example, imagine that an elderly couple wants me to draft their wills, form a trust, manage their investments, and stop by occasionally to see if they need any assistance maintaining their large home that sits on their large farm now surrounded by encroaching suburbs. They have three children out of state who rarely visit. The children have said that they have no interest in keeping the family home and plan on selling it when their parents pass away. As compensation for my work and kindness, the elderly couple wants to give me their farm when they pass away.

As an attorney, I am capable of drafting a will that memorializes this couple's desire to give me their farm when they pass away. The problem with this idea is their children who may be upset when I inherit the property instead of them and the rebuttable presumption that I used undue influence on their parents when, as their fiduciary, I drafted a will that benefited myself. If the elderly couple insists on giving me their farm for my services, I would advise them to seek the advice of another attorney who could ensure that they understand their situation and desires, and have the other attorney draft any documents that might benefit me.

The Defense of Duress

The defense of duress is available when a party enters into a contract under fear or threats that make the party incapable of exercising free will. The threatened act must be wrongful or illegal. The defense would obviously be available if someone held a gun to another's head and said, "Sign the contract." However, the defense would not be available if someone threatened civil litigation to enforce a contract because this threat is neither wrongful nor illegal. This is true even though the threat is likely to cause fear.

Similarly, economic duress alone is usually insufficient as a defense. For example, a business owner may feel that they are under duress and lack free will when they have no other choice but to sign a contract with unfavorable terms. However, they are unlikely to be able to use the defense of duress to get out of their contract unless the other party created the need for an item or service and then demanded an exorbitant price to address the need they created.

The Defense of the Statute of Frauds

Generally speaking, oral and written contracts are equally enforceable. However, there is an exception for contracts that are subject to the Statute of Frauds. If a contract is subject to the Statute of Frauds, a party to the contract can use the defense to argue that the contract should only be enforceable if it is supported by a writing containing all essential terms that is signed by the party against whom enforcement is sought. Notice that this does not say that the contract itself must be in writing—although in practice that is probably always a good idea. It says that these contracts need to be supported by a writing signed by the party against whom enforcement is sought. The writing does not need to be the contract. The writing could be an email to someone who is not even a party to the contract that contains the essential terms and is signed by the party against whom enforcement is sought.

The types of contracts that fall under the Statute of Frauds are contracts that may make us suspicious as to whether someone really intended to be bound to a contract absent some written proof. The types of contracts subject to the Statute of Frauds vary by state, but the seven most common ones can be rememered using the acronym MYLEGS. "My legs" stands for contracts involving Marriage, Years, Land, Executors, Guarantees, and the Sale of Goods over $500.

Marriage

If marriage, separation, or divorce is the consideration for a contract, the contract must be supported by written evidence containing the essential terms signed by the party against whom enforcement is sought. This includes prenuptial agreements. If parents say, "We'll give you a house if you get married," the promise would be unenforceable absent a writing containing the essential terms, signed by the parents.

Years

If a contract, by its own terms, cannot be performed within one year from the day after a contract is formed, it needs to be supported by a writing that will satisfy the Statute of Frauds. A contract to be performed over someone's lifetime is not subject to the Statute of Frauds because according to the terms of the contract, it is not impossible that a lifetime contract could be fully performed within one year. That is, the person could die within the year.

The same is true with projects where it is incredibly unlikely that they will be finished within one year because it is the sort of project that generally takes much longer to complete. The Statute of Frauds applies if the contract *cannot* be performed within one year—not when it is very unlikely that it will be performed within one year.

A contract may also be subject to the Statute of Frauds even if it will only take three months to complete if, based on the terms of the contract, it is impossible for this three-month contract to be completed within one year of when this contract was formed. For example, an oral contract for me to teach a course on Sports Law during a summer semester two years from now would be subject to the Statute of Frauds because the contract could not be performed within 365 days of when the oral contract was formed.

Land

Contracts involving an interest in land are subject to the Statute of Frauds. This includes anything attached to the land like buildings, crops, and minerals. This also includes easements and leases with a duration of more than one year. However, there is an exception to the writing requirement for land when a party has possession of the land plus something else that provides evidence of the contract. Examples of this "something else" that provides evidence of the contract could include payment for the land, paying taxes on it, or grading or bringing in utilities.

For example, imagine we orally agree that I will sell you my house for $1 million. You pay this price in full, but I refuse to move out and give you the deed to my house. If you sue for damages, I would be obligated to give you your money back, but a court would not enforce this contract to sell my house absent a writing that satisfies the Statute of Frauds. However, if you pay me and then move into the house, but I refuse to sign a contract or give you a deed, you have established possession of the house plus a "something else" (that is, payment) sufficient to remove the contract from the Statute of Frauds. In response, a court could transfer title from me to you even absent a writing if this is necessary to avoid injustice.

Executor

An executor is the person who administrates the distribution of property for someone who has died. Contracts of an executor need to be supported by a writing. If an executor tells you that you are going to get your grandfather's gold watch, this will not be an enforceable contract absent a writing that satisfies the Statute of Frauds.

Guarantee

A Guarantee is a promise to pay for the debt of someone else. If you buy a car using credit and then stop making payments on it, the car dealer cannot sue *me* to pay for your car. This is true even if you told the car dealer that I would make the monthly payments for you if you ever failed to make the payments. This would be a guarantee contract, and it would be unenforceable absent a writing signed by me that could satisfy the Statute of Frauds. There is an exception to the writing requirement for guarantees and that is when the main purpose is to protect the guarantor's own economic interest. For example, if I go with you to buy farm equipment that we use on my farm, a court may believe that I was promising to pay for the equipment even absent a writing signed by me.

Sale of Goods of $500 or more

The UCC is the controlling law for the sale of goods. It provides that "a contract for the sale of goods for the price of $500 or more [will] not be enforceable...unless there is some writing sufficient to indicate that a contract for sale has been made between the parties [that is] signed by the party against whom enforcement is sought..." (UCC § 2-201).

Impossibility, Impracticability, and Frustration of Purpose

There are other defense such as the defenses of impossibility, impracticability, and frustration of purpose. The defense of impossibility is available if performing the contract is objectively impossible. The defense of impracticability is available if there is an unforeseen contingency that would result in an increase cost or burden far beyond what either party anticipated. The defense of frustration of purpose is available when the principal purpose of the contract is substantially frustrated, and the nonoccurrence of the event that caused the frustration was a basic assumption of the contract (17A Am. Jur. 2d Contracts, § 638, Applicability of doctrine of frustration of purpose; Restatement (Second) of Contracts § 265).

How to Read a Contract

Now that we have an enforceable contract that consists of an offer, acceptance, consideration and an absence of applicable defenses, we need to examine how to read a contract and what to do if there is a breach.

The starting point for interpreting a contract is to look at the plain meaning of the contract. Courts refer to the **Four Corners of the Contract.** This refers to the four corners of the paper the contract is written on. It asserts that if the written contract is clear, courts should apply the plain meaning of the contract.

However, sometimes contracts are ambiguous. This means they are not clear or may have more than one interpretation. For example, imagine that we enter a contract where I am going to sell you fruit. Our contract states the following:

**Seller shall deliver one million pounds of
fruit to buyer for one million dollars.**

This statement is ambiguous because there are multiple meanings for what I could deliver to satisfy our agreement. I could deliver apples, bananas, oranges, or grapes—just to name a few. All these options satisfy our contract where I promised to deliver one million pounds of fruit. But imagine that I deliver one million pounds of bananas to you, and you refuse to pay me because…you're a winery. You make wine, not smoothies, and the only fruit you want to accept from me is grapes.

When a contractual term is ambiguous, it will often be interpreted against the party that drafted the contract. For example, in *O'Brien v. The Ohio State University* (OSU), OSU argued against enforcing the contract they had formed with their former basketball coach James O'Brien because it was going to force OSU to pay their fired former coach nearly $2.5 million. In response, the court noted, "There is no evidence to suggest OSU lacked a meaningful choice or opportunity to negotiate the contract with O'Brien; morevoer, OSU was the drafting party. OSU is not lacking in sophistication, and has only been prejudiced as a result of being held to its own bargain." Therefore, their contract was enforced.

Regarding our ambiguous fruit delivery contract, the UCC may also look at Course of Performance, Course of Dealing, and Usage of Trade to help resolve an ambiguous term. **Course of Performance** looks at how the parties have performed other transactions within the contract to help define what was meant by the ambiguous term. **Course of Dealing** looks at previous transactions between the parties. **Usage of Trade** looks at terms common to a place, vocation, or trade. All of these can be used to justify an expectation one might have regarding an otherwise ambiguous contractual term.

Material vs. Immaterial Breach

At some point in contract law we need to address what happens when a party to a contract doesn't do what they said they would do. When a party breaks the terms set out in a contract, we say that the party breached the contract. How courts will address a breach of contract varies depending on if the breach was a material breach or an immaterial breach. A material breach is one that cannot be corrected. This makes the contract meaningless. An immaterial breach is one where a contract is still in force, but the non-breaching party may be entitled to recover damages.

The case of *Jacob & Youngs, Inc. v. Kent* involved a dispute over when a breach is material or immaterial. In the case, a general contractor (Jacob) built a residence for Kent. Jacob sued Kent to recover an upaid balance. In response, Kent argued that the contractors were in breach of their contract for failing to comply with the terms of the contract.

The term in dispute was that the contract explicitly stated that Jacob should use pipe from Reading Iron Company. Instead, Jacob used pipe from Cohoes Rolling Mill Company. Kent insisted that Jacob should replace the Cohoes Pipe with Reading Pipe even if it would require demolishing and rebuilding the house. The court determined that the reason for the clause identifying Reading Pipe was to require galvanized steel pipes instead of the cast iron pipes that were common at that time. Both Reading and Cohoes pipes were galvanized steel pipes.

The court argued that the breach was immaterial and that the contractors had substantially performed their duties under the contract. Therefore, their contract was still in force and homeowner Kent was required to pay the contract price for the house minus any financial damages caused by the contractors using Cohoes Pipe instead of Reading Pipe.

For Cause

Many agency contracts, including employment and sponsorship agreements, allow what is called termination "for cause." This is used when a party's poor performance or misconduct amounts to a material breach of the agreement. This would allow, for example, a university to not have to pay its coach for the remaining three years of a multi-year, multi-million-dollar contract if the coach's conduct amounted to a material breach of contract. This is illustrated below in the case of *O'BRIEN v. The OHIO STATE UNIVERSITY* (OSU) (2007-Ohio-4833).

In 1997 OSU hired O'Brien to be their head basketball coach. At the time, the team was not in great shape. They had not been to the Final Four in nearly three decades. In O'Brien's first year as head coach (1997-1998), the team only won eight games. The next year, the team won more games than any other OSU men's basketball team in history. They won the Big Ten conference title, earned an NCAA tournament berth, and advanced to the tournament's Final Four. Jim O'Brien was named the 1999 NCAA Division 1 basketball coach of the year.

As you can imagine, OSU was eager to secure O'Brien to a new contract that would keep him at OSU longer. The new contract significantly increased O'Brien's salary and extended his time at OSU by five years (through 2007). However, the contract stipulated that the salary would not be paid if O'Brien was fired "for cause". The contract then defined "for cause" as one or more of the following:

1) [A] Material breach of the agreement…where the coach fails to remedy the breach within a reasonable time, or

2) [A] Violation of law, policy, rule, or regulation of the NCAA or Big Ten which leads to a 'major' infraction investigation by the NCAA or Big Ten which results in a finding…of lack of institutional control over the men's basketball program or Ohio State being sanctioned.

I'll jump ahead and tell you the end of the story first. O'Brien gets fired about four years and $2.5 million before the end of his five-year contract. If OSU fired him "for cause," he would receive nothing. If OSU did not fire him "for cause," he would be entitled to $2.5 million in damages according to the terms of their contract. OSU fired O'Brien and paid him nothing. In response, O'Brien sued OSU.

Now, here is the background. At the end of the 1997-1998 season— that was O'Brien's first season as coach when OSU won only eight games—a 21-year-old named Alex Radojevic arrived at OSU for an "unofficial recruiting visit." At the time, Radojevic was playing at a community college in Kansas. But in case you think this kid from Kansas might not get noticed on his "unofficial recruiting visit," I should share that Radojevic was a 7'3" Serbian native who would be the number 12 overall selection in the 1999 NBA draft.

O'Brien and his staff started recruiting Radojevic. O'Brien visited him in Kansas where O'Brien learned that Radojevic's father had passed away. Radojevic then returned to OSU for an official visit. Then an individual associated with Radojevic's family asked O'Brien if he could assist Radojevic's mother back in Serbia. In response, O'Brien gave an unmarked envelope containing $6,000 to his assistant with orders to deliver the envelope to a waiter at a restaurant in New York City who went by the name Spomenko "Semi" Patrovic. I am not expecting readers to be experts in late 1990s NCAA regulations, but I am hoping that you sense that it was probably a violation of NCAA rules to slide an unmarked envelope containing $6000 to a guy named "Semi" in New York City for the benefit of a college basketball recruit.

Now fast forward five years to 2003. By this time, O'Brien had coached the team to the 1999 Final Four, the 2000 and 2002 Big Ten regular season co-championships, the 2002 Big Ten tournament Championship, and a school-record four consecutive NCAA tournament appearances (1999-2002). At this time O'Brien also learns about a lawsuit involving an OSU athletics booster that raised questions about Radojevic. This led to a 2004 deposition likely to reveal information about Radojevic and OSU. In response, in April 2004, O'Brien informed the OSU athletic director about the money he sent to Radojevic's mother. The case notes that O'Brien "maintains that the $6,000 was a loan, nothing more, and that he was compelled to offer assistance out of sympathy toward Radojevic's mother."

In May 2004, the athletic director advised O'Brien to retain his own independent legal counsel. In June 2004, OSU fires O'Brien. A year later, the NCAA issued OSU a notice of infractions including six relating to Radojevic. OSU vacated its wins from 1999 to 2002, removed all references to team accomplishments for those years, and paid back all tournament money due to rule violations during O'Brien's tenure.

This was devastating for OSU and its fans and, on the surface, it may seem obvious that OSU would be justified in firing O'Brien "for cause." But remember, O'Brien's contract only identified two situations where he could be terminated "for cause." Let's look at each clause more carefully.

1) [A] Material breach of the agreement...where the coach fails to remedy the breach within a reasonable time.

O'Brien argued that even if there was a material breach, O'Brien was never given an opportunity to remedy the breach within a reasonable time as required by his contract.

2) [A] Violation of law, policy, rule, or regulation of the NCAA or Big Ten which leads to a 'major" infraction investigation by the NCAA or Big Ten which results in a finding...of lack of institutional control over the men's basketball program or Ohio State being sanctioned.

We know that a year after O'Brien was fired, the NCAA issued OSU a notice of infractions regarding Radojevic, but at the time of O'Brien's termination, there was no finding that O'Brien's conduct would lead to a major infraction, or showed a lack of institutional control, or would result in OSU being sanctioned.

It may not seem fair for OSU to pay nearly $2.5 million to the coach that got them punished by the NCAA. But this is contract law where we read the four corners of the contract, and the contract stated that termination "for cause" would only occur in two situations. At the time of O'Brien's termination, neither of these situations had occurred. The court concluded that "The parties agreed that OSU could not fire O'Brien unless a specific condition occurred and, as of June 8, 2004, that condition had not occurred." Therefore, O'Brien was not fired "for cause" and he was entitled to nearly $2.5 million from OSU.

The O'Brien situation forced universities to rethink their coaches' contracts. For example, whereas O'Brien's contract identified only two reasons where he could be fired "for cause", his replacement's contract identified 15 justifications for termination "for cause."

Other Clauses

Contractual clauses are not limited to the topic of termination. For example, the NBA's Uniform Player Contract prohibits "any activity that a reasonable person would recognize as involving or exposing the participant to a substantial risk of bodily injury." These *hazardous activity clauses* often identify specific prohibited activities such as skydiving, hang gliding, snow skiing, and driving or riding on a motorcycle or moped. In 2008, Golden State Warriors player Monta Ellis was suspended 30 games without pay after suffering a torn ligament in a moped accident.

A *morals clause* gives teams, leagues, and companies that endorse athletes the ability to terminate contracts or fine athletes who engage in criminal or "immoral" behavior. For example, the NBA allows its commissioner to suspend or fine a player who "has been guilty of conduct that does not conform to standards of morality or fair play, that does not comply at all times with all federal, state, and local laws, or that is prejudicial or detrimental to the Association." The definition of "standards of morality" is subjective. For example, in 2023, NBA player Ja Morant had several instances where he was caught flashing a gun on Instagram Live. Defenders of Morant argued that having a gun is not illegal. Others argued that, in light of the many deaths caused by gun violence, flashing a gun violates the morals clause as behavior that is detrimental to the reputation of the NBA.

Major League Baseball's constitution contains the *Best Interests of Baseball* clause. This clause allows the commissioner to investigate any act "alleged or suspected to be not in the best interest of the national game of Baseball." In 2020, the Commissioner of Baseball, Rob Manfred, used this power to penalize the Houston Astros for sign-stealing in 2017. The Commissioner suspended the Astro's General Manager and Field Manager from baseball for one year, forfeited the Astro's regular first and second round selections in the 2020 and 2021 Player Drafts, and fined the team $5 million. The Commissioner also granted immunity to the players involved in the scandal—a decision the Commissioner later said he regretted.

Prior to 1975, Major League Baseball contracts had a **reserve clause** where teams retained the rights to trade, sell, or release players. The clause was struck down in arbitration in 1975, leading to widespread free agency in Major League Baseball.

Other clauses include a **weight clause** where an overweight player gets a financial bonus for reporting to training camp under a certain weight, an **attendance clause** where an athlete gets a bonus if spectator attendance exceeds a certain level, and a **no-trade clause** where a player has the right to reject a trade under certain conditions. Pitcher Roger Clemens even had a **freedom clause** with the New York Yankees that allowed him to only show up on days when he was scheduled to pitch.

Personal Service Contracts

As a general rule, parties are free to assign or delegate their rights and duties under a contract to someone else. For example, if we have a contract for me to paint your house for $5,000, I have a duty to paint your house, but I am free to delegate this duty to someone else to perform. Maybe I could find a subcontractor who would paint it for $3,000 and I could pocket $2,000 just to make sure the job is completed. I also have a right to receive $5,000 from you for painting your house, but I could assign this right to another party like a creditor, charity, or friend. Technically speaking, rights are assigned and duties are delegated, but the term "assignment and delegation" is deliberately generic in applying to both.

An exception to the freedom of assignment and delegation occurs in Personal Service Contracts. A **Personal Service Contract** contemplates the unique talents, abilities, and skills of a party to a contract. These cannot be delegated. For example, if you hire me to paint your house because I am a modern-day Picasso or Van Gough, I cannot delegate my duty to paint your house to an average exterior painting contractor. You are paying me because I am a uniquely talented master artist. Similarly, if a soccer team in Miami offers $50-$60 million per year to a specific soccer player named Lionel Messi, Lionel Messi cannot delegate his duty to play to another player even if the other player is younger, stronger, or faster. The contract is personal to Messi for his unique talents, abilities, and skills—perhaps including his ability to draw crowds. This cannot be delegated to anyone else.

However, just because a famous artist or athlete cannot delegate their duty to perform does not mean that the artist or athlete can be forced to perform. Besides the practical desire to avoid the poor performance that could follow paying an athlete to stand on a field or court against the athlete's will, the Thirteenth Amendment of the U.S. Constitution forbids involuntary servitude. This precludes forcing someone to perform their duties under a personal service contract.

Performance and Remedies for Breach

Now that we know what an enforceable contract is and how to read it, we need to look at performance and possible remedies if there is a breach.

Performance

The New York Mets pay former Major League Baseball player Bobby Bonilla $1.19 million every July 1st and they will continue to do so through July 1st, 2035. Why? Because that is what Bonilla's contract with the Mets requires. In 2000, the Mets decided to buy out the $5.9 million remaining on Bonilla's contract. Bonilla and his agent offered the Mets a deal where they could defer payment for a decade and then pay Bonilla $1.19 million every year for 25 years. That is, from 2011 to 2035. Mets ownership at the time accepted the offer thinking they would earn a greater return from the investments they had in what turned out to be a Bernie Madoff ponzi scheme. Now under new ownership since 2020, the Mets embrace their famously unsuccessful contract by celebrating July 1st as Bobby Bonilla Day. Bonilla has a second deferred payment contract with the Baltimore Orioles where he is paid $500,000 every year for 25 years. That contract began in 2004 and will end in 2029.

In 2023, pitcher Shohei Ohtani agreed to a record-breaking 10-year, $700 million contract with the Los Angeles Dodgers. That would be $70 million per year. But in an effort to help the Dodgers free up money for other players—or to avoid California taxes—Ohtani agreed to defer all but $2 million of his annual salary. The remaining $68 million of his $70 million per year contract will be paid, without interest, from 2034 to 2043. I mention California taxes because California Controller Malia Cohen asked Congress to step in to address the $680 million payout that will begin in 2034—when Ohtani may no longer live in California and be subject to its 14.4% state income tax.

After sales of Ohtani's new Dodgers jersey broke the record for the most jerseys sold in a 48-hour period, some suggested that the

Dodgers may make more money selling Ohtani jerseys and the broadcasting rights to watch Ohtani in his native Japan than the $2 million they are paying Ohtani per year. It is true that Ohtani's jersey sales hit a record after the trade was announced and that he is a fan-favorite in Japan. However, the Dodgers don't own the rights to their team's jersey sales or television rights. Major League Baseball owns the rights to both licensed merchandise—like jerseys—and international broadcasting. The league then splits the profits equally among the 30 MLB teams. The Dodgers benefit more exclusively in sales at Dodger Stadium and their own Dodgers Clubhouse stores.

Not only can MLB contracts require teams to pay for players who no longer play the sport, they can also require teams to pay the salaries of players that are playing for other teams. In 2016, the Boston Red Sox signed a seven-year, $217 million deal with pitcher David Price. That was the richest contract ever given to a pitcher at that time. Then in 2020, with three years and $96 million in salary remaining, the Red Sox traded Price to the Los Angeles Dodgers where the Red Soxs were expected to continue paying about half of Price's remaining salary. Why would a team pay half of the salary of a player playing for a different team? One reason could be that it is better to pay half the contract price for a player not meeting expectations than the whole contract price. Another reason could be a desire to reduce salaries to avoid a "luxury tax" penalty imposed on clubs that exceed the league's payroll ceiling.

Specific performance

Specific performance is a contractual remedy in which the court orders a party to perform its promise because monetary damages would be insufficient to fix the harm. This may be an option in forcing the sale of property, but you cannot—and perhaps would not even want to—force an athlete to play for a team they refuse to play for.

Remedies for Breach

When a party to a contract breaches a contract, the non-breaching party may be entitled to financial damages caused by the breach. Contractual damages include Liquidated Damages, Expectation Damages, Consequential Damages, and Incidental Damages.

Liquidated Damages

Liquidated damages are an agreed upon amount of money that a breaching party will owe the non-breaching party in the event of a breach. As with any clause, courts will look to defenses such as the defense of unconscionability to ensure that the clause was not formed by parties with unfair bargaining power creating an unfair result that shocks the conscience of the court. However, a liquidated damages clause will generally be enforceable if the damages would be difficult to ascertain at the time of contracting and the amount of liquidated damages is reasonable.

For example, in *O'Brien v. The Ohio State University* we learned that the contract for Coach O'Brien had a liquidated damages clause that provided that if his contract was terminated for any reason other than "for cause", O'Brien would be entitled to his base salary and normal employee benefits. To compensate for "loss of collateral business opportunities (whether media, public relations, camps, clinics, apparel or similar contracts, sponsorships or any other supplemental or collateral compensation or benefit of any kind) [the liquidated damages clause also entitled O'Brien to]…an amount equal to three and a half (3.5) times the product of (y) the Coach's then current base salary…and (z) the number of years remaining under the term of this agreement."

This liquidated damages clause was enforceable because, at the time of contracting, it was difficult to know what losses O'Brien might suffer as a "loss of collateral business opportunities," and a court may find that three and a half times O'Brien's remaining salary was reasonable.

Expectation Damages

Expectation damages are damages designed to put the non-breaching party in as good of a position as they expected to be in had the other party fully performed the contract. For example, imagine that a city enters into an enforceable contract with a contractor to build a sports stadium for $1 billion. Halfway and $500 million into the project, the contractor abandons the project and the city needs to hire a new contractor to finish the project. The city hires a new contractor who will be able to finish the stadium for $600 million. The result will be a completed stadium for a total cost of $1.1 billion. This is $100 million more than the city expected based on their contract with the original contractor. Therefore, the original contractor would be obligated to pay the city $100 million in expectation damages. Notice that if the second contractor was able to finish the project for under or equal to the originally expected total amount of $1 billion, the original contractor would not owe any expectation damages.

Consequential Damages

Consequential damages are additional damages that are reasonably foreseeable consequences of a breach that were known at the time of contracting. Using an example based on the famous case of *Hadley v. Baxendale*, imagine that my business loses internet service and I contract with a delivery company to deliver hardware necessary to restore my internet service. Our contract makes it clear that the hardware must be delivered tomorrow. But the delivery company does not deliver it tomorrow. They deliver it five days later. As a consequence of the delivery company's breach, I may not be able to run my internet-based business. If my business happens to be Amazon, we could be looking at lost revenue of over $1 billion dollars every day for five days as a consequence of the delivery company's breach. It may be true that I have lost revenue as a consequence of the delivery company's breach, but consequential damages will only be enforceable if the damages were both a reasonably foreseeable consquence of the breach and the consequences were known to the delivery company at the time of contracting.

Incidental Damages

Incidental damages are the additional costs associated with obtaining substitute performance. For example, a breach may require the non-breaching party to interview potential replacement contractors, visit job sites, return defective goods, or pay for the reasonable costs related to mitigating the immediate effects of the breach. These costs add up, and can be included in an award that includes incidental damages.

Punitive and Exemplary Damages

I also want to mention punitive and exemplary damages, but only to let you know that they are generally not awarded in breach of contract cases. These damages are designed to punish or to make an example out of the wrongdoer to deter similar conduct in the future. Punitive and exemplary damages are typically reserved for tort law cases involving intentional misconduct. Where you might see these damages in a contract law case is when a defendant uses fraud not only as a contract defense, but also as a counterclaim for the intentional tort of fraud.

Mitigation

When calculating damages caused by a breach of contract, it is important to note that the non-breaching party has a duty to mitigate its damages. The duty to mitigate requires the non-breaching party to make reasonable efforts to limit the harm caused by the other party's breach. For example, imagine a commercial tenant agrees to pay a landlord $20 million over the next 10 years, but then breaches the contract. The landlord cannot keep the building vacant for 10 years while demanding $20 million from the former tenant. The landlord needs to make reasonable efforts to find a new tenant. If the landlord finds a tenant willing to pay $20 million, the landlord may not have suffered any financial damages other than incidental damages for things like the advertising necessary to find a new tenant. If the landlord's reasonable efforts can only find a tenant willing to pay $15 million, then the landlord's mitigation efforts reduced the damages from $20 million to $5 million. This would reduce the damages owed by the breaching tenant down to $5 million.

Chapter 3: Tort Law

A tort is a civil wrong for which courts may impose liability. It reflects society's understanding of fairness and a belief that when individuals cause harm to others, the individuals who cause the harm should be held responsible for compensating the individuals harmed. The individual who commits a tort is called a tortfeasor.

Tort Law developed in the English Common Law tradition where court cases became precedent for future cases. In this way, a 15th Century English case about a cow getting loose and damaging a neighbor's crops may be a distant predecessor to modern cases about autonomous aerial vehicles getting loose and damaging a neighbor's house. In both cases, tort law seeks financial compensation from the individuals who caused the harm to the victims who were harmed.

We will discuss three categories of torts: Intentional Torts, Unintentional Torts, and Strict Liability. An example of an Intentional Tort in sports is football fans intentionally hitting opposing team coaches with snowballs during the Chargers vs. Giants football game in 1995. This clearly involved the intentional act of throwing a snowball and hitting someone. An example of an Unintentional Tort in sports is ice sliding off the Dallas Cowboys Stadium roof, sending six people to the hospital less than 24 hours before the 2011 Superbowl. In this case, the Cowboys did not intend to hurt anyone, but maybe a court could find them responsible for the foreseeable outcome caused by their failure to warn or prevent injuries from a known danger. Examples of Strict Liability Torts include someone being injured by a defective product or by a team's live tiger mascot. In these cases, society may say that the maker of the defective product or keeper of the dangerous animal should be held responsible for injuries even if they did nothing wrong other than make a defective product or keep a tiger.

Burden of Proof

Tort law is addressed in civil court, not criminal court. Most people are more familiar with criminal law than civil law because of the prevalence of criminal law on the news and TV dramas. In criminal court, there is a prosecutor. The prosecutor is an attorney paid by taxpayers to represent the interest of "the people" and a defendant being charged with a crime. To find the defendant guilty of a crime, the prosecutor needs to prove that the defendant committed every element of the crime to a standard called "**beyond a reasonable doubt**." If the defendant is found guilty, he or she can be forced to go to jail or prison for an amount of time commensurate with the crime committed. The guilty party may also be forced to pay financial damages to the victim or victims of the criminal conduct. Financial damages in criminal court are called restitution.

In civil court, the party that is suing is called the **plaintiff** and the party that is being sued is called the **defendant**. Each party pays for its own legal counsel. Although, plaintiff attorneys are sometimes paid a percentage of the amount recovered in what is called a "contingency fee" arrangement. In this way, plaintiffs sometimes may not feel like they are paying for their legal counsel, but they are. If there is a financial settlement, a percentage of this settlement will go to pay their attorneys.

To find the defendant liable in civil court, the plaintiff needs to prove that the defendant committed every element of the tort to a standard called a "**preponderance of the evidence**." This standard of proof requires proving that "it is more likely than not" that the defendant committed every element of the tort. This is a much lower standard than the criminal standard requiring proof "beyond a reasonable doubt." If the defendant loses a case in civil court, we do not say that the defendant is guilty. Instead, we say that the defendant is liable. The unsuccessful defendant in civil court does not go to jail. Instead, the resolution normally sought in civil court is for the defendant to pay financial damages caused by the defendant's actions or failure to act.

We can compare criminal and civil law in sports by looking at the 1968 Heisman Trophy winner. He was the number one pick in the draft, receiving the largest contract in professional sports history at that time. He was the first player to rush for more than 2,000 yards in a season and is still the only player to rush for 2000 yards in a 14-game season. (The NFL extended the season to 16 games in 1978). He was also in movies, television shows, and commercials. He provided commentary for Monday Night Football and even hosted Saturday Night Live. But this athlete is no longer remembered for his performance on the field. This former football player's name is O.J. Simpson, and he is remembered today for his involvement in the death of his former wife, Nicole Brown Simpson, and her friend Ronald Goldman.

In one of the most publicized trials of the 20th century, O.J. Simpson was charged in criminal court with the crime of murder. He assembled a "dream team" of famous defense attorneys that included Robert Kardashian—a last name now famous because of his daughters. At the criminal trial, Simpson was found not guilty of murder. The families of the deceased then sued Simpson in civil court where he was found liable for the wrongful deaths of Nichole Brown Simpson and Ronald Goldman.

How can someone be found not guilty in criminal court, and then be found liable for essentially the same deaths in civil court? Simpson was found not guilty of murdering Nichole and Ron in criminal court because a jury determined that the prosecution had not proven "beyond a reasonable doubt" that Simpson had murdered the victims. Simpson was found liable for the wrongful death of these same individuals in civil court because a different jury determined that it was more likely than not that O.J. Simpson was liable for their deaths. For this, Simpson was ordered to pay $33.5 million to the family members of the deceased in a 1997 verdict. Simpson appealed the decision, but it was upheld by the California Supreme Court in 2001.

A Word About Elements

I used mathematics to help explain contract law. For tort law, I'll turn to chemistry. Colleagues warned me against using something more complicated to explain something less complicated, but I think talking about elements in chemistry can help us understand elements in law. For example, water is H20. This means that the water molecule contains the elements hydrogen and oxygen with two hydrogen atoms for every one oxygen atom. Hydrogen and oxygen each have their own definitions where hydrogen is an element with one electron and one proton and oxygen is an element with eight electrons and eight protons.

Like water, the crime of murder has two elements. Instead of 1) hydrogen and 2) oxygen, murder has the elements of 1) a homicide and 2) committed with malice aforethought. Then, just as hydrogen was defined, a homicide is defined as the killing of a human being. And just as oxygen was defined, malice aforethought is defined as an intent to kill, intent to do serious bodily harm, or a depraved indifference to human life.

I mention this because if I am thirsty and I ask you for water, you know not to bring me a tank of hydrogen or a tank of oxygen. You even know that although hydrogen peroxide—that is one hydrogen for every one oxygen—may be very similar to water, it definitely will not quench my thirst. Giving me something with elements very similar to water is not the same as giving me water.

Similarly, if there is a homicide—that is, the killing of a human being—but it was not committed with malice aforethought, then we don't have a murder. And if we have malice aforethought, but no homicide, then then there is no murder. This is true even if the person who committed the crime really intended to kill, really intended to cause serious bodily harm, or is seriously depraved. **If you don't have all of the elements of a tort, crime, or contract, then you don't have that tort, crime, or contract.** You might have something else, but if you do not have the exact elements of a specific tort, crime, or contract, then you don't have that tort, crime, or contract.

Intentional Torts

Intentional torts, as you might imagine, all contain the element of intent. When looking at intentional torts, it is important to realize that many torts have the same names as crimes. For example, there are the torts of battery, assault, false imprisonment, and trespassing. You may be more familiar with these as crimes with definitions that vary by state. In criminal law, a prosecutor could seek jail time for someone who is found guilty beyond a reasonable doubt of committing one of these crimes. In civil law, we are seeking financial damages from the person who is found liable, by a preponderance of the evidence, of committing one of these torts.

Battery

The tort of battery protects against contact to an individual's body without that individual's consent. It exists to protect one's bodily integrity and personal dignity. For example, an unwelcomed and uninvited kiss has been found to be a battery. A hard foul against a basketball player going up for a layup during a game would likely not be a battery because there is implied consent to any contact that is a reasonably foreseeable part of the game.

The tort of battery contains the following four elements:

1) A Voluntary Act
2) Intentionally Causing
3) Harmful or Offensive Contact
4) To a Victim's Person or Something Closely Associated Thereto

All these elements must exist to find someone liable for the tort of battery. Let's walk through each element.

---

1) A Voluntary Act

A voluntary act is a conscious act. It is not an epileptic seizure. It is not sleepwalking. If you kick someone while sleepwalking, you should not be found liable for the tort of battery because the contact was not the result of your voluntary act. This element does not come up in most real-life fact patterns, but I include it for anyone studying for a Bar exam. If an act is not voluntary, there should be no liability for an intentional tort.

2) Intentionally Causing

All intentional torts require the existence of a voluntary, intentional act. The element of intent can be satisfied when someone either:

1) Desires the Consequences of their Actions, or
2) Knows to a Substantial Certainty That the Consequences Will Occur.

For battery, the act that must be intended is harmful or offensive contact to another person. For the element of intent, it is not necessary to prove that the defendant intended to cause this harmful or offensive contact. We just need to see that the defendant intended to make contact and this contact ended up being harmful or offensive.

The first definition for intent—desiring the consequences of their actions—is usually obvious. If someone tries to throw a snowball at someone and ends up hitting someone, we have intent. The second definition—knowing to a substantial certainty that the consequences will occur—requires more attention. As an example, imagine that I run out of an empty library and accidentally run into someone. Did I desire to run into anyone? No. Did I know to a substantial certainty that I would run into someone? Remember, I said the library was empty. There was no one around, and so I would not know to a substantial certainty that I would run into someone. In this case, I should not be found liable for the tort of battery because I did not intend to make contact with a person. That is, I did not desire to hit anyone, and I did not know to a substantial certainty that I would hit someone.

Let's change the scenario and imagine that I am a football player who wants to improve my ability to avoid tackles. For practice, I am going to put on my helmet and pads and run down a crowded New York City sidewalk as fast as I can while trying to avoid pedestrians. I do not desire to hit anyone. I'm trying to avoid everyone. However, the intent element would still be satisfied because I would know to a substantial certainty that I will make contact with someone when I run down a crowded New York City sidewalk as fast as I can.

Similarly, imagine someone shoots a rifle at a crowded moving passenger train. The shooter does not desire to hit anyone on the train, but it is a crowded passenger train. The element of intent could be satisfied even if the shooter did not desire to hit anyone because the shooter would know to a substantial certainty that a person would be hit if he shoots at a crowded passenger train.

But what if the shooter is an Olympic athlete shooting at hay bales as they pass through the desert on a cargo train, and, unbeknownst to the shooter, a trespasser jumped onto a train car, hides in the hay bales, and gets shot by the shooter. Did the shooter desire to hit a person? No. Did the shooter know to a substantial certainty that someone would get shot? In this case, the Olympian was shooting at a cargo train—not a passenger train—and would not know to a substantial certainty that someone would be hiding in the hay bales and get shot. Therefore, the intent element would not be satisfied, and the shooter should not be found liable for the tort of battery because the Olympian did not desire to hit anyone and would not know to a substantial certainty that someone would be hit.

As a public service announcement, please let me remind you that just because someone is not liable for one specific tort or crime doesn't mean that they won't be liable for one or many other torts or crimes. These examples are for illustration purposes only and no one should shoot at trains.

3) Harmful or Offensive Contact

The tort of battery requires harmful or offensive contact to a person. Remember, the defendant does not need to intend to make harmful or offensive contact. It is also not required that the plaintiff is harmed. The defendant just needs to intend to make contact that ends up being harmful or offensive.

For example, imagine that fans of the Philadelphia Eagles football team want to toughen up their players by hitting them in the stomach every time they walk by. The players may not be harmed by amateurs hitting them in the stomach. They may even benefit from these surprise workouts of being randomly hit by fans as they walk down their city sidewalks. The only harm may be to a few fans who injure their hands while hitting a player. Nevertheless, this contact still violates a player's right to bodily integrity and personal dignity. In this scenario, the harmful or offensive contact element is still satisfied even if the players were not harmed by the contact.

Whether or not the contact is offensive will be judged objectively, not subjectively. That is, we will not ask if the defendant or victim thought the contact was offensive. Their personal, subjective beliefs about what is or is not offensive is not the standard. Instead, the plaintiff must prove that the contact in question offends a reasonable sense of personal dignity (RESTATEMENT (THIRD) OF TORTS: INTENTIONAL TORTS TO PERSONS § 3(b)).

For example, in *Patricia K. Cohen and Joe Cohen v. Roger Smith* (269 Ill. App. 3d 1087; 648 N.E.2d 329; 1995), Patricia Cohen was admitted to St. Joseph Memorial Hospital to deliver her baby. After an examination, Cohen was informed that she would need a cesarean section. Cohen and her husband informed her physician, who in turn advised the Hospital staff, that the couple's religious beliefs prohibited Cohen from being seen unclothed by a male. Cohen's doctor assured her husband that their religious convictions would be respected. But during Cohen's cesarean section, Roger Smith, a male nurse on staff at the Hospital, allegedly observed and touched Cohen's naked body.

Let me pause here and add that there are no facts to suggest that the touching involved anything different than what medical professionals would do in the course of performing a cesarean section birth to deliver a healthy baby. But the question for battery is not if the defendant meant the contact to be offensive, but whether a reasonable person would find the contact offensive. In this case, the defendant knew of the plaintiff's particular sensitivity—indeed prohibition—to contact, and the defendant contacted her anyway. This satisfied the contact element of battery.

4) To a Victim's Person or Something Closely Associated Thereto

The final element of battery requires contact with the victim's person, or something closely associated thereto. This includes directly contacting a person or causing something to make contact with a person. For example, hitting someone, spitting on someone, throwing and hitting someone with a rock, urinating in the office coffee, or blowing smoke in the face of an anti-smoking activist (Leichtman v. WLW Jacor Communications, Inc. 634 N.E.2d 697 (1994)) could all be considered offensive contact.

The definition includes contact not only to the person, but also contact to "something closely associated thereto." This does not refer to some object that may be sentimentally connected to a person. We are still talking about contact that affects the bodily integrity of a person. For example, hitting the horse someone is riding on, knocking off someone's hat, or kicking out the cane someone is using to walk, could all count as contact to something closely associated to the plaintiff. Whether contact with the car one is driving satisfies this element varies by jurisdiction and, perhaps, by the type of car and contact. For example, in protecting one's bodily integrity and personal dignity from unwanted touching, it makes sense that contact to the horse, wheelchair, or motorcycle one is riding on affects that person's sense of bodily integrity. By analogy, maybe the driver's side door or window of certain cars in certain jurisdictions would count as a battery too. However, it seems unlikely that someone kicking the back right tire of a monster truck affects the bodily integrity of the driver sufficient to find the defendant liable for the tort of battery.

Transferred Intent

The doctrine of transferred intent allows us to satisfy the intent element by shifting the intent from an intended victim to an unintended victim, and from one intentional tort to another intentional tort. For example, with transferred intent, I cannot avoid liability for hitting a coach with a snowball by arguing that I did not intend to hit the coach because I was aiming for the referee standing next to the coach. We will transfer the intent I had to hit the referee to satisfy the intent element necessary for finding me liable for battery against the coach. We will also transfer the intent between intentional torts. This means that I could not avoid liability for battery by arguing, "But I didn't intend to commit a battery. I intended to commit an assault." The intent to commit the assault will satisfy the intent element required for battery.

Assault

The tort of assault also protects one's bodily integrity and personal dignity, but it takes it a step further than the tort of battery. Whereas the tort of battery requires contact to the person, assault protects against the reasonable apprehension of an imminent battery, even if there is no contact.

The tort of assault contains the following six elements:

1) A Voluntary Act
2) Intentionally Causing
3) The Victim's Reasonable Apprehension
4) Of an Imminent
5) Harmful or Offensive Contact
6) To a Victim's Person or Something Closely Associated Thereto

Notice that the first and last two elements for assault are identical to the elements already discussed for the tort of battery. The result is that assault exists where the victim has a reasonable apprehension of an imminent battery. Think of someone pointing an unloaded gun at another person and pulling the trigger. This is horrible, but if there is no contact, there is no battery. The same is true of someone firing a loaded gun at someone and missing. Society will not tolerate this behavior and tortfeasors of this conduct can be found responsible for compensating victims of the tort of assault.

Like the tort of battery, assault requires a defendant who acts 1) voluntarily and 2) intentionally. This brings us to element number three: the Victim's Reasonable Apprehension.

3) The Victim's Reasonable Apprehension

The tort of assault requires the victim's reasonable apprehension. Apprehension includes fear, but also the anxiety that something bad or unpleasant will happen. For example, imagine an old man throws a rock at you as you pass by his house on the public sidewalk every morning. You are young and agile and confident that you will be able to dodge the old man's weak throw. Plus, even if the rock hits you, you doubt the weak throw would hurt you. Therefore, you might not say that you're afraid of the contact, but it would still be reasonable to have some apprehension or anxiety about getting hit with a rock. That would be enough to satisfy the reasonable apprehension element for assault.

4) Of an Imminent

The reasonable apprehension must be of an imminent harmful or offensive contact. If someone says, "Give me all of your money or I'll come back tomorrow and hurt you," there is no apprehension of an imminent harmful or offensive contact. Similarly, let's assume that you have brown hair, and someone threatens you by saying, "If you didn't have brown hair, I'd throw a rock at you." You do not have apprehension of an imminent harmful or offensive contact because the threat was conditioned on characteristics that did not apply to you.

The remaining elements, the harmful or offensive contact to a victim's person or something closely associated thereto, are shared with battery.

Battery and assault are often claimed together when someone has a reasonable apprehension of harmful or offensive contact (assault) that results in the person being contacted (battery). Situations where there is an assault without a battery exist when a victim has apprehension of an imminent contact that does not result in contact. For example, someone throwing a rock at someone and missing could be an assault if the victim had a reasonable apprehension of being hit by the rock. Situations where there is a battery, but no assault exist when the victim is contacted without being aware of the imminent contact. This could occur when someone is hit in the back of the head by a snowball without any warning, or when someone is contacted while asleep or sedated for surgery.

False Imprisonment

The tort of false imprisonment exists to defend an individual's freedom of movement.

The tort of false imprisonment contains the following four elements:

1) A Voluntary Act
2) Intentionally Causing
3) The Victim's Confinement into a Bounded Area by Force or Threat of Force
4) The Plaintiff Knows of the Confinement or is Injured by the Confinement

Intent

The intent element is the same as other intentional torts. It can be satisfied where one desires the outcome or knows to a substantial certainty that the outcome will occur. It is important to recognize that this does not require an evil intent. For false imprisonment, it does not matter if the defendant had a good or bad motive to confine someone. The question is only whether the defendant acted volitionally and intentionally to confine the plaintiff.

For example, imagine that you have a friend who is an alcoholic who has been sober for 150 days, and you are worried that your friend will return to alcohol tonight because your friend's favorite team just won the championship. You lock your friend in a comfortable room to prevent your friend from going to the bar to celebrate with other friends. Locking your friend in the room was an intentional, volitional act to confine your friend. This satisfies the intent element of the tort of false imprisonment even if you had an honorable motive to confine your friend.

In contrast, if you accidentally lock your friend in a room when you were closing your office for the night, you did not intend to confine your friend and therefore you would not be found liable for false imprisonment. The tort of false imprisonment requires the defendant's intent to confine a plaintiff.

Confinement into a Bounded Area by Force or Threat of Force

To be liable for the tort of false imprisonment, the plaintiff must have been confined into a bounded area by force or threat of force without a reasonable means of escape. An unreasonable means of escape is one likely to cause physical injury or serious reputational harm. Therefore, confinement could include locking someone in a room where the only escape is jumping out of a third story window. It could also include stealing someone's clothing while they are in the shower if this left walking naked through a crowded gymnasium as the victim's only means of escape.

The confinement must be by force or threat of force. Reputational threats are generally insufficient. Therefore, a threat to kill someone or a close family member if they leave a room would obviously be a threat of force. Threatening to reveal an embarrassing secret would not be a sufficient threat of force.

It does not matter how large or nice the bounded area may be. It could be a beautiful estate garden behind an ancient castle wall. It just needs to be an identifiable area to which the plaintiff is confined without a reasonable means of escape. For example, if I lock you out of my office, you cannot say that I have confined you to the world outside of my office. However, if I lock you inside a huge office with a comfortable couch, nice view, and open bar, I could still be found liable for the tort of false imprisonment because I have confined you into a bounded— albeit nicely appointed—area.

The Plaintiff Knows of the Confinement or is Injured by the Confinement

The goal of the tort of false imprisonment is to protect one's freedom of movement. If your roommate locks the door on you while you are sleeping and then unlocks it before you awake, your roommate did not restrict your freedom of movement. You were not even aware of the confinement. The tort of false imprisonment requires that the plaintiff knows of the confinement or is injured by the confinement.

Situations where a plaintiff does not know of the confinement, but is injured by the confinement include cases where infants are locked in a room or car. The infant may be too young to be aware of the confinement, but if the infant suffers dehydration or any harm, this harm will replace the requirement that the plaintiff must know of the confinement. If the plaintiff does not know about the confinement, and is not injured by the confinement, there is no false imprisonment.

There is no duration requirement for the confinement. If the defendant intentionally confines the plaintiff into a bounded area against the plaintiff's will with the plaintiff's knowledge or injury, there is false imprisonment. A longer duration could be used to impose greater financial damages, but a short duration does not excuse the defendant from liability.

False imprisonment is also a crime, occasionally making headlines with athletes involved in domestic disputes. Sometimes the crime is coupled with kidnapping because the crime of kidnapping can be defined as the crime of false imprisonment plus any movement of the victim. Therefore, if a couple is arguing in a car and the defendant locks the car door and moves the car, there could be criminal charges for not only false imprisonment but kidnapping as well.

Coaches and athletic directors should be aware that locking athletes into weight rooms or locker rooms or the team bus by force or threat of force without a reasonable means of escape can lead to liability for the tort of false imprisonment.

Defamation

The tort of defamation exists to protect plaintiffs from false statements that cause plaintiffs reputational harm. In 2023, Pro Football Hall of Fame quarterback Brett Favre sued the Mississippi state auditor and sportscasters for defamation after they made statements alleging that Favre had stolen money for speaking fees that belonged to the Mississippi Department of Human Services. Also in 2023, after jury selection but before trial, Fox News paid Dominion Voting $787.5 million to settle a defamation lawsuit alleging that Fox News commentators made knowingly false comments about Dominion Voting machines in the 2020 U.S. presidential election. Also in 2023, a jury found then former president Donald Trump liable for defamation for statements that he made about writer E. Jean Carroll in 2019 after she went public with claims that Trump had raped her decades earlier. In 2024, a federal judge rejected Trump's bid to throw out the $83.3 million verdict.

When defamation is oral, it is referred to as slander. When defamation is in writing, it is referred to as libel.

The tort of defamation contains the following five elements:

1) False
2) Defamatory
3) Statement of Fact
4) Of or Concerning the Plaintiff
5) Published to a Third Party.

1) False and 2) Defamatory

Notice that the first element of defamation is that the statement must be false. If someone says something that hurts your reputation that is true, there will be no liability for the tort of defamation. The next requirement is that the statement must be defamatory. A statement that is defamatory is one that subjects the plaintiff to scorn or ridicule or lowers the plaintiff's reputation. If someone makes false statements about another person that are flattering or full of praise, the statements are not defamatory and therefore there will be no liability for defamation.

3) Statement of Fact

In order for a false, defamatory statement to be defamation, it needs to be a statement of fact. This contrasts with a statement of opinion. A statement of fact is one that can be proved to be true or false. An opinion cannot be proved to be true or false. For example, saying that you don't think your favorite athlete was trying hard enough or didn't want to win is an opinion because it cannot be proven to be true or false. Saying that an athlete bet against his own team is a statement of fact because it could be proved to be true or false.

4) Of or Concerning the Plaintiff and 5) Published to a Third Party

Finally, the false, defamatory, statement of fact must be of or concerning the plaintiff and published to a third party. This tort is about a plaintiff's reputational harm. If the false statements are not about the plaintiff or are not communicated to a third party, it does not hurt the plaintiff's reputation. Remember, defamation can be written or oral. This means that when the legal definition refers to "published to a third party," it is not just referring to written publications, but to any communication of a false, defamatory, statement of fact, of or concerning the plaintiff made to a third party.

Privileges

There are times when liability for defamation is limited or even erased. These are called privileges. Privileges can be absolute or qualified. An absolute privilege provides complete immunity against defamation. A qualified privilege provides immunity only in certain situations and can be lost if the defendant's conduct exceeds the qualified privilege. For example, there is a qualified privilege for employers who make false, defamatory, statements of fact on employee evaluations. The qualification is that the statements must be made in good faith and publication must be limited to those with a legitimate interest. If the statements are made in good faith and the publication is limited to those with a legitimate interest, there will no liability for defamation. For example, if an employer writes on an evaluation that an employee missed seven days of work without an excuse when the employee only missed four days without an excuse, the employer may have made a false defamatory statement of fact. However, if the statement was made in good faith and publication was limited to those with a legitimate interest, the employer will not be liable for defamation.

The U.S. Speech or Debate Clause of the U.S. Constitution provides absolute immunity for statements that are made as part of the legislative deliberative process. The legislative deliberative process is when members of Congress are debating potential legislation. For example, a congressperson could say, "We need to pass this legislation to protect children from pedophiles likes my opponent," while specifically identifying their opponent. Let's assume this is false and it is clearly defamatory and published, but it will not be defamation if it was said as part of the legislative deliberative process. This means that when people share a video clip of their favorite politicians making statements during the legislative process, they may be sharing their favorite politicians enjoying their absolute privilege to lie during the legislative process.

For example, imagine that senators are questioning a witness who is testifying under oath to tell the truth or face the penalty of perjury. The senators can make false statements as they examine the witness and not be subject to liability for defamation or perjury. The only person who has any consequences for lying during these senate hearings is the individual sworn-in and testifying under oath. This legislative privilege does not apply to a legislator's statements at press conferences, in newsletters, or in phone calls, because they are not part of the "deliberative process" (*Hutchinson v. Proxmire*, 443 U.S. 11 (1979)). Therefore, when questioned by the press about false comments made during the legislative process, legislators often simply state that they have "no further comment." If they did make a comment, they could be subject to defamation litigation.

The scope of defamation litigation was significantly limited in the United States in the 1964 U.S. Supreme Court case *New York Times Co. v. Sullivan.* This case arose after the *New York Times* printed an advertisement soliciting funds for Martin Luther King Jr. The advertisement stated that Alabama police had arrested King seven times when King had been arrested "only" four times. Therefore, saying he had been arrested seven times, was false. In response, Montgomery police commissioner L.B. Sullivan sued the Times for defamation in an Alabama county court. The court found the Times liable and awarded Sullivan $500,000.

At the time, many newspapers feared the threat of litigation and were reluctant to report on civil rights issues. The threat was real. Southern officials had filed nearly $300 million in libel actions against the press by the time the Supreme Court decided *New York Times Co. v. Sullivan* in 1964 ((Kagan, 1993). A libel story: Sullivan then and now (reviewing Anthony Lewis, *Make no law: The Sullivan case and the First Amendment*, [1991]). *Chicago Unbound*, University of Chicago Law School). Some feared that these lawsuits were having a chilling effect on the First Amendment's right to a free press, and so the United States Supreme Court agreed to hear the case of *New York Times Co. v. Sullivan*.

The Supreme Court ruled in favor of the *New York Times*, holding that the First Amendment protects the publication of all statements, even false ones, about the conduct of public officials except when statements are made with actual malice. Actual malice refers to statements made with knowledge that they are false or in reckless disregard to their truth or falsity. "After *New York Times v. Sullivan*, it became difficult for a public official to win a defamation lawsuit against the press because, in addition to proving that the statement was false, the public official now needed to prove that the statement was made by someone who knew it was false, or who at least showed reckless disregard to the statement's truth or falsity" (Kealy, D. M. (2022). Defamation Coverage in the Commercial General Liability Insurance

Policy. Pathways to Research in Business & Economics BUS014, 1-10).

Another limitation on liability for defamation was passed into law in Section 230 of the Communications Decency Act of 1996 (47 US Code § 230). The Act states that "no provider or user of an interactive computer service shall be treated as the publisher or speaker of any information provided by another information content provider" (47 u.s.c. § 230(c)(1),2011). Section 230 makes it unlikely that online platforms like YouTube, TikTok, Facebook, X, or Yelp will be held liable for content uploaded to their platforms by others.

Fraud
The tort of fraud, also called misrepresentation and deceit, contains the following elements:

1) Intentional Material Misrepresentation of a Past or Present Fact
2) Knowing the Statement Is False (Also Called Scienter)
3) Made with the Intent to Induce Another Party to Rely on the Misrepresentation
4) The Other Party Justifiably Relies on the Misrepresentation
5) Causing the Plaintiff Damages

As an example, you can think about someone selling you a used car. If the salesperson is lying about a present or past material fact to get you to buy something, and you buy it in reliance on this lie, and this causes you damages, the salesperson may be liable for fraud.

The first element requires the false statement to be a material misrepresentation. A material misrepresentation is one that goes to the basis of the bargain. If the car salesperson is lying to you about a truck's engine, but you would have bought the truck anyway because you're just buying the truck to use the truck bed to make a trailer, then the lie about the engine was not a material misrepresentation. Examples of fraud in sports include lies about age, resume, grades, and even identity. For example, in 2010 a 16-year-old named Jerry Joseph who led Permian High School to the Texas state basketball playoffs turned out to be a 22-year-old from Florida named Guerdwich Montimere.

Invasion of Privacy
The tort of invasion of privacy is an umbrella term used for torts involving privacy. The tort of invasion of privacy includes Intrusion into

Seclusion, Public Disclosure of a Private True Fact, False Light, and Commercial Misappropriation.

Intrusion into Seclusion exists when a plaintiff has a reasonable expectation of privacy with which the defendant interferes in a way that would be objectionable to a reasonable person. **Public Disclosure of a Private True Fact** exists when there is disclosure of a private fact that would be highly offensive to a reasonable person and the statement is not newsworthy. Notice that this is like the tort of defamation except that the statement being disclosed is true. **False Light** exists when a defendant is at fault for disseminating false information about a plaintiff that is offensive to a reasonable person, but not necessarily defamatory. Notice that this is like defamation except that the statement being disclosed is not defamatory. For example, lying about someone having a terminal illness would hopefully not subject that person to scorn or ridicule, but disseminating such a lie could be offensive to a reasonable person. **Commercial Misappropriation**, also called *Misappropriation of Likeness* or a *Right of Publicity*, acknowledges that individuals own the right to their name, image, and likeness. For example, a business cannot imitate the voice of the late James Earl Jones—if that is even possible—in an advertisement to imply his endorsement without his estate's consent. This would also apply to a business using the face, silhouette, or likeness of an individual in an advertisement without consent.

Using an athlete's likeness without consent was litigated in *Ed O'Bannon v. NCAA*. O'Bannon was a former basketball player who led UCLA to the 1995 NCAA championship before being drafted ninth overall by the New Jersey Nets. Years later, O'Bannon was working as car salesman in Las Vegas, Nevada when he saw his likeness on a video game that his friend's child was playing. At first, O'Bannon said he was flattered, but then he realized that his friend had paid for the video game and O'Bannon had never been compensated or even asked for his permission to use his likeness in the video game. In response, lawyers for O'Bannon reached a $40 million settlement with video game maker EA Sports and the Collegiate Licensing Company. O'Bannon also filed an antitrust lawsuit against the NCAA challenging the NCAA's use of the image and likeness of former NCAA student-athletes for commercial purposes. The court ruled in O'Bannon's favor, paving the way for NCAA students to get paid for their name, image, and likeness (*O'Bannon v. NCAA*, 802 F.3d 1049 (9th Cir. 2015). See the chapter on Antitrust Law for more details.

Wrongful Interference with Contractual Relations

The tort of wrongful interference with contractual relations, also called tortious interference with contractual relations, contains the following elements:

1) A Valid, Enforceable Contract Exists Between Two Parties
2) A Third Party Knows That This Contract Exists
3) The Third Party *Intentionally Induces* a Party to the Contract to Breach the Contract

At first glance, it may seem unbelievable that this is an enforceable tort when you think of phone companies poaching customers from other phone companies and sports teams poaching players from other teams. Don't they know that the individual has a contract with another carrier or team and aren't they intentionally inducing a party to the contract to breach the contract? To avoid liability, it is common to see the new organization pay the amount remaining on the prior contract. In this way, T-Mobile is not inducing customers to breach their contract with AT&T. They are offering a new contract and will buy out the remainder of the customer's existing contract with AT&T.

It is also possible that a former team will pay to have someone play for a different team. For example, when pitcher David Price was transferred from the Boston Red Sox to the Los Angeles Dodgers, the Red Sox continued to pay about half of Price's remaining salary. In this way, moving from the Red Sox to the Dodgers did not create a breach of contract. It reduced the salary the Red Sox were obligated to pay according to their contract.

With athletes, there is also the practical limitation of the inability to enforce the remedy of specific performance. Specific performance is a contractual remedy in which the court orders a party to perform its promise because monetary damages would be insufficient to fix the harm. This may be an option in forcing the sale of property, but you cannot—and perhaps would not even want to—force an athlete to play for a team they refuse to play for.

It may be difficult to impose specific performance on athletes, but it is not difficult to impose financial damages on businesses that are liable for tortious interference with contractual relations. For example, former Dallas Cowboys wide receiver Dez Bryant signed a contract with Official Brands, Inc. (Official Brands) authorizing Official Brands "to utilize Dez Bryant's name, nickname, initials, autograph, facsimile signature, photograph, likeness, video, and/or endorsement in connection with the advertisement, marketing, promotion, and sale of" Bryant's brand, called 'Throw up the X'" (*Off. Brands, Inc. v. Roc Nation Sports, LLC*, No. 3:15-CV-2199-B, 2015 WL 8915804, at *1 (N.D. Tex. Dec. 15, 2015)). Their contract was drafted to run from 2014 until 2016, but Bryant terminated the contract in 2015 to join Jay Z's Roc Nation Sports instead. In response, Official Brands sued Roc Nation for tortious interference with contractual relations, arguing that Roc Nation "embarked upon a scheme to...unlawfully induce Dez Bryant to terminate [the]...contract with Official Brands." *Id.*

Roc Nation then filed a motion of summary judgment to dismiss the case. The court denied this motion stating that "the Court has determined that Official Brands successfully stated a claim for tortious interference with contractual relations" because the facts revealed that 1) There was an enforceable contract between Bryant and Official Brands, 2) Roc Nation knew of this contract, and 3) Roc Nation intentionally induced Bryant to breach his contract with Official Brands and move to Roc Nation. Thus, the elements of the tort were satisfied and Roc Nation's motion to dismiss the case was denied.

Trespass to Land
The tort of trespass to land contains the following elements:

1) Voluntary and Intentional
2) Entry or Causing Something or Someone to Enter
3) Plaintiff's Land
4) Without Permission

The intent element for trespass to land does not require defendants to intend to trespass. The defendants need only to intend to enter the plaintiff's land without permission. The defendants may reasonably believe they have permission to enter the land or even believe they own the land.

When do we see trespassing in sports law? We see it when someone runs onto a sports field, court, or pitch to get attention. We also see it when a player, coach, or spectator is ejected from a game and refuses to leave. If individuals no longer have permission to be on the plaintiff's land, they may be liable for trespassing. In this chapter we are just discussing torts, but trespassing can also violate criminal laws and land someone in jail.

Trespass to Personal Property (Trespass to Chattels)

The tort of trespass to personal property, also called trespass to chattels, contains the following elements:

1) Intent
2) Interference, Intermeddling
3) With the Victim's Right to Possession of Personal Property
4) Causing Harm to the Property

This tort protects an individual's right to their possessions. If someone takes your jersey or racecar before your game or race, someone has interfered with your right to possess your personal property. If they cause harm to the property, they could be liable for the tort of trespass to personal property and be forced to pay the costs associated with their interference with the property. Trespass to personal property can turn into the tort of conversion when the interference with the personal property becomes more severe.

Conversion

The tort of conversion contains the following elements:

1) Intent
2) Dominion and Control
3) With the Victim's Right to Possession of Personal Property
4) Causing Substantial Interference with the Personal Property

At some point the damage to the personal property becomes so severe or the defendant's behavior is so bad that it becomes conversion. In the tort of conversion, the defendant intentionally exercises dominion or control to such a degree that it leads to a substantial interference with the victim's right to possession of personal property. Using the example above, if someone takes your jersey or racecar and destroys it or does not return it, they have exercised dominion and control over your personal property and caused substantial interference with your rights to it. They would be liable for the tort of conversion and may be forced to pay the costs to replace the jersey or car that they took from you.

Unintentional Torts

Now we move from intentional torts to the unintentional tort of negligence.

Negligence

The tort of negligence contains the following elements:

1) Duty
2) Breach
3) Causation
4) Damages.

To find a defendant liable for the tort of negligence, the plaintiff must prove by a preponderance of the evidence that the defendant owed a duty to another party, the defendant breached the duty owed, and this breach caused damages to the plaintiff.

Duty

To find a defendant liable for negligence, the plaintiff must first establish that the defendant owed a duty to the plaintiff. When engaged in any risk creating endeavor, defendants owe a duty to all foreseeable plaintiffs in the zone of danger. This eliminates plaintiffs that are too far removed from the conduct of the defendant. For example, imagine that you are at fault in a car accident. Everyone is okay, but the accident caused a windshield to break and there is shattered glass everywhere. Somehow, a single shard of glass is picked up by a tornado. The tornado spins the glass around and then shoots it out, injuring a particularly unlucky person two miles away from your accident. The person injured by the glass two miles away sues you for negligence. The zone of danger for a car accident is the area around the car, not two miles away. You did not owe a duty to the plaintiff two miles away. Since you did not owe the injured person a duty, a judge should dismiss the negligence case that was filed against you.

In the Common Law tradition, there was also no duty to rescue another person unless you caused the harm or had a special relationship with the plaintiff. Individuals with a special relationship with the plaintiff that might require a duty to rescue could include a parent, teacher, or lifeguard. Some jurisdictions have changed this by statute requiring someone to intervene to help in certain situations. Many jurisdictions also have Good Samaritan Laws that protect individuals who may accidentally injure someone while intervening to rescue someone. For example, the New Mexico Good Samaritan Statute states that no person shall be held liable for administering emergency care in good faith except for gross negligence, and except when care "is rendered for remuneration or with the expectation of remuneration" or "rendered by a person or agent of a principal who was at the scene of the accident or emergency because he or his principal was soliciting business or performing or seeking to perform some services for remuneration" (N.M. Stat. Ann. § 24-10-3. C).

Standard of Care

The discussion on duty often focuses not on whether the defendant owed a duty, but on what duty the defendant owed. The duty that a defendant owes a plaintiff is referred to as the **standard of care** that the defendant owes a plaintiff. There are three main standards of care that apply to negligence lawsuits: 1) the basic standard of care, 2) the professional standard of care, and 3) the child standard of care.

The Basic Standard of Care

The basic standard of care requires the defendant to act as a reasonable person. You can think of the reasonable person as an imaginary person that a jury creates during jury deliberations. This imaginary person has all the life experiences of the jury members. It has the jury's history of making good decisions, and the jury's history of making bad decisions. Once created, the jury then asks how this imaginary person would have behaved if put in the situation faced by the defendant on trial. Did the defendant behave like, or better, than our imaginary reasonable person? Or, did the defendant fail to act like a reasonable person?

The Professional Standard of Care

The professional standard of care asks if the defendant complied with the customary practice of other professionals in good standing. Notice that this standard does not ask if the professional was reasonable. It asks if the defendant followed the customary practice of similar professionals in similar circumstances.

The professional standard applies to professions like medical doctors, attorneys, and engineers. These are professions with advanced education and certification requirements. In these situations, a jury may not be well-suited to judge the reasonableness of the professional's conduct. For example, medical staff may shock someone's heart with a defibrillator, throw someone into a tub of ice to reduce a fever, or poke a hole in someone's throat as an emergency tracheotomy. These actions may not seem reasonable to me, but they may be appropriate life-saving measures followed by medical professionals. Therefore, we do not ask if the medical staff were reasonable. We apply the professional standard of care and ask if the professionals complied with the customary practices of other professionals in good standing. Expert witnesses are often required to explain to the jury the standard practices in the field and assess whether the professional adhered to these standards.

The Child Standard of Care

The child standard of care asks if a child acted like other children of similar age, experience, and intelligence. It also considers the individual child's own experience and intelligence. For example, imagine a seven-year-old shoots someone in the leg with a rifle or bow and arrow. Maybe most children of a similar age, experience, and intelligence would not know what to do with a rifle or bow and arrow, but imagine this seven-year-old is on the U.S. Junior Olympic archery or rifle team. Ordinarily, the Junior Olympian would not be liable if they were acting like children of the same age, experience, and intelligence, but in this case, we could find a breach of the standard of care if this particular child knew better.

Breach

The element of breach is satisfied when the defendant fails to meet the applicable standard of care. If the basic standard of care applies, then there is a breach when the defendant fails to act like a reasonable person would have acted in the given situation. If the professional standard of care applies, then there is a breach when the defendant fails to comply with the customary practice of other similar professionals in good standing. If the child standard applies, then there is a breach if the child failed to act like other children of the same age, experience, and intelligence, or because the child failed to act according to that child's unique experience and intelligence.

For example, imagine that it looks like an athlete suffered a concussion during a game. If a coach decides that the athlete is fine and should continue playing, and as a result suffers injuries, we would use the basic standard of care to determine if the coach acted unreasonably. If a physician is on the sidelines and determines that the athlete is fine and should continue playing, and as a result suffers injuries, we would use the professional standard to ask if the physician failed to comply with the customary practices of other physicians in good standing.

Negligence Per Se

The concept of *negligence per se* allows plaintiffs to use the defendant's violation of a statute as a rebuttable presumption that the defendant breached their duty. This is available when there is a statute that was designed to protect the plaintiff from a certain kind of harm, the defendant violated the statute, and the plaintiff suffered the kind of harm the statute was designed to address. For example, California passed a law requiring Automated External Defibrillators (AEDs) at fitness centers (HSC § 104113). These are designed to help those experiencing sudden cardiac arrest. If a fitness center does not have an AED as required by statute, and a customer suffers a sudden cardiac arrest that would have been less severe had the fitness center complied with the statute, then the plaintiff could use *negligence per se* to prove the fitness center breached the duty they owed. Notice that if a customer at the fitness center breaks a leg, the customer could not use violation of the AED statute to prove a breach because the statute was designed to address sudden cardiac arrest, not broken legs.

Causation

There are two types of causation discussed in negligence: 1) Actual cause and 2) Proximate cause.

Actual Cause

The Actual cause is sometimes referred to as the "*but for*" cause. For example, the plaintiff would not have been hit in the head by a rock "*but for*" the defendant throwing a rock towards the plaintiff. The actual cause is the link between the defendant's breach and the damages suffered by the plaintiff. For example, imagine that you run a red light and you hit an ambulance in the intersection. Let's assume that reasonable drivers do not run red lights and so you breached your duty of acting like a reasonable person when you ran through the red light. Everyone is okay except that there was a person who died in the back of the ambulance. The family of this person sues you for negligence. Before you panic, here is an interesting additional fact for your attorney: the person who died in the back of the ambulance died twenty minutes before the accident. The deceased was just being transported by the ambulance. Do you still need psychological counseling? Yes, it is still a horrible day for you and the family of the deceased. However, you should not be found liable for negligently causing the death of the person who was in the back of the ambulance because you did not cause this person's death. You cannot say that the person would be alive *but for* you running the red light. There is no causal link between your breach of the duty to act like a reasonable person and the damages suffered by the family. Without the plaintiff proving causation, the defendant cannot be found liable for the tort of negligence.

Proximate Cause

The second type of causation is called proximate cause. Proximate cause requires a foreseeable link between the defendant's breach and the plaintiff's damages. Proximate cause helps prevent causation from getting ridiculous in the hands of creative lawyers and philosophers. For example, in science you may have heard about the chaos theory. The chaos theory has also been called the "butterfly effect." The idea is that the small impact of a butterfly flapping its wings could disturb the air enough to move a leaf. The moving leaf could scare a monkey and make the monkey jump. The monkey jumping could cause a branch to move, which could cause a tree to sway, which could cause an updraft. The updraft could cause cloud formation, causing rain, causing rivers to flood, causing ocean warming, causing a hurricane to form and damage the Southern United States.

It may be interesting to philosophize about how small actions can make large impacts in our world, but this is too difficult to trace for the courtroom. We need to limit causation to that which is foreseeable. Without requiring foreseeability, you might sue me for negligence, arguing that I wrote a boring book that caused you to fall asleep, which caused you to drop my book, which knocked over your drink, which stained your carpet. You could argue that this satisfies the actual cause requirement because there is an unbroken chain of events between my conduct of writing the book and your carpet damage. However, this would not satisfy the proximate cause requirement. Proximate cause eliminates damages that are so unforeseeable that it would not be fair to say that the defendant's actions caused the plaintiff's damages.

Res Ipsa Loquitor

Res Ipsa Loquitor is Latin for "the thing speaks for itself." It is available to plaintiffs in situations where it should be obvious that the defendant breached the duty that was owed.

Here are the elements of Res Ipsa Loquitur:

1) This sort of thing typically does not happen absent negligence.
2) The harm causing instrumentality is under the defendant's control.
3) The plaintiff did not contribute to his or her own injury.

Res Ipsa Loquitor is not its own tort. It is merely a way to address the element of breach in the tort of negligence. When *Res Ipsa Loquitor* applies, we shift the burden of proof from forcing the plaintiff to prove the defendants breached, to forcing the defendants to prove they did not breach.

For example, in *Byrne v. Boadle*, a barrel of flour fell from a second-story loft, hitting a plaintiff on the head. All the plaintiff might know is that he was hit in the head and he's lying on the ground, covered in flour, with a broken barrel next to him. In this case, he also knows that this happened in front of a flour business. How could the plaintiff prove that it was the flour business that caused his injuries?

Well, barrels tend not to fall on peoples' heads absent someone's negligence, the barrel was in the defendant's control, and the plaintiff did not contribute to his own injury. Similarly, imagine that a patient discovers that a medical professional accidentally left a utensil inside the patient's body during surgery. The patient was unconscious during surgery, and likely unable to prove which professional was responsible. But, again, this is not the sort of thing that happens absent someone's negligence, and it seems likely that it was caused by the negligence of the defendants who were in the room during surgery. With *Res Ipsa Loquitor* we shift the burden from the plaintiffs having to prove that the defendants breached their duty, to the defendants having to prove that they did not breach their duty.

Damages

The final element of negligence is damages. To successfully sue someone for negligence, you need to show that the defendant caused the plaintiff damages. Note that for many of the intentional torts, the plaintiff did not need to prove financial damages. For example, imagine that a baseball player spits on an opposing coach every time the player is within spitting distance of the coach. This is gross, but imagine that the spit never causes the coach to get sick and never damaged the coach's clothing. The coach just wipes the spit off of his face. In this case, there are no financial damages, but we do not require financial damages for the tort of battery. The elements of the tort of battery are satisfied when there is a voluntary, intentional, harmful or offensive contact to a person or something closely associated thereto, even if there are no financial damages. Unlike the tort of battery, the tort of negligence requires proof of damages.

Compensatory Damages

The most common form of damages in negligence cases is **compensatory damages**. These are damages designed to compensate the plaintiff for the losses the plaintiff suffered.

Compensatory damages are divided into special damages and general damages. **Special damages** are a specific dollar amount that can represent medical bills, lost income, etc. **General damages** are a subjective dollar amount to cover intangible losses such as pain and suffering.

Punitive Damages

In addition to compensatory damages, there can be punitive damages designed to punish the wrongdoer and deter the conduct in the future. For example, in 1992, 79-year-old Stella Liebeck bought a cup of coffee at a McDonald's drive-thru in Albuquerque, spilled it on her lap, suffered burns, and a jury awarded her nearly $3 million in punitive damages. Some people have pointed to the judgment as an example of ridiculously high jury awards.

However, what was missing from some of the headlines was that Mrs. Liebeck suffered third-degree burns and required skin grafts, and McDonald's had received more than 700 previous reports of injury from hot coffee, including other third-degree burns. She offered to settle the case for $20,000 to cover her medical expenses and lost income. McDonald's never offered more than $800.

The jury found that Mrs. Liebeck was partially at fault for her injuries and reduced her compensatory damages accordingly. But it was the jury's punitive damages that made headlines. Upset by McDonald's unwillingness to correct a problem that was causing hundreds of injuries, the jury awarded Liebeck the equivalent of two days' worth of McDonald's coffee revenue. This amount was reduced by 80 percent by the judge, and to avoid years of appeals, Mrs. Liebeck and McDonald's reached a confidential settlement.

Nominal Damages

Nominal damages are a small, symbolic amount awarded to a plaintiff when a legal wrong occurred, but no significant financial loss resulted from the wrong. For example, imagine that a defendant is trespassing on the plaintiff's land, but not causing any damage to the land. The plaintiff may still want to go to court to establish the land's boundaries. In response, the court could find that the defendant is liable for trespassing and award the plaintiff nominal damages of $1. This would serve to recognize that the plaintiff's rights were violated, even if there was no actual financial harm suffered. Nominal damages alone are generally not considered sufficient to establish a claim for the tort of negligence.

The Egg-Shell Plaintiff

The concept of the egg-shell plaintiff acknowledges that defendants take their plaintiffs as they find them. A defendant may accidentally hit a plaintiff with a thick skull, or a defendant may accidentally hit a plaintiff with a skull as thin as an eggshell. The person with the thick skull may suffer no injuries. The person with the thin skull may be severely injured. The susceptibility to injury makes no impact on the defendant's liability. If the defendant was negligent in causing the person with the thin skull injuries, the defendant is liable for the injuries even if another plaintiff would have suffered no injuries.

Negligence Examples in Sports

Whenever someone breaches a duty owed and this is the cause of damages, there could be a lawsuit for the tort of negligence. Examples can include an outbreak of an infectious disease (MRSA, norovirus, rabies, Covid-19), concussions and brain injuries, stampedes caused by pre and post game celebrations, negligent supervision of operations (like snow falling off a roof and injuring people), negligent hiring or training, mascot misconduct, failure to properly train, providing improper equipment, improper maintenance of playing fields, or even unequal matching of opponents.

Sharing the Blame

As we saw in the case of Mrs. Liebeck and McDonald's, sometimes both sides are at least partially at fault. When this happens, how do we divide the blame? States have answered this question in three different ways: contributory negligence, comparative fault, and modified comparative fault.

Contributory Negligence

The Common Law tradition held that if a plaintiff is in any way at fault for the plaintiff's damages, the plaintiff is barred from recovery. This means the plaintiff is prevented from recovering any monetary compensation from the defendant. In a jurisdiction that follows this tradition, Mrs. Liebeck would be barred from recovery because she contributed to her injuries when she spilled the coffee on herself even if the coffee was unreasonably hot. The only remaining contributory fault jurisdictions in the U.S. are Alabama, Maryland, North Carolina, Washington D.C., and Virginia.

Comparative Fault

In a move to soften the harsh bar to recovery in a strict contributory negligence system, some states have moved to a comparative fault system. In a state that applies comparative fault, the plaintiff's recovery is reduced in proportion to the plaintiff's percentage of fault.

For example, imagine that an athlete and coach both suspect that the athlete suffered a concussion, but the athlete stays in the game, and this causes injuries that would have been avoided if the athlete was removed from the game. We could argue that the coach is liable, but we may also argue that the athlete was aware of the concussion risks and wanted to stay in the game. In a contributory fault jurisdiction, the athlete would be barred from recovery, meaning the athlete would receive nothing. In a comparative fault jurisdiction, the athlete's recovery would be reduced in proportion to the athlete's percentage of fault. If there were $100,000 in damages and a jury determines that the athlete was 50% at fault, then the athlete's recovery would be reduced to $50,000.

Comparative fault is often criticized in situations where a plaintiff is mostly at fault. For example, imagine that trespassers suffer $1 million in damages when they are injured while breaking into a fitness center and a jury determines that the trespassers were 90% at fault for their own injuries. In a comparative fault jurisdiction, the trespassers' recovery would be reduced by 90%–that's $900,000—but would be entitled to the remaining $100,000. Comparative fault is used by the majority of jurisdictions including some of the most populous states like California, New York, and Florida. It is also used in New Mexico where the *Liebeck v. McDonalds* case was heard. Of course, there would be no liability for the tort of negligence if the fitness center did not owe the trespassers a duty of care, and defendants generally do not owe a duty of care to unknown trespassers.

Modified Comparative Fault

Some states have determined that contributory fault is too harsh in completely barring a plaintiff from recovery when the plaintiff is at *any* fault, but too generous to plaintiffs who are mostly at fault. In response, some states use a modified comparative fault system. This system bars plaintiffs from recovery if the plaintiff is more at fault than the defendant. For example, in Texas a "claimant may not recover damages if his percentage of responsibility is greater than 50 percent" (*Texas Civil Practice and Remedies Code*, Section 33.001 Proportionate Responsibility). If the plaintiff is 50 percent or less at fault, comparative fault applies. This means that trespassers who are 90% at fault would receive nothing, and an elderly woman who is 50% or less at fault for spilling coffee on herself would receive her recovery minus her percentage of fault. The maximum percentage of liability allowed in modified comparative fault jurisdictions varies by state.

Strict Liability

In certain situations, a defendant can be held strictly liable for a plaintiff's damages even if the defendant did not act intentionally—that is, there was no intentional tort—and the defendant did not even breach a duty of care owed to the plaintiff. That is, there was no negligence either. Strict liability can apply when the defendant is engaged in an unreasonably dangerous activity or when the defendant makes or distributes a defective product.

Unreasonably Dangerous Activities

Unreasonably dangerous activities can include using explosives or keeping wild animals. For example, imagine a sports team has a live tiger for a mascot. If the tiger injures someone, we will not ask if the defendant acted reasonably. We will ask if the defendant kept a tiger. This would be an unreasonably dangerous activity and the defendant would be held strictly liable for any damages caused by the tiger.

Defective Product

Strict liability also applies to defective products. This liability extends to anyone in the stream of commerce from manufacturers, wholesalers, and retailers. The types of product defects are manufacturing defects, design defects, and warning defects.

Manufacturing Defect

A manufacturing defect exists when a manufacturer fails to assemble, test, or check the quality of a product resulting in a product that departs from its intended design. For example, a percentage of U.S. coins are minted incorrectly and become desired by collectors. If a similar manufacturing process created a product that was not like the others, this would be a manufacturing defect.

Design Defect

A design defect exists when the product conforms to the design specifications, but the design poses a foreseeable risk of harm. The Restatement (Third) of Torts provides that a design defect occurs "when the foreseeable risks of harm posed by the product could have been reduced or avoided by the adoption of a reasonable alternative design by the seller or other distributor, or a predecessor in the commercial chain of distribution, and the omission of the alternative design renders the product not reasonably safe."

To evaluate a design defect, plaintiffs can use the Risk-Utility Analysis or the Consumer Expectation Test. The **Risk-Utility Analysis** asks if the risk of harm from the product as designed outweighs its utility to the user and to the public. For example, we have power lines that provide electricity to homes and businesses. The risk of their design is that they sometimes cause fires when knocked down during high winds. The utility is that they provide electricity to our homes and businesses. In a Risk-Utility Analysis, we would weigh the utility of the power lines providing electricity against the risk that the powerlines sometimes cause fires.

The **Consumer Expectation Test** asks what an ordinary consumer would expect of the product. This test was used in *Wilson Sporting Goods Co. v. Hickox*, 59 A.3d 1267, 1277 (D.C. 2013). In the case, we learn that Wilson Sporting Goods designed a new throat guard for its baseball umpire mask. Edwin Hickox purchased the mask and was wearing it while umpiring a game when he was struck by a ball that caused a concussion and permanent hearing loss. Hickox and his wife sued Wilson for product liability and won. The court held that "an ordinary consumer would have expected the mask to perform more safely than it did."

Here is an excerpt from *Wilson Sporting Goods Co. v. Hickox* (2013). **In the words of the Court:**

> Finally, liability for design defect requires proof that the defect proximately caused the plaintiff's injury. *Warner Fruehauf,* 654 A.2d. Wilson argues that the Hickoxes failed to present sufficient causation evidence, because they did not show that additional product testing by Wilson would have uncovered the design defect. We are doubtful that such proof was required, because proof that a product was designed defectively under the consumer-expectations test does not appear to require proof that the defect was reasonably foreseeable, whether through testing or otherwise. *See Caterpillar Tractor,* 593 P.2d at 885 ("[T]he plaintiff need only show, for strict liability to apply, that he used the product in an intended or reasonably foreseeable fashion and the product failed to perform in that capacity as safely as expected."); *Ontai v. Straub Clinic & Hosp., Inc.,* 66 Haw. 237, 659 P.2d 734, 739 (1983) ("It is enough

that the plaintiff demonstrates that because of its manufacture or design, the product does not meet the reasonable expectations of the ordinary consumer or user as to its safety."). In any event, there was sufficient evidence that testing would have revealed the defect, because Dr. Paul testified that Wilson would have discovered the defect if it had conducted testing to measure the force exerted by the mask on the wearer's head after impact by a baseball. Combined with Dr. Paul's testimony that Mr. Hickox would not have suffered the same injury if he had worn an alternative mask, this evidence was sufficient to establish proximate causation. *Wilson Sporting Goods Co. v. Hickox*, 59 A.3d 1267, 1277 (D.C. 2013)

Warning Defect

A warning defect in strict product liability occurs when a product is unreasonably dangerous to consumers because it lacks adequate instructions or warnings. This defect can lead to injuries that could have been avoided if proper warnings or instructions had been provided.

Who can be liable for a defective product is spelled out in the Restatement (Second) of Torts Section 402A.

It states the following:

SPECIAL LIABILITY OF SELLER OF PRODUCT FOR PHYSICAL HARM TO USER OR CONSUMER.

Subsection 1: One who sells any product in a defective condition unreasonably dangerous to the user or consumer or to his property is subject to liability for physical harm thereby caused to the ultimate user or consumer, or to his property, if:
(a) the seller is engaged in the business of selling such a product, and
(b) it is expected to and does reach the user or consumer without substantial change in the condition in which it is sold.
Subsection 2: The rule stated in Subsection (1) applies though:
(a) the seller has exercised all possible care in the preparation and sale of his product, and
(b) the user or consumer has not bought the product from or entered into any contractual relation with the seller.

Defenses to Torts

After a plaintiff proves that a defendant committed all elements of a tort, defendants can offer defenses to explain why their conduct should be excused. Defenses can limit or even prevent liability for a tort. Defendants must prove these defenses to a preponderance of the evidence.

Consent

If a defendant can prove that the plaintiff consented to the tort, then the defendant should not be held liable for committing the tort. For example, throwing and hitting someone in the head with a baseball could technically be a battery because it involves someone committing a voluntary, intentional act that caused harmful or offensive contact to a person. However, if a plaintiff is playing catch with the defendant and simply misses a catch and gets hit in the head, it seems inappropriate that the defendant should be held liable for the tort of battery.

Consent can be either expressed or implied. Expressed consent exists when there are words—oral or in writing—stating that the victim consents to the conduct that would otherwise be a tort. For example, if someone plays paintball, they often need to sign a waiver providing expressed consent to getting hit by paintballs. Consent can also be implied by conduct or by law. Consent implied by conduct could exist in our baseball example. Maybe your friend did not expressly say that you could throw a ball at him. Instead, he simply raised his glove indicating that you should throw the baseball to him.

Consent can also be implied by law. For example, imagine an unconscious person is touched by emergency medical personnel seeking to help the unconscious person. Although this contact may be harmful, the law will likely find that this should not be a battery because it will find there was implied consent to this necessary emergency treatment.

Assumption of the Risk

The defense of assumption of the risk is available when a plaintiff knows of a risk, understands the risk, and still voluntarily elects to encounter the risk. Assumption of the risk can be expressed by the plaintiff's words—either written or oral—or implied by the plaintiff's conduct. For example, modern parkour athletes seem to jump off, around, and between buildings. If they know and understand the risk of jumping off buildings and then voluntarily elect to jump off a building, a defendant could argue that the injured plaintiff assumed the risk of injury when the plaintiff jumped off the building.

Contact Sports Exception

The case of *Nabozny v. Barnhill* established the contact sports exception. In this case, the plaintiff, Nabozny, was a soccer goalie who was injured when an opposing player kicked Nabozny's head, causing permanent damage to Nabozny's skull and brain. Nabozny sued Barnhill for negligence. During the trial, experts agreed that the game rules prohibited all players from contacting the goalkeeper when he is in possession of the ball in the penalty area. However, the court determined that negligence is not enough to find liability in a contact sport. Instead, participants in contact sports will only be held liable for injuries to other players if their conduct is "willful or with a reckless disregard for the safety of the other player so as to cause injury to that player" (*Nabozny v. Barnhill*, 31 Ill. App. 3d 212, 215, 334 N.E.2d 258, 261 (1975). **Recklessness** requires proof that the defendant consciously disregarded a substantial risk of harm. That is a standard much higher than the basic negligence standard of merely breaching a duty of acting like a reasonable person.

This is how the contact sports exemption was articulated in *Pfister v. Shusta* (657 N.E. 2d 1013 (1995)).

In the words of the court:
The contact sports exception strikes the appropriate balance between society's interest in limiting liability for injuries resulting from physical contact inherent in a contact sport and society's interest in allowing recovery for injuries resulting from willful and wanton or intentional misconduct by participants. Those who participate in soccer, football, softball, basketball, or even a spontaneous game of can kicking, choose to play games in which physical contact among participants is inherent in the conduct of the game. Participants in such games assume a greater risk of injury resulting from the negligent conduct of coparticipants. Justice Green accurately reviewed the policy reasons supporting the contact sports exception in his dissent in the case at bar:
"The exposure of one participant to liability to another participant for merely negligent bodily contact, even under the disorganized situation here, will cause more harm than good.... [I]n common understanding, football, wrestling, and boxing, among others, are clearly recognized as contact sports. Basketball, hockey, and soccer all permit some bodily contact and, in actual practice, more

---

contact is permitted than a reading of the rules would indicate. In all of the above sports, players regularly commit contact beyond that which is permitted by the rules even as applied. In basketball, such an illegal contact is described as a foul for which a sanction is imposed. Sometimes the player fouled is injured. This is to be expected. If every time a negligent foul resulted in injury, and liability was imposed, the game of basketball as we know it would not be played." 256 Ill.App.3d at 191-92, 194 Ill. Dec. 618, 627 N.E.2d 1260 (Green, J., dissenting).

Commonly Known Dangers

In product liability there is the defense of commonly known dangers. For example, in 1957, Marguerite Jamieson was injured when an elastic exercise rope slipped off her foot and struck her in the eye. It detached her retina. Jamieson claimed that the manufacturer should be liable because it had failed to warn users that the rope might slip off a foot and strike you in the eye. The court disagreed, arguing that there are certain commonly known dangers for which a manufacturer should not be liable.

In the words of the court:

> A manufacturer cannot manufacture a knife that will not cut or a hammer what will not mash a thumb or a stove that will not burn a finger. The law does not require him to warn of such common dangers. On the other end of the spectrum of practicalities, a manufacturer should not be permitted to market without protection to the user a spray which would kill trees if used at the wrong time, as in McClanahan, or a skirt which would otherwise ignite if brushed by a lighted cigarette, as in Noone. A manufacturer might be liable for failure to provide a shield or an emphatic warning to users of an electric power saw, but he would not be liable if he failed so to provide in respect to a kitchen knife. *Jamieson v. Woodward & Lothrop,* 247 F.2d 23, 26 (D.C. Cir. 1957)

Perhaps akin to product liability's "commonly known dangers" is a pitcher in baseball hitting a batter with a ball. Some casual spectators may think that this act is just an accident and so would not constitute the intentional tort of battery. It also would not satisfy the elements for negligence if there are no damages. However, real fans know that this conduct is not always an accident. Sometimes the pitchers intend to hit the batter, and then hit the batter. Could this be a battery? The short answer is no. In 2006, a judge ruled that a pitcher intentionally hitting a batter with a ball will not be a battery because intentionally hitting a batter is a fundamental part of the game of baseball (*Avila v. Citrus Cmty. Coll* (Cal. 2006)).

Statutes of Limitation and Repose

States have also limited liability by passing statutes of limitation and statutes of repose. A **statute of limitation** is a legal rule that sets the maximum time within which a plaintiff must initiate legal proceedings after an alleged offense. For example, if a state requires plaintiffs to sue within two years of an injury or within one year from the date the injury was discovered, then the plaintiffs must initiate legal proceedings before these deadlines. If they wait beyond the deadlines, they will be barred from recovery. Whereas statutes of limitation are tied to the date when a potential plaintiff suffers harm, **statutes of repose** are often tied to the date when a defendant sold a product or did some work. For example, Texas has a two-year statute of limitation for product liability cases and a 15-year statute of repose. This means that if you are injured by a product in Texas, you would need to initiate legal proceedings within two years of your injury and within 15 years of when the product was sold.

Chapter 4: Criminal Law

Whereas tort law often seeks to provide a monetary remedy to the plaintiff, criminal law seeks to punish, rehabilitate, and/or prevent wrongdoers from committing more crimes.

In criminal court, there is a prosecutor who is an attorney paid by taxpayers to represent the interest of "the people" and a defendant being charged with a crime. You do not have to go out and hire an attorney to sue someone who commits a crime against you. You call the police and the prosecutor's office will decide whether to prosecute. Prosecutorial discretion is the term used to describe a prosecutor's ability to decide whether to charge a person for committing a crime, and what criminal charges to file.

To find the defendant guilty of a crime, the prosecutor needs to prove that the defendant committed every element of the crime to a standard called "beyond a reasonable doubt." If the defendant is found guilty, he or she can be forced to go to jail or prison for an amount of time commensurate with the crime committed. The guilty party may also be forced to pay financial damages to the victim or victims of the criminal conduct. Financial damages in criminal court are called restitution.

There are state crimes and federal crimes. If a defendant is accused of a state crime, the trial will be held in state court with a state prosecuting attorney and a state judge. Punishment would be in a state prison, and any appeals would go to the state appellate court. If a defendant is accused of a federal crime, the trial is in federal court with a federal prosecuting attorney and a federal judge. Punishment would be in a federal penitentiary, and any appeals would go to the federal appellate court. Of course, both state and federal cases can ultimately be appealed to the United States Supreme Court.

U.S. criminal law developed as part of the English Common Law tradition where court precedent created the criminal law definitions. For example, through court decisions, Common Law burglary became defined as breaking and entering a dwelling place at night with the intent to commit a felony therein. Notice that this addresses a specific threat that wouldn't apply if someone broke into your shed or house to get out of the rain because your shed isn't your dwelling place and getting out of the rain isn't a felony. Each state then passed their own laws to define the various crimes and punishments for their state. To provide greater uniformity in criminal law, the American Law Institute published the Model Penal Code (MPC) in 1962. The MPC is not legally binding on states, but most states have enacted criminal codes that at least borrow heavily from the MPC. Variations still exist. Therefore, individuals should refer to their specific state statutes to find their state's criminal definitions.

States are free to make their own criminal laws as long as they don't violate the U.S. Constitution or their own state constitutions. The most likely U.S. constitutional objections to state law are from the Fourteenth Amendment of the U.S. Constitution. This provides that no state can deprive any person of life, liberty, or property without due process of law. The due process requirement of the Fourteenth Amendment is usually satisfied by a fair trial which the Sixth Amendment requires for all criminal prosecutions. Due process also requires that laws should be reasonably clear to provide a fair warning to citizens. It also prevents legislatures from making ex post facto laws. **Ex post facto** laws are laws that make something a crime or increases the punishment for a crime after a crime has been committed.

Other important amendments relating to criminal law are the Fourth Amendment, preventing unreasonable search and seizure, and the Fifth Amendment. The Fifth Amendment prevents someone from having to answer for a crime unless indicted, having to be tried for the same crime twice, or having to be a witness against oneself. It also prevents individuals from being deprived of life, liberty, or property by the federal government without due process of law. Although the Fourth Amendment and Fifth Amendment were originally written as limitations on the Federal Government, these now apply to the states through their incorporation in the Fourteenth Amendment's prohibition against depriving any person of life, liberty, or property without due process of law.

Criminal Procedures and a President, Q&A

Although not a sport, it seems that politics has become one of America's favorite pastimes. Lucky for law students, this provides an easy way to review criminal procedures. Below is a Q&A about a criminal case involving classified documents that were found at President Donald Trump's personal residence while Joe Biden was president.

Q: Was there any risk of a foreign national accessing classified documents at then Former President Trump's Mar-a-Lago residence?

A. Yes, in 2019 a Chinese National was sentenced to prison for entering the restricted grounds at Mar-a-Lago and lying to U.S. Secret Service agents. Prosecutors say they found multiple electronic devices in her hotel room, including a signal detector that can seek out and detect hidden cameras, another cell phone, nine USB drives and five SIM cards. This occurred prior to the demands that Trump return classified documents.

Q. On August 5, 2022, a search warrant was issued to search Mar-a-Lago. On August 8, 2022, the search was executed. Why does law enforcement need a **search warrant**?

A. Because of the Fourth Amendment to the U.S. Constitution.

Q. What does the Fourth Amendment say?

A. The Fourth Amendment of the U.S. Constitution states, "The right of the people to be secure in their persons, houses, papers, and effects, against unreasonable searches and seizures, shall not be violated, and no Warrants shall issue, but upon **probable cause,** supported by Oath or affirmation, and particularly describing the place to be searched, and the persons or things to be seized.

Q. The Fourth Amendment states that no warrants shall be issued without "probable cause." How has the Supreme Court defined "probable cause?"

A. In *Carroll v. United States*, the Supreme Court defined "probable cause" as an officer's reasonable belief, based on circumstances known to that officer, that a crime has occurred or is about to occur. (*Carroll v. United States*, 267 U.S. 132, 149 (1925)).

Q. On June 8, 2023, Trump was indicted on 31 counts of violating the Espionage Act in connection with documents discovered at Mar-a-Lago. Why does there need to be an **indictment**?

A. Because of the Fifth Amendment to the U.S. Constitution.

Q. What does the Fifth Amendment say?

A. The Fifth Amendment states, "No person shall be held to answer for a capital, or otherwise infamous crime, unless on a presentment or indictment of a Grand Jury, except in cases arising in the land or naval forces, or in the Militia, when in actual service in time of War or public danger; nor shall any person be subject for the same offence to be twice put in jeopardy of life or limb; nor shall be compelled in any criminal case to be a witness against himself, nor be deprived of life, liberty, or property, without due process of law; nor shall private property be taken for public use, without just compensation."

Q. The Fifth Amendment states that "no person shall be held to answer for a capital, or otherwise infamous crime, unless on a presentment or indictment of a Grand Jury." What is a grand jury?

A. A **grand jury** is an impartial group of citizens that listens to the prosecutor and witnesses, and then votes in secret on whether they believe enough evidence exists to charge the person with a crime.

Q. What if a grand jury decides there is insufficient evidence to prosecute the defendant?

A. If a grand jury decides not to charge an individual based upon the evidence, no indictment would come from the grand jury.

Q. Are the grand jury discussions public?

A. No, all proceedings and statements made before a grand jury are sealed, meaning that only the people in the room have knowledge about who said what about whom.

Q. Does getting indicted imply that someone must have done something illegal?

A. No. In our legal system there is a presumption of innocence which means that any defendant in a criminal trial is assumed to be innocent until they have been proven guilty.

Q. If you sense that there is a bias in the indictment for one side, for which side would you suspect there is a bias?

A. The indictment is written by the prosecution. Therefore, you should expect that it is written in a light most favorable to the prosecution.

Q. If the prosecution drafts the indictment, should we assume that the allegations in the indictment are false?

A. No, in civil court, Rule 11 of the Federal Rules of Civil Procedure requires that any pleading, written motion, or other paper submitted to the court must be based on facts that have evidentiary support or are likely to have evidentiary support after a reasonable opportunity for further investigation or discovery. In criminal law, prosecutors must:

1) Refrain from prosecuting a charge they know is not supported by probable cause.
2) Make reasonable efforts to ensure the accused has been advised of the right to, and the procedure for obtaining, counsel.
3) Disclose evidence that negates the guilt of the accused or mitigates the offense.

Q. What did the indictment in the classified documents case against Trump allege?

A. The indictment alleges that after leaving office, Trump stored classified documents in boxes at his residence and some of these included information regarding defense and weapons capabilities of both the United States and foreign countries; United States nuclear programs; potential vulnerabilities of the United States and its allies to military attack; and plans for possible retaliation in response to a foreign attack. It further alleges that Trump showed and described a "plan of attack" to a publisher and two members of his staff—none of whom possessed a security clearance. He told them that the plan was "highly confidential" and "secret," adding "as president I could have declassified it," and, "Now I can't, you know, but this is still secret."

Q. In recent years, classified documents were found at the residences of President Trump, former Vice President Pence, and former President Biden, but only Trump was charged with having classified documents. Does this show a bias against Trump?

A. Trump was not charged with possession of classified documents. He was charged with willfully retaining national defense information, withholding and concealing documents, committing a conspiracy to obstruct justice, and making false statements. When Pence and Biden discovered classified information, they notified federal law enforcement to have them take custody of the documents. When the grand jury issued a subpoena requiring that Trump turn over all documents with classified markings, the indictment says, "Trump endeavored to obstruct the FBI and grand jury investigations and conceal his continued retention of classified documents."

Q. After Trump officially announced that he was running for president in 2024, Attorney General Garland announced the appointment of Jack Smith as special counsel in the classified documents case. Why?

A. The government appoints a special counsel to investigate or prosecute cases where there might be a conflict of interest for the usual prosecuting authority or where it may be in the public interest to have an independent investigator. The special counsel operates with a degree of independence from the Department of Justice. The president serves as head of the Executive Branch and the Attorney General reports to the president. Once Trump announced that he was running for president, a special counsel was appointed to prosecute the case so that the prosecution was not being directed by the Attorney General, who reports directly to Trump's then political opponent, President Biden.

Q. On July 15, 2024, Judge Cannon dismissed the classified documents case. Why?

A. Judge Cannon dismissed the case arguing that the appointment of a special counsel is unlawful.

Q. When Judge Cannon dismissed the case, did that mean that the case was closed forever?

A. No, in August 2024, Special Counsel Jack Smith filed an appeal to the 11th Circuit Court of Appeals, challenging Judge Cannon's dismissal.

Q. Had anyone before Trump ever run for president after being convicted of a crime?

A. Yes. Eugene Debs was the Socialist Party presidential candidate in 1904, 1908, and 1912. He was sentenced to 10 years in prison for violating the Espionage Act and ran for president from prison in 1920. President Harding commuted his sentence in December 1921 after Debs had already served nearly five years in prison.

Q. What are the potential consequences for violating the Espionage Act?

A. In 1953, Julius and Ethel Rosenberg were executed for sharing nuclear secrets in violation of the Espionage Act. They were 35 and 37 years old. They left two young sons. Michael Meeropol grew up to become a professor of economics. His younger brother is an anthropologist.

Trump's election in 2024 effectively ended the federal prosecution against him. The president, after all, is head of the Executive Branch which is tasked with enforcing the law. Special Counsel Jack Smith resigned in 2025 before Trump took office.

Mens Rea and *Actus Reus*

Most crimes require the combination of a guilty mind (*mens rea*) plus a guilty act (*actus reus*). For example, the crime of murder requires a homicide committed with malice aforethought. The guilty mind would be the malice aforethought which is defined as an intent to kill, intent to do serious bodily harm, or depraved indifference to human life. The guilty act would be the homicide which is the killing of a human being. If a defendant does not have the mental state required for a specific crime, the defendant cannot be found guilty of the crime. Similarly, if the defendant had the *mens rea*, but did not commit the act, the defendant cannot be found guilty of the crime no matter how guilty and depraved the defendant's mind might be.

We should note that just because individuals do not have the *mens rea* and *actus rea* for one crime does not mean that they will walk away free from all consequences. The defendant may still be guilty of a different crime. For example, at Common Law, if you remove the *mens rea* from murder, you get the crime of manslaughter which was defined as an unlawful homicide committed without malice aforethought. The mental state for manslaughter could include recklessness which requires proof only that the defendant consciously disregarded a substantial risk of harm. That is far less than malice aforethought's intent to kill, intent to do serious bodily harm, or depraved indifference to human life.

Many states have also added degrees to crimes—like murder in the first degree or murder in the second degree—to align more serious consequences with more serious offenses. For example, Common Law murder in many statutes is referred to as Murder in the Second Degree. Murder in the First Degree is then reserved for those murders where the defendant's malice aforethought also included premeditation and deliberation.

Attempt Crimes

There are also crimes where attempting a crime is a crime in itself. For example, attempted murder is a crime. To be found guilty of an attempt crime, one must have the specific intent to commit the completed offense plus an act that is less than what is needed for the completed offense. This means that for attempted murder, one must have the specific intent to commit a homicide. This is a higher *mens rea* requirement than required for the crime of murder because the *mens rea* for murder also includes the intent to do serious bodily harm or depraved indifference to human life. These mental states would be insufficient for the crime of attempted murder because attempted murder requires the specific intent to kill.

Mens Rea + *Actus Reus* = Completed Offense Crime
Mens Rea + Less than *Actus Reus* = Attempted Offense Crime

State of Washington v. Jason P. Shelley

To illustrate various elements of criminal law in sports, let's jump into the case of the *State of Washington v. Jason P. Shelley*. Notice that even by the title you have a hint that this is going to be a criminal case because we have the state of Washington as the moving party against an individual. States can also sue individuals in a civil case, but it is not as common.

This case involves a pick-up basketball game at the University of Washington's Intramural Activities Building. The parties are Jason Shelley and a victim named Mario Gonzalez. We learn in the case that Gonzalez had a "reputation for playing overly aggressive defense." We learn that during a game between Shelley and Gonzalez, Gonzalez tried to hit the ball from Shelley and then "scratched Shelley's face and drew blood." This caused Shelley to briefly leave the game.

But remember, this case has Shelley as the defendant, not Gonzalez. What did Shelley do? Shelley returned to the game and struck Gonzalez, breaking his jaw in three places. For this Shelley "was convicted of assault in the second degree after the State successfully argued to the jury that Shelley intentionally punched [Gonzalez]."

In the case, we learn that when police detectives interviewed Shelley, Shelley said he "had been getting mad" at Gonzalez and the scratch was "the final straw." If you learn anything from this chapter, please remember that you have the right to remain silent and should contact an attorney instead of admitting to the police that you had the *mens rea* necessary for the *actus reus* you committed.

Shelley appealed his conviction to the Washington Court of Appeals arguing that the wrong standard for consent was used in his conviction. The trial court had defined consent in contact sports as "conduct within the rules of the game." Shelley's attorneys argued that the better definition would define consent as any "reasonably foreseeable hazards of joint participation in an athletic contest." The court agreed that the "reasonably foreseeable hazards" was the better standard. After all, committing a hard foul in basketball against someone going up for a layup is technically against the rules, but the remedy is a trip to the foul line, not jail time for battery.

Even though the appeals court agreed that there is implied consent in contact sports to "the conduct and harm that are the reasonably foreseeable hazards of joint participation in an athletic contest," they still found that there was no consent to Shelley's conduct because it "was not a reasonably foreseeable hazard of their game."

Here is an excerpt from *State of Washington v. Jason P. Shelley*. **In the words of the Court:**

> During a rough basketball game, Jason Shelley struck another player and broke his jaw in three places. He was convicted of assault in the second degree after the State successfully argued to the jury that Shelley intentionally punched the other player. On appeal, Shelley claims that he was entitled to argue that the victim consented to the possibility of injury when he decided to play pickup basketball. While we agree that consent may be a defense to assault in athletic competitions, Shelley has failed to establish a factual basis for that defense. Further, while we hold that the consent defense is not limited to conduct within the rules of the games, rather it is to the conduct and harm that are the reasonably foreseeable hazards of joint participation in an athletic contest, we conclude that Shelley's conduct was not a reasonably foreseeable hazard.

> On March 31, 1993, Jason Shelley and Mario Gonzalez played "pickup" basketball on opposing teams at the University of Washington Intramural Activities Building (the IMA). Pickup games are not refereed by an official; rather, the players take responsibility for calling their own fouls. During the course of three games, Gonzalez fouled Shelley several times. Gonzalez had a reputation for playing overly aggressive defense at the IMA. Toward the end of the evening, after trying to hit the ball away from Shelley, he [Gonzalez] scratched Shelley's face, and drew blood. After getting scratched, Shelley briefly left the game and then returned. [Dwight Kealy's commentary: This means Shelley had time to "cool off"].

Shelley and Gonzalez have differing versions of what occurred after Shelley returned to the game. According to Gonzalez, while he was waiting for play in the game to return to Gonzalez's side of the court, Shelley suddenly hit him. Gonzalez did not see Shelley punch him. According to Shelley's version of events, when Shelley rejoined the game, he was running down the court and he saw Gonzalez make "a move towards me as if he was maybe going to prevent me from getting the ball." The move was with his hand up "across my vision." Angry, he "just reacted" and swung. He said he hit him because he was afraid of being hurt, like the previous scratch. He testified that Gonzalez continually beat him up during the game by fouling him hard. [Dwight Kealy's commentary: He's trying to use the defense of self-defense].

A week after the incident, a school police detective interviewed Shelley and prepared a statement for Shelley to sign based on the interview. Shelley reported to the police that Gonzalez had been "continually slapping and scratching him" during the game. Shelley "had been getting mad" at Gonzalez and the scratch on Shelley's face was the "final straw." As the two were running down the court side by side, "I swung my right hand around and hit him with my fist on the right side of his face." Shelley asserted that he also told the detective that Gonzalez waved a hand at him just before throwing the punch and that he told the detective that he was afraid of being injured. [Dwight Kealy's commentary: Again, there's the Fifth Amendment protection against self-incrimination. Shelley just admitted that he was getting mad, it was the final straw, and he swung and hit the victim].

Gonzalez required emergency surgery to repair his jaw. Broken in three places, it was wired shut for six weeks. His treating physician believed that a "significant" blow caused the damage.

During the course of the trial, defense counsel told the court he intended to propose a jury instruction that: "A person legally consents to conduct that causes or threatens bodily harm if the conduct and the harm are reasonably foreseeable hazards of joint participation in a lawful, athletic contest or competitive sport." Although the trial court agreed that there were risks involved in sports, it stated that "the risk of being intentionally punched by another player is one that I don't think we ever do assume." The court noted, "In basketball...you consent to a certain amount of rough contact. If they were both going for a rebound and Mr.

Shelley's elbow or even his fist hit Mr. Gonzalez as they were both jumping for the rebound and Mr. Gonzalez'[s] jaw was fractured in exactly the same way...then you would have an issue." Reasoning that "our laws are intended to uphold the public peace and regulate behavior of individuals," the court ruled "that as a matter of law, consent cannot be a defense to an assault." The court indicated that Shelley could not claim consent because his conduct "exceed[ed] what is considered within the rules of that particular sport[:]"

[C]onsent is to contact that is contemplated within the rules of the game and that is incidental to the furtherance of the goals of that particular game.

If you can show me any rule book for basketball at any level that says an intentional punch to the face in some way is a part of the game, then I would take another—second look at your argument. I don't believe any such rule book exists.

Later Shelley proposed jury instructions on the subject of consent:

An act is not an assault, if it is done with the consent of the person alleged to be assaulted.

It is a defense to a charge of second degree assault occurring in the course of an athletic contest if the conduct and the harm are reasonably foreseeable hazards of joint participation in a lawful athletic contest or competitive sport.

The trial court rejected these and Shelley excepted. The trial court did instruct the jury about self-defense.

Consent
First, we hold that consent is a defense to an assault occurring during an athletic contest. This is consistent with the law of assault as it has developed in Washington. A person is guilty of second degree assault if he or she "[i]ntentionally assaults another and thereby recklessly inflicts substantial bodily harm." One common law definition of assault recognized in Washington is "'an unlawful touching with criminal intent.'" At the common law, a touching is unlawful when the person touched did not give consent to it, and was either harmful or offensive. As our Supreme Court stated in *State v. Simmons,* "'where there is consent, there is no assault.'" The State argues that because *Simmons* was a sexual assault case, the defense consent should be limited to that realm. We decline to apply the defense so narrowly. Logically, consent must be an issue in sporting events because a person participates in a

game knowing that it will involve potentially offensive contact and with this consent the "touchings" involved are not "unlawful."

Our review of the cases and commentary on the issue of consent reveals that although the defense of consent is applied in the realm of sexual assault, it has been sparingly applied by the courts in other areas. The rationale that courts offer in limiting it is that society has an interest in punishing assaults as breaches of the public peace and order, so that an individual cannot consent to a wrong that is committed against the public peace. Urging us to reject the defense of consent because an assault violates the public peace, the State argues that this principle precludes Shelley from being entitled to argue the consent defense on the facts of his case. In making this argument, the State ignores the factual contexts that dictated the results in the cases it cites in support.

When faced with the question of whether to accept a school child's consent to hazing or consent to a fight, or a gang member's consent to a beating, courts have declined to apply the defense. Obviously, these cases present "touchings" factually distinct from "touchings" occurring in athletic competitions.

If consent cannot be a defense to assault, then most athletic contests would need to be banned because many involve "invasions of one's physical integrity." Because society has chosen to foster sports competitions, players necessarily must be able to consent to physical contact and other players must be able to rely on that consent when playing the game. This is the view adopted by the drafters of the Model Penal Code:

There are, however, situations in which consent to bodily injury should be recognized as a defense to crime.... There is...the obvious case of participation in an athletic contest or competitive sport, where the nature of the enterprise often involves risk of serious injury. Here, the social judgment that permits the contest to flourish necessarily involves the companion judgment that reasonably foreseeable hazards can be consented to by virtue of participation.

The more difficult question is the proper standard by which to judge whether a person consented to the particular conduct at issue.

The State argues that "when the conduct in question is not within the rules of a given sport, a victim cannot be deemed to have consented to this act." The trial court apparently agreed with this approach. Although we recognize that there is authority supporting this approach, we reject a reliance on the rules of the games as too limiting. Rollin M. Perkins on Criminal Law explains:

The test is not necessarily whether the blow exceeds the conduct allowed by the rules of the game. Certain excesses and inconveniences are to be expected beyond the formal rules of the game. It may be ordinary and expected conduct for minor assaults to occur. However, intentional excesses beyond those reasonably contemplated in the sport are not justified.

Instead, we adopt the approach of the Model Penal Code which provides that:

(2) **Consent to Bodily Injury.** When conduct is charged to constitute an offense because it causes or threatens bodily injury, consent to such conduct or to the infliction of such injury is a defense if:

. . . . .

(b) the conduct and the injury are reasonably foreseeable hazards of joint participation in a lawful athletic contest or competitive sport or other concerted activity not forbidden by law.

The State argues the law does not allow "the victim to 'consent' to a broken jaw simply by participating in an unrefereed, informal basketball game." This argument presupposes that the harm suffered dictates whether the defense is available or not. This is not the correct inquiry.

The correct inquiry is whether the conduct of defendant constituted foreseeable behavior in the play of the game. Additionally, the injury must have occurred as a by-product of the game itself. In construing a similar statutory defense, the Iowa court required a "nexus between defendant's acts and playing the game of basketball." In *State v. Floyd,* a fight broke out during a basketball game and the defendant, who was on the sidelines, punched and severely injured several opposing team members. Because neither defendant nor his victims were voluntarily participating in the game, the defense did not apply because the statute "contemplated a person who commits acts during the course of play, and the exception seeks to protect those whose acts otherwise subject to prosecution are committed in furtherance of the object of the sport." As the court noted in *Floyd,* there is a "continuum, or sliding scale, grounded in the circumstances under which voluntary participants engage in sport...which governs the type of incidents in which an individual volunteers (*i.e.,* consents) to participate[.]"

The New York courts provide another example. In a football game, while tackling the defendant, the victim hit the defendant. After the play was over and all of the players got off the defendant, the defendant punched the victim in the eye. The court in *People v. Freer* held that this act was not consented to:

Initially it may be assumed that the very first punch thrown by the complainant in the course of the tackle was consented to by defendant. The act of tackling an opponent in the course of a football game may often involve "contact" that could easily be interpreted to be a "punch". Defendant's response after the pileup to complainant's initial act of "aggression" cannot be mistaken. Clearly, defendant intended to punch complainant. This was not a consented to act. *People v. Freer,* 86 Misc.2d 280, 381 N.Y.S.2d 976, 978 (1976).

As a corollary to the consent defense, the State may argue that the defendant's conduct exceeded behavior foreseeable in the game. Although in "all sports players consent to many risks, hazards and blows," there is "a limit to the magnitude and dangerousness of a blow to which another is deemed to consent." This limit, like the foreseeability of the risks, is determined by presenting evidence to the jury about the nature of the game, the participants' expectations, the location where the game has been played, as well as the rules of the game.

Here, taking Shelley's version of the events as true, the magnitude and dangerousness of Shelley's actions were beyond the limit. There is no question that Shelley lashed out at Gonzalez with sufficient force to land a substantial blow to the jaw, and there is no question but that Shelley intended to hit Gonzalez. There is nothing in the game of basketball, or even rugby or hockey, that would permit consent as a defense to such conduct. Shelley admitted to an assault and was not precluded from arguing that the assault justified self-defense; but justification and consent are not the same inquiry.

Related to his consent argument, Shelley claims that the assault statute is vague when applied to sports altercations because it fails to provide either adequate notice of proscribed conduct, or standards to prevent arbitrary enforcement as to athletes who believe they can be rough because they are accustomed to unprosecuted rough play. A statute is void for vagueness if it either "does not define the criminal offense with sufficient definiteness that ordinary people can understand what conduct is proscribed" or if it fails to "provide ascertainable standards of guilt to protect against arbitrary enforcement." Because his claim does not implicate any First Amendment rights, Shelley cannot claim the statute is facially vague; he may only argue that it is vague as applied to him.

Our holding that a defendant is entitled to argue that another player may legally consent to conduct that causes or threatens bodily harm if the conduct and the harm are reasonably foreseeable hazards of joint participation in a lawful, athletic contest or competitive sport cures any problem with vagueness. With this defense, an ordinary person should understand that intentionally punching a person in an athletic competition may result in criminal prosecution. Accordingly, the crime is defined with sufficient definiteness. Additionally, the statute did not invite arbitrary enforcement by law enforcement on the facts of this case given that breaking another's jaw in three places satisfies the substantial bodily harm element of RCW 9A.36.021(1)(a).

We affirm (*State v. Shelley*, 85 Wash. App. 24, 25–34, 929 P.2d 489, 490–94 (1997)).

Private Justice

In addition to state and federal prosecution for criminal acts, leagues and referees also impose their own penalties to guide athlete behavior. For example, "victims" get a trip to the free throw line, a penalty kick, or in football, sometimes 15 yards and an automatic first down. "Perpetrators" risk fouling out, ejection, or in hockey, "time-out" in a penalty box.

Leagues impose penalties for both on and off-field behavior. For example, in 2014 the NFL initially suspended Baltimore Ravens running back Ray Rice for two games after his arrest on domestic violence charges. After TMZ released a video of Rice knocking his fiancée unconscious in a hotel elevator, the NFL suspended him indefinitely and Baltimore released him from the team. The NFL reinstated Rice after 12 games, but no team ever signed him again.

In 2019, the NFL suspended Oakland Raiders linebacker Vontaze Burfict for the remainder of the season after his helmet-to-helmet hit on Indianapolis tight end Jack Doyle in a Week 4 game. The consequences of a personal foul are usually just a 15-yard penalty or ejection, but it appears that the NFL considered Burfict's history of violations and, perhaps, the footage of him laughing about the hit after he was ejected from the field.

In 2023 a bench-clearing brawl between the Chicago White Sox and Cleveland Guardians resulted in a six-game suspension for the players who threw punches at each other (Tim Anderson of the White Sox and José Ramírez of the Guardians). A variety of managers and coaches also received one-game suspensions.

Throughout the 2021-2022 NBA season Kyrie Irving, the former first overall draft pick of 2011, was fined over $16 million for refusing to receive the COVID-19 vaccine as required by New York City. Despite remaining unvaccinated, later in the season the Nets allowed Irving to play in games outside New York and Toronto. The Nets suspended Irving again during the 2022-23 season. This time, it was for his failure to "unequivocally say he has no antisemitic beliefs" after posting a link to an antisemitic work on his Twitter (now X) feed.

In 2020 Major League Baseball fined the Houston Astros $5 million—the maximum allowable under MLB's constitution—and imposed one-year suspensions to General Manager A.J. Hinch and former Assistant General Manager Brandon Taubman for stealing signs during the 2017 and 2018 seasons. The Astros were also forced to forfeit their first and second round draft picks for two years. To encourage truthful testimony, players were given full immunity—a decision that then commissioner Rob Manfred later said he regretted. In spite of this "private justice," the Astros went on to win the World Series in 2022.

The Malice at the Palace

In 2004 a fight broke out between players and fans at an NBA game between the defending champion Detroit Pistons and the Indiana Pacers. The press labeled the fight "The Malice at the Palace" because the game was held at The Palace of Auburn Hills in Michigan. With only 45.9 seconds left in the game and the Pacers leading 97-82, Pacers forward Ron Artest committed a hard foul against Pistons center Ben Wallace as Wallace attempted a layup. Wallace responded by shoving Artest and a fight broke out between players. The players were then separated. Artest decided to lie down quietly on the scorer's table where he was hit by a drink thrown by a fan named John Green. Artest responded by rushing into the stands to retaliate. A scene of thrown punches and drinks ensued.

Here is an excerpt from the commentators watching the scene unfold:

> Commentator 1-Now Artest has jumped over the scorer's table and is trying to get down to the bench. Artest is in the stands. Oh this is awful. Fans are getting involved. [Pacers player Stephen] Jackson's in the fans. Rasheed Wallace's going into the stands. The Security's trying to somehow restore order. Fans and players are going at it and the players are trying to help each other out.
>
> Commentator 2-This is a disgrace.
>
> Commentator 1-All the players, now, they're jumping in there to try to get the other players out because the fans have become involved.
>
> Commentator 2-What a sad scene here at the palace. And now another fight is breaking out in front of the Pistons' bench. It's a fan on the court. This is very, very dangerous.... You wonder if the officials are going to let this game continue. Now they're throwing bottles down onto the floor. They're trying to get the Pacers to go back to the locker room. What was maybe you could call a hard foul at best has turned into, just an ugly, ugly scene. (Midwest Sports Network (2019, May 21) *Pacers and Pistons Brawl – 2004 Original* https://www.youtube.com/watch?v=ghtDbOisWtA)

In the end, five players and five Detroit fans faced criminal charges for throwing punches, drinks, and even a chair. The players were sentenced to a year of probation and community service. In addition to the criminal charges, the five fans were banned from attending Pistons home games for life and the league imposed the following sanctions on players:

Player	Suspension by the NBA	Salary lost
Ron Artest (IND)	Remainder of the season (86 games; 73 regular season and 13 playoff)	$ 4,997,500
Stephen Jackson (IND)	30 games	$ 1,750,000
Jermaine O'Neal (IND)	15 games (originally set at 25 games, reduced on appeal)	$ 4,115,000
Ben Wallace (DET)	6 games	$ 400,000
Anthony Johnson (IND)	5 games	$ 122,222
Reggie Miller (IND)	1 game	$ 61,111
Chauncey Billups (DET)	1 game	$ 60,611
Derrick Coleman (DET)	1 game	$ 50,000
Elden Campbell (DET)	1 game	$ 48,888

St. Pius High School

In 1996, a football game between St. Pius High School of Albuquerque and Albuquerque Academy was stopped after five players from Albuquerque Academy were cut—one so badly that he required 12 stitches to his forearm. The cause: the Center for St. Pius, junior Mike Cito, had a chin strap that was "sharp enough to shred a magazine cover" (Associated Press. (1996, October 23). *Father Turns Son Into a Weapon by Sharpening Buckle on Helmet*). His father, dentist Stephen Cito, later admitted that he sharpened a buckle on the chin strap "because game officials had failed to penalize players for roughing up his son in an earlier game" (Ibid).

In court, the younger Cito admitted, "I wore a helmet with a buckle that had been altered...It was sharpened." Asked why, the teen told the judge, "It was sharpened to protect me from harm." "By whom," the judge asked. "My father," the boy replied (Washington Post. (1996, December 23). Father, son sentenced for football incident. The Washington Post).

It is not clear to me if the younger Cito was answering that the helmet was sharpened by his father, or if he was concerned about being harmed by his father, or both.

Both father and son were charged with conspiracy to commit aggravated assault. The charge normally carries a sentence of 18 months. The two were sentenced to community service and probation. The father also received a two-day jail sentence while the son was expelled from St. Pius High School and banned from competitive sports for a year.

Julio Castillo

In our discussion of torts, we mentioned that although causing a voluntary, intentional contact with someone can be a battery, a pitcher intentionally hitting a batter will not be a battery because intentionally hitting a batter was found to be a fundamental part of the game of baseball (*Avila v. Citrus Cmty. Coll* (Cal. 2006)). However, in 2009, as part of a bench-clearing brawl, minor league pitcher Julio Castillo threw a baseball at full speed not toward a batter, but toward the opposing team's dugout. The ball ended up going high and hitting a fan in the stands in the head. For this, Castillo was convicted of felonious assault causing serious physical injury. The charge carries a maximum sentence of 8 years in prison. Castillo was sentenced to 30 days in jail and three years probation (Associated Press. (2009, August 6). *Castillo gets jail, probation.* ESPN).

A decade later, Sporting News reported that "Castillo never pitched another inning in the U.S. and returned to the Dominican Republic when his work visa was revoked. He was 20 [years old] at the time of the incident and [according to the Dayton Daily News, he] did not know how to read or write" (Bernstein, D. (2019, June 24).

Regina v. Maki and Green

Before talking about the cases of *Regina v. Maki* and *Regina v. Green* we should ask why a criminal law case starts with "Regina v." instead of "The People v." or "The State v." Here's a hint, this is a hockey case. If you need another hint, what country loves hockey? Canadians love hockey and this is a Canadian criminal law case. In Canada, the queen or king of England is the personification of the state, and "regina" is Latin for "queen." During the reign of Queen Elizabeth II from 1952 until her death in 2022, it was common to see Canadian criminal cases titled "Regina v." the defendant just as you would see "The People" or "The State" v. the defendant in the United States. After King Charles III became king upon the queen's death on September 8th, 2022, new Canadian criminal cases may be named "Rex v." the defendant, with "rex" being Latin for "king."

Regina v. Maki and *Regina v. Green* were criminal cases against hockey players Wayne Maki of the St. Louis Blues and Ted Green of the Boston Bruins. They were charged with assault after hitting each other with their sticks during a pre-season game in Ottawa, Canada.

Maki shoved Green into the boards. Green responded by shoving Maki to the ice. Maki, while down on the ice, speared Green in the groin with his hockey stick. Green responded by swinging his stick like a baseball bat, hitting Maki on the arm. "Green then turned away from Maki to go to the penalty box when Maki struck Green on the head. The blow crushed part of Green's skull, leaving Green partially paralyzed and immediately causing his speech to slur" (Mooney, H. (2021, December 30). *Wayne Maki and Ted Green: A Gruesome Night in Hockey History.*

A 2021 article from the Sports History Network quoted the Blues' play-by-play man Dan Kelly describing the incident as "one of the most horrifying, most violent exchanges I've ever seen in hockey."

"I could see right away that Green was badly hurt," Kelly told legendary hockey broadcaster Brian MacFarlane years afterward. "When he tried to get up, his face was contorted, and his legs began to buckle under him. It was dreadful. I almost became physically ill watching him struggle because I knew this was very, very serious. I remember it like it happened yesterday (ibid).

The court decided that Maki acted in self-defense and commented that there was no evidence to show that he intended to injure Green. Green was acquitted on an implied consent doctrine, calling his injury to Maki an 'inherent risk of the game'" (Wyatt M. Hicks, *Preventing and Punishing Player-to-Player Violence in Professional Sports: The Court System Versus League Self-Regulation*, 11 J. Legal Aspects Sport 209, 223 (2001)).

Regina v. Ciccarelli

It would not be until 1988 when we would see the first criminal conviction of a professional hockey player for an on-ice incident. The charges resulted from Minnesota North Stars right wing, and future NHL Hall of Famer, Dino Ciccarelli striking Toronto Maple Leafs' rookie Luke Richardson multiple times in the head with his stick. The judge agreed that "when one engages in a hockey game, one accepts that some assaults which would otherwise be criminal will occur, and consents to such assaults" (Gregory Schiller, Are Athletes Above the Law? From A Two-Minute Minor to A Twenty-Year Sentence: Regina v. Marty Mcsorley, 10 Sports Law. J. 241, 262 (2003)). However, the court held that "to engage in a game of hockey is not to enter a forum to which the criminal law does not extend. To hold otherwise would be to create the hockey arena a sanctuary for unbridled violence to which the law…could not apply" (ibid). The judge concluded that, "it is time now that a message has to go forth from the courts that unprovoked violence, whether in a hockey game or for that matter under any other circumstances, is not tolerated in our society" (ibid). The words may seem strong, but the verdict was not. Ciccarelli was sentenced to one day in jail and a $1000 fine.

Michael Vick

Michael Vick was the fastest ever NFL quarterback, running the 40-yard dash in 4.33 seconds. He set records for the most quarterback rushing yards in a career (6,109) and in a season (1,039 in 2006). The per season record would drop in 2019 and the career record would drop in 2024—both to Lamar Jackson. But Michael Vick is no longer remembered just for his yards on the field. A search warrant as part of a drug investigation into one of Vick's cousins led to the discovery of evidence of unlawful dog fighting activities at a property owned by Vick. For this, Vick was charged with violating the federal Racketeer Influenced and Corrupt Organizations Act, or RICO.

RICO is a federal law designed to combat organized crime by targeting criminal enterprises involved in "racketeering activities" *such as* illegal gambling, bribery, kidnapping, murder, money laundering, counterfeiting, embezzlement, drug trafficking, etc. To convict a defendant under the federal RICO statute (18 U.S.C. § 1962), the Government "must prove (1) the existence of an enterprise that affects interstate or foreign commerce, (2) that the defendant was employed by or associated with the enterprise, (3) that the defendant participated in the conduct of the enterprise's affairs, and (4) that the participation was through a pattern of racketeering activity." *United States v. Posada–Rios,* 158 F.3d 832, 855 (5th Cir.1998), *United States v. Nieto*, 721 F.3d 357, 365–66 (5th Cir. 2013). Vick pleaded guilty to conspiracy to travel in interstate commerce in aid of unlawful activities and to sponsor a dog in an animal fighting venue. For this, Vick spent 18 months in prison.

In response, people accused Vick of being a murderer. Former Fox News commentator Tucker Carlson even said Vick "should have been executed." Of course, the definition of murder requires a homicide, and homicide is defined as the killing of a person, and dogs are not persons, but we love our pets. Vick received a harsher sentence than defendants who have attacked people. Hockey players Maki and Ciccarelli are lucky that they did not kill the victims they struck over the head with their sticks. For this Ciccarelli served one day in jail and Maki, who crushed his opponent's skull leaving him partially paralyzed and immediately causing his speech to slur, was acquitted. The Albuquerque dentist who sharpened his son's helmet buckle and sent him into a game to slice his opponents served two days. Charges against Ray Rice for knocking his fiancée unconscious were dismissed after he "completed a one-year program that included anger management." Meanwhile, Vick spent 18 months in prison after pleading guilty to conspiracy to travel in interstate commerce in aid of unlawful activities and to sponsor a dog in an animal fighting venue. Again, we love our pets.

Many states have enacted their own RICO laws with slight variations. For example, Georgia's RICO statute includes attempting or soliciting in the definition of racketeering activities. In 2023 then former President Donald Trump was indicted along with 18 co-defendants for violating Georgia's RICO statute for allegedly being part of a conspiracy that committed two or more acts of racketeering in an attempt to change the outcome of the 2020 presidential election in favor of Trump. An indictment is a formal charge of criminal activity. In the Georgia case, the indictment followed the recommendation from a group of 23 citizens impaneled on a grand jury who reviewed evidence and determined that there was probable cause to support the indictment. Four co-defendants pleaded guilty including attorneys Sidney Powell, Kenneth Chesebro, and Jenna Ellis.

Theft Crimes: Larceny, Embezzlement, and Robbery

The theft crimes of larceny, embezzlement, and robbery each have their own definitions. At common law, larceny was the unlawful taking and carrying away of the tangible personal property of another with the specific intent to permanently deprive the victim of the property. Embezzlement was the unlawful conversion of the personal property of another by a defendant who was in lawful possession of the property. Robbery was the unlawful taking and carrying away of the tangible personal property of another from a victim's presence by force or threat of force. These crimes continue today with variations based on state statutes.

Larceny

I question the appropriateness of the nickname "Lucky" given to Rodney Darnell "Lucky" Whitehead Jr. In 2015, Whitehead signed as a free agent with the Dallas Cowboys where he played wide receiver until 2017 when headlines announced that he had been charged with petty larceny for shoplifting at a convenience store in Virginia. The charge was larceny because it involved someone unlawfully taking and carrying away the tangible personal property of another with the specific intent to permanently deprive the victim of the property. It was called "petty" larceny in Virginia because it was for an amount less than $200.

On July 24, 2017, NFL.com reported that "Police responded to a call made by a convenience store employee who said Whitehead ran out of the store without paying for some merchandise. Police located Whitehead in the parking lot and arrested him a short time later." The article stated that the theft occurred in Prince William County Virginia at 1:30 a.m. on June 22nd. "Whitehead [then] failed to show up for his scheduled arraignment on July 6 and a warrant was issued for his arrest" (NFL.com. (2017, July 24). Lucky Whitehead arrested on petty larceny charge).

By the next day, July 25th, the Cowboys had released Whitehead. Then the Prince William County Police Department announced that the man charged with shoplifting in June was not Whitehead. As ESPN reported, "The Prince William County Police Department said the man who was arrested didn't have identification with him. He verbally provided the name, date of birth and Social Security number of Rodney Darnell Whitehead Jr. to police officers, who checked the information through the Virginia Department of Motor Vehicles database." The article continues that the "Police also compared the DMV photo on file with the man in custody and 'acted in good faith that, at the time, the man in custody was the same man matching the information provided" (ESPN.com. (2017, July 25). Police say Lucky Whitehead was misidentified; arrested man gave false information).

Of all the possible sports larceny examples I could choose from, I choose this one to emphasize that in our legal system, individuals are presumed innocent until proven guilty beyond a reasonable doubt in a court of law.

The next day, July 26, 2017, Whitehead was claimed by the New York Jets. Less than a month later he suffered a fractured foot in practice. He was released by the Jets and in 2019 Whitehead moved to the Canadian Football League where he played with the Winnipeg Blue Bombers until moving to the British Columbia Lions in 2021. Then, while second in the league in receiving yards for the season, Whitehead broke his hand in a Week 9 loss to his former team the Blue Bombers. He returned after missing two games and was named as a CFL All-Star for the season with 60 receptions, 932 yards, and four touchdowns in just 12 games played.

Embezzlement

Embezzlement is the unlawful conversion of the personal property of another by a defendant who was in lawful possession of the property. Where do we see this in sports? We see it in youth sports. When the treasurer or parent of the little league team, cheerleading squad, or booster club collects tens of thousands of dollars in donations from businesses and parents, they have lawful possession of the money. When they take the money for themselves, they commit embezzlement.

For example, Robert Reischauer pleaded guilty to stealing over $100,000 from a St. Paul, Minnesota suburb's athletic association where he worked as the finance manager from its founding in 1976 until 2013 when the association conducted an audit. Joshua Paul Nowack, the former treasurer of the Tijeras Creek Little League in Orange County, California, was sentenced to six months in jail and ordered to pay $87,517.97 in restitution for embezzlement that took place between 2014 and 2017. Carey Chesser and Shannon Wenzel pled guilty and faced up to six to 12 months in prison and an order to pay $17,500 in restitution after stealing from the Milford (Ohio) Youth Basketball Association. The two had purchasing authority to buy concession supplies to be sold during games. An investigation uncovered that "while making those purchases, they were adding items for their own personal use and paying for those items with the association funds" (Chaney, C. (2015, September 24). Two women plead guilty to grand theft from Milford Youth Basketball Association).

A former Director of Pop Warner Football in New Jersey, David Marshall, was sentenced to 27 months in prison and ordered to pay $559,841 in restitution. According to documents filed with the court, "Between 2005 and 2011, Marshall performed work for Pop Warner on a voluntary basis and held various positions. From 2006 through 2011, Marshall was the regional director for the Eastern Region of Pop Warner. He was responsible for handling the finances of the Eastern Region and had access to its bank and credit card accounts. Marshall used his authority to steal hundreds of thousands of dollars from Pop Warner. He improperly used funds from Pop Warner bank accounts to pay off personal debts and make cash withdrawals. Marshall also used a Pop Warner credit card to purchase personal items and other things unrelated to Pop Warner" (FBI. (2014, July 30). Former Director of Pop Warner Sentenced to 27 Months in Prison for Stealing Hundreds of Thousands of Dollars from the Organization).

To help avoid embezzlement, organizations should consider requiring two signatures to authorize any spending, insist on full transparency of finances, conduct regular audits, and institute term limits for those with access to finances.

Robbery

In 2007 former football player O.J. Simpson led a group of men who broke into sports memorabilia dealer Bruce Fromong's Las Vegas, Nevada hotel room. They held him at gun point and stole memorabilia from him. This would satisfy the Common Law definition of robbery as the unlawful taking and carrying away of the tangible personal property of another from a victim's presence by force or threat of force. On October 3, 2008, exactly 13 years after Simpson was acquitted of the murders of his ex-wife and her boyfriend, Simpson was found guilty of robbery and sentenced to 33 years in prison with eligibility for parole in nine years. He was granted parole in 2017. He died in 2024 at the age of 76.

Point Shaving

The practice of intentionally changing the score of a game without changing who wins is called "point shaving." During the 1993-1994 season, two Arizona State University basketball players accepted $50,000 to keep the score between ASU and the University of Texas at El Paso (UTEP) within 10 points. ASU won the game by 8 points. The basketball players were paid $50,000. Those who wagered to have ASU win by less than 10 points won millions of dollars. The level of gambling activity alerted the FBI which resulted in the arrest of five individuals. Among those indicted was ASU's then Number 3 all-time leading scorer, Stevin "Hedake" Smith. Smith pleaded guilty to conspiracy to commit sports bribery. For more details, I recommend the Netflix series *Bad Sports*, Episode 1, Hoop Schemes.

Criminal Trespass of Pitch Invaders

What at first glance may look like 15 minutes of fame running around the field of play could lead to a year in jail and a $25,000 fine. This is the penalty for what has been called New York City's "Calvin Klein" law. The law is named in honor of designer Calvin Klein who in 2003 got up from his New York Knicks courtside seat to grab the arm and start a conversation with shooting guard/forward Latrell Sprewell as Sprewell was trying to in-bound the ball. Security eventually escorted Klein back to his seat. With more fans rushing courts and fields, there is a need for greater security presence to ensure the safety of the athletes. I'll admit that sometimes it's humorous. For example, after a fan was tackled by security at an NFL game, the play-by-play commentators suggested, "The last person I would want to run into is a New Jersey State Trooper. Did you see that tackle? They're actually hitting harder than the Jet's defense" (NFL Savage Fans on the Field, https://www.youtube.com/watch?v=Fd9ojWDRIMI).

Parents and Youth Sports

In 2003, New Jersey passed the Violent Fan's Law which states that "A person who commits a simple assault...in the presence of a child under 16 years of age at a school or community sponsored youth sports event is guilty of a crime of the fourth degree. The defendant shall be strictly liable upon proof that the offense occurred, in fact, in the presence of a child under 16 years of age. It shall not be a defense that the defendant did not know that the child was present or reasonably believed that the child was 16 years of age or older. The provisions of this subsection shall not be construed to create any liability on the part of a participant in a youth sports event or to abrogate any immunity or defense available to a participant in a youth sports event" (P.L. 2002, CHAPTER 53, VIOLENT FAN'S LAW). The law was passed after a man was convicted of involuntary manslaughter for beating another man to death at their sons' hockey practice. The fatal fight was witnessed by a team full of children, including the perpetrator's son and the victim's three children.

Barry Bonds, Perjury, and Obstruction of Justice

Barry Bonds finished his career in baseball in 2007 with 14 All-Star appearances, eight Gold Gloves, winning the National League MVP seven times, being named Major League Player of the Year three times, and receiving the Silver Slugger award 12 times. He was the only player with at least 500 home runs and 500 stolen bases. He holds the record for the most home runs in a season at 73 in 2001, and the most home-runs in a career at 762. During Bond's final year, he was also indicted on several counts of perjury under 18 U.S.C. §1623 (2006), and one count of obstruction of justice under 18 U.S.C. § 1503 (2006). These charges were based on him testifying to a grand jury in 2003 that "he had never knowingly used anabolic steroids or human growth hormone" (Harms, Rob (2015, July 21). *Justice Department Drops Case Against Barry Bonds. The New York Times*).

The crime of perjury is an offense for knowingly making a false statement in court after taking an oath or affirmation to tell the truth. The prosecution eventually dropped the perjury charges against Bonds, choosing only to pursue the obstruction of justice charge for which Bonds was convicted by a federal jury in 2011. Bonds appealed the decision and in 2015 the 9th Circuit Court of Appeals reversed his conviction stating that there was "insufficient evidence" that Bonds' "rambling, non-responsive answer to a simple question during a grand jury proceeding" was material as required under the federal obstruction of justice statute (18 U.S.C. § 1503) (*United States v. Barry Lamar Bonds,* 11-10669, 3:07-cr-00732-SI-1 (9th Cir. 2014).

Chapter 5: Sports and Religion

When I teach this chapter on religion and sports to my undergraduate students at a public, federal land grant institution, I sometimes start class by asking if they think it would be okay if I started class with prayer. I then stare out at a room full of students staring back at me. After a pause, a head shifts and an eyebrow raises. I can tell they're asking themselves, "Did he just ask us a question about praying?

I then add that I didn't say I was *going* to start class with prayer. I just asked if it would be okay *if* I started class with prayer. Life returns. Some eyes squint with heads shaking sideways, suggesting, "No, it would not be appropriate." A few students usually add that they personally would not have a problem with it, but the consensus has always been: No, it would not be okay for a college professor at a state school to begin a class about sports or business law, with prayer.

Of course, as a college professor, I have to ask more questions like, "Why not?" and "When you say it wouldn't be okay, do you mean to say it would violate someone's constitutionally protected rights or it just wouldn't be appropriate?" Does it matter that we are a state university instead of a private university? Could a public high school coach pray with students at the 50-yard line after a game? Could a coach pray with students before a meal on a school-sponsored trip? Does it matter if the conversation about religion is at an elementary school or at university? Could a school broadcast a prayer over the school's public announcement system? Would it matter if the prayer is led by a student? Does it matter if the prayer sounds like a generic 'God Bless America' or a prayer that invites the audience to 'repeat this prayer after me' to convert to a particular religion?

These are the questions we will dive into in this chapter. But first, I like to remind people that religious beliefs are deeply personal. Our goal is not to humiliate an opposing viewpoint. Our goal is to examine the legal issues. One of the great things about discussing these topics within the context of the law is that we need thoughtful attorneys on both sides of controversial issues. The Supreme Court once held that in order to even have standing to sue—that is, the ability to sue in court—a party must have "such a personal stake in the outcome of the controversy as to assure that concrete adverseness which sharpens the presentation of issues upon which the court so largely depends for illumination of difficult constitutional questions" (Baker v. Carr, 369 U.S. 186 (1962)).

Imagine arguing over who is the greatest basketball player of all time with someone who just doesn't care about sports. You cite statistics and break out your database in the sports bar. You start comparing players until realizing that it's pointless to argue with someone who doesn't know or care about the topic. We refine our arguments and gain clarity when we discuss issues with individuals who are smart, prepared, disagree with us, and care about the issues. This means that if you encounter someone with whom you really disagree, this person is not your enemy. This person just provided the "concrete adverseness which sharpens the presentation of the issues" that you would need to have standing to have your controversy heard by a court. I share this introduction as a reminder that in this chapter—and in every chapter—our goal is not to convert or crush the other side. Our goal is to learn how to identify issues and apply the law to the facts in an effort to find logical answers to our legal questions.

The U.S. Constitution

The starting point for our conversation on law and religion is the First Amendment of the U.S Constitution. It states:

First Amendment:

Congress shall make no law respecting an establishment of religion, or prohibiting the free exercise thereof; or abridging the freedom of speech, or of the press; or the right of the people peaceably to assemble, and to petition the government for a redress of grievances.

Zooming in on religion, we find what are referred to as the Establishment Clause and the Free Exercise Clause.

The **Establishment Clause** tells us that Congress shall make no law respecting an establishment of religion.

The **Free Exercise Clause** tells us that Congress shall make no law prohibiting the free exercise of religion.

When we read that "Congress shall make no law," this is a limitation on the federal government. This makes historical sense for several reasons. First, many early U.S. settlers came from countries that had fought wars to determine which religion would be the established religion of the country. Fleeing to what would become the United States was often a good alternative to staying in place and suffering as a religious minority.

For example, to this day, England has an established church called the Church of England. You may also hear it referred to as the Anglican Church. It began in 1527 when England's King Henry VIII wanted a male heir. King Henry VIII—and by extension England—was Catholic at the time and so the king asked Pope Clement VII to annul his marriage so that he could marry someone else. When the Pope refused, a separate Church of England was formed and King Henry VIII was declared the Supreme Head of the Church of England. Henry then allied himself with Protestants who had been previously viewed as heretics. Then in 1553, Henry VIII's daughter Mary became Queen of England. Queen Mary I reversed her father's Protestant reforms and burned over 280 religious dissenters at the stake during what has been called the Marian persecutions. This earned her the nickname "Bloody Mary" by her Protestant opponents. With this as a backdrop, you can imagine the appeal of a trip to the New World to avoid religious persecution.

A second reason for states to insist on preventing Congress from establishing a religion is the fact that some states had already established their own state religions. For example, the Congregationalist Church was the established church of Connecticut until 1818. The state of New Hampshire's constitution required all state legislators to be Protestant until the requirement was deleted in1877. Remember, the U.S. Constitution was a limitation on what the federal government could do—not on what state governments could do. The Tenth Amendment also specifically stated that any "power not delegated to the United States by the Constitution, nor prohibited by it to the States, are reserved to the States." This left states the ability to establish their own religions.

Freedom of Religion and the States

Does this mean that the First Amendment of the U.S. Constitution only applies to the federal government and the states are still free to establish their own religions? Not anymore. After the Fourteenth Amendment was passed in 1866, key portions of the Bill of Rights—that is the first 10 amendments—were said to be incorporated into the Fourteenth Amendment and now apply to the states. The doctrine of applying portions of the first 10 amendments to the states through the Fourteenth Amendment is called the "Incorporation Doctrine."

The Free Exercise Clause and States

The United States Supreme Court first applied the Free Exercise Clause to states in the 1940 decision *Cantwell v. Connecticut*. In the opinion the court states:

> We hold that the statute, as construed and applied to the appellants, deprives them of their liberty without due process of law in contravention of the Fourteenth Amendment. The fundamental concept of liberty embodied in that Amendment embraces the liberties guaranteed by the First Amendment. The First Amendment declares that Congress shall make no law respecting an establishment of religion or prohibiting the free exercise thereof. The Fourteenth Amendment has rendered the legislatures of the states as incompetent as Congress to enact such laws (Cantwell v. Connecticut, 310 U.S. 296 (1940)).

The Establishment Clause and States

The Establishment Clause was first applied to the states in the 1947 case of *Everson v. Board of Education*. In the opinion the court states:

> The 'establishment of religion' clause of the First Amendment means at least this: Neither a state nor the Federal Government can set up a church. Neither can pass laws which aid one religion, aid all religions or prefer one religion over another. Neither can force nor influence a person to go to or to remain away from church against his will or force him to profess a belief or disbelief in any religion. No person can be punished for entertaining or professing religious beliefs or disbeliefs, for church attendance or non-attendance. No tax in any amount, large or small, can be levied to support any religious activities or institutions, whatever they may be called, or whatever form they may adopt to teach or practice religion. Neither a state nor the Federal Government can, openly or secretly, participate in the affairs of any religious organizations or groups and vice versa. In the words of Jefferson, the clause against establishment of religion by law was intended to erect 'a wall of separation between Church and State.' [...] The First Amendment has erected a wall between church and state. That wall must be kept high and impregnable. 330 U.S. 1, 15-16 and 18.

State Constitutions

When looking at state laws that may affect religion, you need to remember to look at not only the U.S. Constitution, but also to a specific state's constitution. This is because the U.S. Constitution provides a baseline of protections for individual liberties. It does not prevent a state from providing even greater liberties to its citizens. For example, whereas the U.S. Constitution states that "Congress shall make no law respecting an establishment of religion," the state of New Mexico's Constitution adds that, "No person shall be required to attend any place of worship or support any religious sect or denomination; nor shall any preference be given by law to any religious denomination or mode of worship" (NM Const art II § 1).

With this in mind, imagine that a megachurch has the best auditorium and sound system in town and a public high school wants to use the auditorium for a required presentation. Depending on the facts, this may not violate the U.S. Constitution's Establishment Clause, but requiring students to attend "any place of worship" could arguably violate New Mexico's state constitution.

State Action Requirement

The bottom line when it comes to lawsuits involving the First Amendment of the U.S. Constitution is that you need State Action. State Action "refers to the requirement that in order for a plaintiff to have standing to sue over a law being violated, the plaintiff must demonstrate that the government (local, state, or federal), was responsible for the violation, rather than a private actor" (Cornell Law School. (n.d.). State action requirement. Legal Information Institute).

Private sports teams are not the government—even if the city government assists with the financing of the stadium. Private schools are also not the government. I have two professor colleagues who teach at private universities. One is at a more progressive, secular private institution. The other is at a more conservative, religious private institution. Both worry about free speech and freedom of religion from different perspectives. The colleague at the secular university was told that he should not say anything about his faith in class. If he does, he could be fired. The colleague at the religious private institution fears that the university is going to require all professors to sign a new statement of faith that includes language with which he does not agree. If he refuses to sign it, he could get fired. If these professors are fired, could they sue their institutions for violating their first amendment rights to free speech or free exercise of religion? The short answer is no. Their employers are private institutions. As private institutions, they are not proper defendants for a First Amendment lawsuit.

Here is an exam question that I have used to test student understanding of the state action requirement:

> Copyright 2022 Dwight M. Kealy. Before entering the stadium of the Los Angeles Dodgers, I am stopped at a security checkpoint where a private security officer checks to make sure that I'm not bringing in anything dangerous. The officer asks me to remove my head-covering. I tell the officer that wearing the head-covering is a requirement of my sincerely held religious beliefs. And this is true. The officer won't let me in the stadium without checking under my head covering. I feel that I do not have any choice, and remove my head covering for the inspection. I later sue the Dodgers and their security company for violating my First Amendment (Free Exercise of Religion) and Fourth Amendment (unreasonable search and seizure) rights. What is the likely outcome?

The correct answer is, "I will lose because the First and Fourth Amendments do not apply to this case." The question is based on *Stark v. Seattle Seahawks* where Seahawks season ticketholders Fred and Kathleen Stark argued that the pat-down searches required prior to entry into National Football League games was an unreasonable search in violation of the Fourth Amendment.

There are times when a private entity can be subject to liability as a state actor. The *Stark v. Seattle Seahawks* case outlines that a private entity could be liable for state action when the private entity serves a public function "traditionally exclusively reserved to the state" (*Jackson v. Metro. Edison Co.*, 419 U.S. 345, 352 (1974). It found that "courts have recognized traditional state functions include administering elections (*Terry v. Adams*, 345 U.S. 461 (1953); and running a company-owned town, (*Marsh v. Alabama* 326 U.S. 501 (1946)." However, it also noted that the Supreme Court found that "operating an event center...does not rise to the level of a traditional state function" (*Jackson v. Metro. Edison Co.*, 419 U.S. 345, 352 (1974). The Supreme Court also "held that a privately owned school that received up to 99% of its funding from public sources and was subject to significant public regulation did not perform a traditionally exclusive public function" (*Rendell-Baker v. Kohn*, 457 U.S. at 842). Based on these precedents, the Seattle Seahawks was found to be a private actor—not a state actor—and the Fourth Amendment case against them was dismissed.

It is important to remember the state actor requirement when you hear sports headlines about private teams firing athletes for exercising their

First Amendment right to free speech when kneeling in protest during the national anthem. This is what former NFL player Colin Kaepernick and midfielder for the U.S. Women's Soccer Team, Megan Rapinoe, did before games in 2016. Firing someone for their speech may sound like a violation of the individual's First Amendment rights, but if the team is a private actor, the First Amendment does not apply.

Now that we know who or what is not a state actor, we should ask, "Who is a state actor?" Obviously, the federal or state governments cannot pass laws to violate the Establishment or Free Exercise Clauses. This includes state schools. As stated in *Tinker v. Des Moines*, "The Fourteenth Amendment, as now applied to the States, protects the citizen against the State itself and all of its creatures— Boards of Education not excepted. These have, of course, important, delicate, and highly discretionary functions, but none that they may not perform within the limits of the Bill of Rights" (*Tinker v. Des Moines School Dist.*, 393 U.S. 503 (1969). Therefore, unlike a private university, a state university could be a proper defendant in a First Amendment lawsuit.

Establishment Clause Tests

Prior to 2022, the Supreme Court offered three tests for determining whether governmental action violates the Establishment Clause: The Coercion Test, the Lemon Test, and the Endorsement Test. In the 2022 opinion for *Kennedy v. Bremerton School District*, the United States Supreme Court added a "History and Tradition Test."

1. The Coercion Test

"The coercion test looks at whether the government is "coerc[ing] anyone to support or participate in religion or its exercise...." *Lee v. Weisman*, 505 U.S. 577, 587, 112 S.Ct. 2649, 120 L.Ed.2d 467 (1992)."

This test comes from *Lee v. Weisman* where the Supreme Court determined that including clergy to offer prayers as part of an official public high school graduation ceremony violates the Establishment Clause.

Here is an excerpt. **In the words of the court:**

> "The school district's supervision and control of a high school graduation ceremony places subtle and indirect public and peer pressure on attending students to stand as a group or maintain

respectful silence during the invocation and benediction. A reasonable dissenter of high school age could believe that standing or remaining silent signified her own participation in, or approval of, the group exercise, rather than her respect for it. And the State may not place the student dissenter in the dilemma of participating or protesting. Since adolescents are often susceptible to peer pressure, especially in matters of social convention, the State may no more use social pressure to enforce orthodoxy than it may use direct means" (ibid).

In response to the argument that the prayers were not a big deal, the court argued, "The embarrassment and intrusion of the religious exercise cannot be refuted by arguing that the prayers are of a *de minimis* character, since that is an affront to the rabbi and those for whom the prayers have meaning, and since any intrusion was both real and a violation of the objectors' rights" (ibid).

The court concludes, "Although our precedents make clear that proof of government coercion is not necessary to prove an Establishment Clause violation, it is sufficient. Government pressure to participate in a religious activity is an obvious indication that the government is endorsing or promoting religion." In a concurring opinion, three justices stated more bluntly, "I join the whole of the Court's opinion, and fully agree that prayers at public school graduation ceremonies indirectly coerce religious observance" (ibid).

Chaudhuri v. State of Tennessee (130 F. 3d 232, 6th Cir. (1997)

Unlike *Lee v. Weisman* where prayer at a high school graduation was found to violate the Establishment Clause, the 6th Circuit Court of Appeals found a different outcome at the university level in *Chaudhuri v. State of Tennessee* (130 F. 3d 232, 6th Cir. (1997)). Tennessee State University (TSU) had a practice of including a nonsectarian, non-proselytizing prayer at the university's graduation ceremony. The court held that "a prayer may serve to dignify or to memorialize a public occasion.... Quoting County of *Allegheny v. American Civil Liberties Union*, 492 U.S. 573 (1989)." The court noted that prayers can "solemnize public occasions, express confidence in the future, and encourage the recognition of what is worthy of appreciation in society." *Chaudhuri v. State of Tenn.*, 130 F.3d 232, 236 (6th Cir. 1997)

The difference between allowing the prayer at a university graduation in *Chaudhuri* and not allowing it in *Lee* may be rooted in the relative ages of the participants. The Supreme Court has noted that "there are heightened concerns with protecting freedom of conscience from subtle coercive pressure in the elementary and secondary public schools" because "prayer exercises in public schools carry a particular risk of indirect coercion"; *Grand Rapids Sch. Dist. v. Ball*, 473 U.S. 373 (1985). The court noted "The symbolism of a union between church and state is most likely to influence children of tender years, whose experience is limited and whose beliefs consequently are the function of environment as much as of free and voluntary choice" (*Lee v. Weisman*, 505 U.S. 577).

2. The Endorsement Test

A school district also violates the Establishment Clause if "a reasonable observer familiar with the history and context of the display would perceive the display as a government endorsement of religion." *Modrovich v. Allegheny County*, 385 F.3d 397, 401 (3d Cir.2004); see also *County of Allegheny v. Am. Civil Liberties Union Greater Pittsburgh Chapter*, 492 U.S. 573, 596, 109 S.Ct. 3086, 106 L.Ed.2d 472 (1989) (adopting the endorsement test)." We see this in the case of:

Santa Fe Independent School District v. Doe, 530 U.S. 290 (2000)

In *Santa Fe Independent School District [of Texas] v. Doe* the Supreme Court ruled against a school district policy that had a student, who had been elected by students, deliver a prayer over the public address system before home varsity football games. The case centered around a district policy where students voted to determine if there should be a prayer before football games. They then held a separate election where "students selected a student to deliver the prayer at varsity games." The district's attempt to hold a vote may seem fair, but the court noted that the whole idea of voting is to perpetuate the perspective of the majority. They stated, "the majoritarian process implemented by the District guarantees, by definition, that minority candidates will never prevail and that their views will be effectively silenced." The court concluded that "The [District's] policy involves both perceived and actual endorsement of religion." Adding, that the Constitution does "not permit the District 'to exact religious conformity from a student as the price' of joining her classmates at a varsity football game."

Borden v. School District of E. Brunswick (2008)

Borden v. School District of E. Brunswick (2008) applied the endorsement test to determine if a coach praying with students violated the Establishment Clause.

Here is an excerpt. **In the words of the court:**

> Marcus Borden, the head football coach at East Brunswick High School, would like to engage in the silent acts of bowing his head during his team's pre-meal grace and taking a knee with his team during a locker-room prayer.... We hold that Borden's silent acts violate the Establishment Clause because, when viewing the acts in light of Borden's twenty-three years of prior prayer activities with the East Brunswick High School football team during which he organized, participated in, and even led prayer activities with his team, a reasonable observer would conclude that Borden was endorsing religion when he engaged in these acts.

We will revisit the question of whether a coach praying with students violates the Establishment Clause when we discuss *Kennedy v. Bremerton Sch. Dist.* (2022).

3. The Lemon Test

The case of *Lemon v. Kurtzman* created The Lemon Test. It created the following rules to use to determine if a government's law violates the Establishment Clause:

> 1) The law should have a secular purpose. That is, the law's aim should not be to aid religion.
> 2) Even if there is a secular purpose, the primary effect should not be to aid or inhibit religion.
> 3) The law should not foster an excessive entanglement between the government and religion.

The importance of discussing *Lemon v. Kurtzman* when talking about the Establishment Clause is akin to the importance of discussing *Roe v. Wade* when talking about abortion laws. Both *Lemon v. Kurtzman* and *Roe v. Wade* were decided in the early 1970s—Lemon in 1971 and Rowe in 1973. And, although both were effectively overturned in the summer of 2022, both still shape the vocabulary of their respective topics. *Roe v. Wade* was overturned by *Dobbs v. Jackson Women's Health Organization* in June 2022. Although *Lemon v. Kurtzman* was not technically overruled, its influence was decimated by the July 2022 decision in *Kennedy v. Bremerton Sch. Dist.* I say that *Kennedy* did not technically overrule *Lemon* because the majority opinion in *Kennedy* did not say that it was overturning *Lemon*, but you can see the impact of *Kennedy* on *Lemon* by reading the minority's dissent. It states:

Today's decision goes beyond merely misreading the record. The Court overrules *Lemon v. Kurtzman*, 403 U.S. 602 (1971), and calls into question decades of subsequent precedents that it deems "offshoot[s]" of that decision. In the process, the Court rejects longstanding concerns surrounding government endorsement of religion and replaces the standard for reviewing such questions with a new "history and tradition" test (*Kennedy v. Bremerton Sch. Dist.*).

4. The History and Tradition Test

Kennedy v. Bremerton Sch. Dist. (2022)

The case of K*ennedy v. Bremerton* revisits the question of a football coach praying with a team—this time at the 50 yard-line in the middle of the field after a game. Plaintiff Joseph Kennedy was a high school football coach in the public school district in Bremerton, Washington. Immediately after each game, he went to the middle of the field to pray. He was soon joined by players.

Worried that the practice of prayer would violate the Establishment Clause, "the District issued an ultimatum. It forbade Mr. Kennedy from engaging in 'any overt actions' that could 'appea[r] to a reasonable observer to endorse... prayer... while he is on duty as a District-paid coach.' The District did so because it judged that anything less would violate the Establishment Clause" (*Kennedy v. Bremerton Sch. Dist.*, 597 U.S. 507 (2022)).

Kennedy continued the practice of prayer after games. The District responded by placing Kennedy on paid administrative leave. "In a letter explaining the reasons for this disciplinary action, the superintendent criticized Mr. Kennedy for engaging in "public and demonstrative religious conduct while still on duty as an assistant coach" by offering a prayer following the games on October 16, 23, and 26" (*Kennedy v. Bremerton Sch. Dist.*, 597 U.S. 507, 519–20, 142 S. Ct. 2407, 2419, 213 L. Ed. 2d 755 (2022)).

After the season, Kennedy's performance reviews dropped from "'uniformly positive evaluations' every other year of his coaching career" to an evaluation that "advised against rehiring Mr. Kennedy on the grounds that he 'failed to follow district policy' regarding religious expression and 'failed to supervise student-athletes after games'" (*Kennedy v. Bremerton*). Mr. Kennedy did not return for the next season. Instead, he filed a lawsuit in federal court "alleging that the

District's actions violated the First Amendment's Free Speech and Free Exercise Clauses."

The school district argued that, as a coach, Mr. Kennedy "wielded enormous authority and influence over the students," and students might have felt compelled to pray alongside him. To support this argument, the District submits that, after Mr. Kennedy's suspension, a few parents told District employees that their sons had "participated in the team prayers only because they did not wish to separate themselves from the team" (*Kennedy v. Bremerton Sch. Dist.*, 597 U.S. 507(2022)).

Coach Kennedy argued that his conduct was "a private prayer between God and myself and I don't think anybody in America should have to worry about their faith and their job."

At the federal appeals court level, prior to the case making it to the Supreme Court, the school district described the prayer as far less than private.

In the words of the court:

> BSD [Bremerton School District] stated that this demonstration of support for Kennedy involved "people jumping the fence" to access the field, and BSD received complaints from parents of students who had been knocked down in the stampede. Principal John Polm said that he "saw people fall[.]" Principal Polm testified that "when the public went out onto the field, we could not supervise effectively," resulting in "an inability to keep kids safe." A photo of this scene is in the record, and it depicts approximately twenty players in uniform kneeling around Kennedy with their eyes closed, a large group of what appear to be adults standing outside the ring of praying players, and several television cameras photographing the scene. (*Kennedy v. Bremerton Sch. Dist.,* 991 F.3d 1004, 1013 (9th Cir. 2021)).

A Private Stampede

So, did the case involve a private prayer between a coach and his god or a stampede? Based on what the Supreme Court decided, maybe we can call it a "private stampede." The Supreme Court ruled that the coach's prayer was protected as private speech. As private speech, it was not government speech. And therefore, it did not violate the Establishment Clause.

To understand the case, we need to realize that when the court talks about private speech, they are not talking about someone praying silently in a closet. Instead, they are making a distinction between private speech and government speech, much like we discussed in the distinction between a private school and a public school.

In the Words of the Court:

The First Amendment's protections extend to "teachers and students," neither of whom "shed their constitutional rights to freedom of speech or expression at the schoolhouse gate." *Tinker v. Des Moines Independent Community School Dist.*

At the first step of the...inquiry, the parties' disagreement centers on one question: Did Mr. Kennedy offer his prayers in his capacity as a private citizen, or did they amount to government speech attributable to the District?

When the coach prayed after the game, the court argued that "he was not engaged in speech 'ordinarily within the scope' of his duties as a coach."

If a public employee speaks "pursuant to [his or her] official duties," this Court has said the Free Speech Clause generally will not shield the individual from an employer's control and discipline because that kind of speech is—for constitutional purposes at least—the government's own speech.

Applying these lessons here, it seems clear to us that Mr. Kennedy has demonstrated that his speech was private speech, not government speech. When Mr. Kennedy uttered the three prayers that resulted in his suspension, he was not engaged in speech "ordinarily within the scope" of his duties as a coach. *Lane*, 573 U.S. at 240, 134 S.Ct. 2369. He did not speak pursuant to government policy. He was not seeking to convey a government-created message. He was not instructing players, discussing strategy, encouraging better on-field performance, or engaged in any other speech the District paid him to produce as a coach. See Part I–B, supra. Simply put: Mr. Kennedy's prayers did not "ow[e their] existence" to Mr. Kennedy's responsibilities as a public employee. *Garcetti*, 547 U.S. at 421, 126 S.Ct. 1951.

The timing and circumstances of Mr. Kennedy's prayers confirm the point. During the postgame period when these prayers occurred, coaches were free to attend briefly to personal matters—everything from checking sports scores on their phones to greeting friends and family in the stands. App. 205; see Part I–B, supra. We find it unlikely that Mr. Kennedy was fulfilling a responsibility imposed by his employment by praying during a period in which the District has acknowledged that its coaching staff was free to engage in all manner of private speech.

This Court has since made plain, too, that the Establishment Clause does not include anything like a "modified heckler's veto, in which...religious activity can be proscribed" based on "'perceptions'" or "'discomfort.'" *Good News Club v. Milford Central School*, 533 U.S. 98, 119, 121 S.Ct. 2093, 150 L.Ed.2d 151 (2001)

...there was "no evidence that students [were] directly coerced to pray with Kennedy."

Naturally, Mr. Kennedy's proposal to pray quietly by himself on the field would have meant some people would have seen his religious exercise. Those close at hand might have heard him too. But learning how to tolerate speech or prayer of all kinds is "part of learning how to live in a pluralistic society," a trait of character essential to "a tolerant citizenry." *Lee*, 505 U.S. at 590, 112 S.Ct. 2649.

In *Santa Fe Independent School Dist. v. Doe*, the Court held that a school district violated the Establishment Clause by broadcasting a prayer "over the public address system" before each football game. 530 U.S. 290, 294, 120 S.Ct. 2266, 147 L.Ed.2d 295 (2000). The Court observed that, while students generally were not required to attend games, attendance was required for "cheerleaders, members of the band, and, of course, the team members themselves." Id., at 311, 120 S.Ct. 2266. None of that is true here. The prayers for which Mr. Kennedy was disciplined were not publicly broadcast or recited to a captive audience. Students were not required or expected to participate.

Here, a government entity sought to punish an individual for engaging in a brief, quiet, personal religious observance doubly protected by the Free Exercise and Free Speech Clauses of the First Amendment.

Now I would like to share some excerpts from the Dissent. These are helpful in determining the outcome of future cases, but the majority opinion above is the current law of the land.

In the Words of the Court:

As the majority tells it, Kennedy, a coach for the District's football program, "lost his job" for "pray[ing] quietly while his students were otherwise occupied." The record before us, however, tells a different story.

Before the homecoming game, Kennedy made multiple media appearances to publicize his plans to pray at the 50-yard line, leading to an article in the Seattle News and a local television broadcast about the upcoming homecoming game. In the wake of this media coverage, the District began receiving a large number of emails, letters, and calls, many of them threatening.

After the issues with Kennedy arose, several parents reached out to the District saying that their children had participated in Kennedy's prayers solely to avoid separating themselves from the rest of the team. No BHS students appeared to pray on the field after Kennedy's suspension.

The Court also distinguishes *Santa Fe* because Kennedy's prayers "were not publicly broadcast or recited to a captive audience." This misses the point. In *Santa Fe*, a student council chaplain delivered a prayer over the public-address system before each varsity football game of the season. 530 U.S. at 294, 120 S.Ct. 2266. Students were not required as a general matter to attend the games, but "cheerleaders, members of the band, and, of course, the team members themselves" were, and the Court would have found an "improper effect of coercing those present" even if it "regard[ed] every high school student's decision to attend...as purely voluntary." Id., at 311–312, 120 S.Ct. 2266. Kennedy's prayers raise precisely the same concerns.

Today, the Court once again weakens the backstop. It elevates one individual's interest in personal religious exercise, in the exact time and place of that individual's choosing, over society's interest in protecting the separation between church and state, eroding the protections for religious liberty for all. Today's decision is particularly misguided because it elevates the religious rights of a school official, who voluntarily accepted public employment and the limits that public employment entails, over those of his students, who are required to attend school and who this Court has long recognized are particularly vulnerable and deserving of protection. In doing so, the Court sets us further down a perilous path in forcing States to entangle themselves with religion, with all of our rights hanging in the balance. As much as the Court protests otherwise, today's decision is no victory for religious liberty. I respectfully dissent (*Kennedy v. Bremerton Sch. Dist.*, 213 L. Ed. 2d 755, 142 S. Ct. 2407, 2451 (2022)).

After reading the majority and dissenting opinions in *Kennedy v. Bremerton*, I ask my students again if they think it would be okay if I started class with prayer. The Lemon Test's question about excessive entanglement is no longer the first consideration. Now it would be a question of whether I was speaking as a private person or in my role as a government employee. The students agree that it would be inappropriate for me to pray during class, but what about after class? After class, I may check sports scores on my phone or communicate with friends and family just like Coach Kennedy after his game. So far, students have unanimously agreed that after *Kennedy v. Bremerton*, I *could* pray after class in the middle of the classroom and students would be free to join or not join. Some suggest that it should be quiet, but I remind them that, based on *Kennedy*, I can call the press and there's a chance students may get trampled in a stampede. Although permitted, I conclude that this is not a practice I would do or encourage for several reasons. 1) It is inconsistent with what I feel is my mission of teaching law to a diverse student body at a secular university, and 2) An attorney once joked that in the United States everyone is guaranteed their "decade in court." And I have no interest in spending a decade in court.

Weinbaum v. City of Las Cruces, N.M., 541 F.3d 1017 (10th Cir. 2008)

The 2008 case of *Weinbaum v. City of Las Cruces, N.M.* provides a preview of how courts may apply *Kennedy v. Bremerton*'s "history and tradition" test. For full disclosure, the beautiful city of Las Cruces is my hometown and the hometown of my employer, New Mexico State University. My Business Law colleague Professor Matthew Holt served as counsel for the defendant in this case.

In *Weinbaum v. City of Las Cruces, N.M.*, the plaintiff argued that the city's symbol consisting of Christian or Latin crosses—that is, a cross with three equal arms and a longer foot—violated the Establishment Clause by endorsing Christianity. The City of Las Cruces is located about 225 miles south of Albuquerque, New Mexico, at the intersection of what was the East/West Butterfield Overland Mail Route—a trail from San Antonio, Texas to California—and the North/South Spanish El Camino Real de Tierra Adentro ("the Royal Road to the Interior

Lands"). As such, plaintiffs argued that the city should be described as the crossing point between these two major trails without any reference to the Latin cross that the district court noted has a legacy that while "humbling, inspiring, or empowering to some, [also] intimidates, inflames, or unnerves others."

In response, the court looked at the history and tradition of the name "Las Cruces."

In the words of the court:

C. Origin of the Name "Las Cruces"

By 1598, El Camino Real de Tierra Adentro ("the Royal Road to the Interior Lands") passed through the area where Las Cruces was eventually founded. However, because of the area's aridity and the local Native Americans' hostility, very few settlers inhabited the area until the late 1840s. By 1849, though, a village about fifteen miles north of present-day Las Cruces had become overcrowded. The mayordomo of that village sought the help of the U.S. Army in resettling some of his townspeople elsewhere. To alleviate the overcrowding, a U.S. Army Lieutenant, Delos Sackett, "laid out a grid of streets using a rawhide rope" at the site of present-day Las Cruces and thereby founded a new town.

Historians have offered two theories regarding the origin of that new town's name, "Las Cruces." Some have argued that the settlement came to be called "Las Cruces" because the Butterfield Overland Mail Route—a trail from San Antonio to California—crossed El Camino Real in present-day Las Cruces. As such, Las Cruces was the "crossing" point of the two major trails. In his expert report, however, Dr. Hunner convincingly contends that this account is flawed. Indeed, this account appears anachronistic because the Butterfield Trail did not pass through present-day Las Cruces until the 1850s, a few years after Las Cruces was named.

Instead, Dr. Hunner and other historians argue that the City's name is rooted in the appearance of memorials to the victims of a series of massacres in the area. Dr. Hunner notes that, "[i]n a tradition that continues to this day, crosses have been placed in New Mexico at the site of tragic deaths." Present-day Las Cruces and its surrounding area had a series of such deaths. Thus, Susan Shelby Magoffin, a settler, described the Las Cruces area in a diary entry from February 1847 [writing]: "Yesterday, we passed over the spot where a few years since a party of Apaches attacked Gen. Armijo as he returned from the Pass with a party of troops, and killed some fourteen of his men, the graves of whom, marked by a rude cross, are now seen." By 1849, it seems, a "forest of crosses" stood in the area. Hence, the City's founding as El Pueblo del Jardin de Las Cruces ("the City of the Garden of the Crosses").

On the basis of this evidence, Dr. Hunner concludes that "the newly created town in 1849 was named after the crosses that marked the graves of the travelers on the historic trail." Despite Dr. Hunner's conclusions, Plaintiffs–Appellants persisted before the district court in claiming that "Las Cruces" can be translated as "the crossings." See Las Cruces, 465 F.Supp.2d at 1172. With a nifty bit of forensic etymology, the district court cemented Dr. Hunner's conclusion. The district court noted that the use of the feminine definite article "las" rather than the masculine definite article "los" confirms the fact that "cruces" was intended to be the plural form of "cruz" (a feminine noun meaning "cross"), rather than "cruce" (a masculine noun meaning "crossing"). Id. Accordingly, "if the village had been named for crossroads or crossings, it would have been named Los Cruces, and not Las Cruces." Id. A second linguistic clue accords with Dr. Hunner's account: The district court noted that El Pueblo del Jardin de Las Cruces is a Spanish euphemism for a cemetery. Id. at 1173 n. 5.

F. The District Court's Opinions

In the City symbol case, the court exhaustively explicated the history of the Latin cross as a symbol, the City's history, and the City's use of the contested symbol. With this factual foundation settled, the court turned to the Lemon test, as shaped by subsequent Supreme Court cases. First, the district court held that the City's secular justifications for using its symbol were persuasive because the symbol "literally reflects the name [of the City], Las Cruces," 465 F.Supp.2d at 1178. As such, the symbol did not have the "ostensible and predominate purpose of advancing religion." Id. at 1179. Second, the historical context persuaded the court that the symbol does not have the effect of endorsing religion. Id. at 1179–80. Finally, because the City's contested conduct did not involve it with a religious institution, the court held that use of the symbol did not excessively entangle the City with religion. Id. at 1180.

1. The Las Cruces City Symbol

The issue here is whether the City's symbol has the effect of endorsing Christianity. We first consider the objective perception of the symbol's purpose because purpose may lend some evidentiary weight to an inquiry of effect. Effects are most often the manifestations of a motivating purpose. As background, we note that the evidence regarding the City's adoption of the symbol is indeterminate, but there is no evidence that the City's purpose was to advance religion. However, the City offered various secular justifications for the symbol, including identification of City property and identification with the City's unique historical name. We presume, then, that an objective observer would not conclude that the City adopted the symbol with the purpose of endorsing Christianity.

Here, Las Cruces's unique history explains why the City's name translates as "The Crosses" and, relatedly, why the City uses crosses in its symbol. Dr. Hunner—the Rule 706 expert—established that the City's name derives from its founding near the site of a make-shift cemetery. Thus, the City's name derives from the "forest of crosses" that once memorialized those massacred in the area. This history is not arcane; in fact, the City has made these historical facts readily available in an explanatory brochure, "History of the Crosses: How Las Cruces Got Its Name," which Dr. Hunner's report substantiates. See O'Connor, 416 F.3d at 1228 (noting that [a] "reasonable observer" would consider [a] readily available explanatory brochure). The brochure explains that clusters of crosses stood in the area to commemorate "the gravesites [sic] of people who traveled through or populated the area nearly two centuries ago." Because a city's symbol is shorthand for the entity itself—a pictograph of sorts—the use of crosses makes intuitive sense for a city named "The Crosses." Thus, the City's unique history militates against the argument that the symbol's effect is to endorse Christianity.

It is also important here to observe the widespread use of multiple crosses throughout the community to signify a connection to the City. Rather than being a unique effort by the City to advance religion, it appears that symbols containing multiple crosses identify many secular businesses within the Las Cruces community. The use of crosses, by all accounts, is common in Las Cruces, even setting aside the City's use of its symbol. As such, our concern that the City's imprimatur attends the symbol's religious imagery dissipates. In this context, the objective observer would not be struck by the City's incorporation of crosses into its symbol and would not see that symbol as an endorsement of Christianity.

Unless one were to attack the very name of the City itself—an attack which is not advanced here—it is hardly startling that a City with the name "The Crosses" would be represented by a seal containing crosses. And indisputable evidence showed that even the name of the City reflected merely the cemetery, representing the violence in the area rather than proselytizing forces in general or a particular faith. So here, unlike in Robinson or Friedman, we have a secular symbol, which could be, and was, understood to be secular by the residents of the City.

What makes this case close is the City's use of three crosses, and the fact that the middle cross stands taller than the outside crosses. Still, the effect of the seal is not to endorse Christianity. First, because the City is called "The Crosses," of course, the use of multiple crosses makes sense. Questioning the exact number of crosses or their layout would "immerse [us] in the minutiae of graphic design," Murray, 947 F.2d at 170 (Goldberg, J., dissenting), an untenable position we have pledged to avoid, see Robinson, 68 F.3d at 1233. Second, we return to the fact that the Las Cruces community uses the crosses the way Palo Alto uses the tall green tree. The effect of these symbols is to identify the cities by referring (via pictographic shorthand) to the cities' names. In light of Las Cruces's name and history, we conclude that the symbol does not have the effect of endorsing Christianity.

Unequivocally, the City and District are currently displaying symbols and artwork that might be constitutionally suspect in some other American communities or in other contexts. But, Las Cruces is the "City of Crosses" and the use of crosses as a symbol therein is not a religious statement. As such, the City and District's religious symbols "are not minor trespasses upon the Establishment Clause to which [we] turn a blind eye. Instead, their history, character, and context prevent them from being constitutional violations at all." Newdow, 542 U.S. at 37, 124 S.Ct. 2301 (O'Connor, J., concurring) *Weinbaum v. City of Las Cruces*, N.M., 541 F.3d 1017, 1039 (10th Cir. 2008)

NCAA's BYU Rule

Brigham Young University (BYU) is sponsored by the Church of Jesus Christ of Latter-day Saints as a "university [that] seeks to provide a high-quality, competitive education in an atmosphere conducive to the beliefs and standards of the Church." One way this commitment is reflected in sports is their policy against competing on Sundays. This created a scheduling conflict when the BYU baseball team could not compete in the College World Series in 1958 and 1961. In response, the NCAA created what has been called the "BYU Rule."

NCAA "BYU Rule":

31.1.4.1 Institutional Policy. If a participating institution has a written policy against competition on a particular day for religious reasons, it shall submit its written policy to the governing committee on or before September 1 of each academic year in order for it or one of its student-athletes to be excused from competing on that day. The championship schedule shall be adjusted to accommodate that institution, and such adjustment shall not require its team or an individual competitor to compete prior to the time originally scheduled.

Some suspected that this policy against playing on Sundays affected BYU's seeding in the 2024 NCAA Basketball tournament. BYU was the highest-rated number 5 seed by the NCAA selection committee, but was given the number 6 seed to open the tournament. Why would this matter? Because, as one sports commentator noted, "Every 5-seed in the field either plays in a Friday-Sunday regional, or feeds into a Friday-Sunday second weekend. The selection committee didn't acknowledge BYU's no-Sunday play policy, but it's easy to see how it could have played a role" (Walker, S. (2024, March 18). Did BYU's no-Sunday policy play a role in NCAA Tournament 6-seed? *KSL.com*).

NCAA Five-Year Rule

Another NCAA policy likely influenced by BYU's religious tradition is the Five-Year Rule. Student-athletes are only eligible to compete for five years beginning with the first semester or quarter the student-athlete first registers as a full-time college student. This can be a problem for BYU athletes who often spend 18 months to two years on a religious mission with their church during their eligibility years. In 2023, 64 players on BYU's football roster served missions in 29 different countries. To prevent these student-athletes from losing eligibility, the NCAA's five-year rule specifically excludes years spent on official religious missions.

12.8.1 Five-Year Rule. A student-athlete shall complete the student-athlete's seasons of participation within five calendar years from the beginning of the semester or quarter in which the student-athlete first registered for a minimum full-time program of studies in a collegiate institution, with time spent in the armed services, on official religious missions or with recognized foreign aid services of the U.S. government being excepted. For international students, service in the armed forces or on an official religious mission of the student's home country is considered equivalent to such service in the United States.

Eli Herring, BYU

A number of BYU players have gone on to play in the National Football League—which plays on Sundays—including Hall of Fame quarterback Steve Young. But one BYU player stands out as a player who refused to play on Sundays even after leaving BYU. He is former BYU Offensive Tackle, Eli Herring.

At 6'8" and weighing 330 pounds, Herring stands out in any crowd. He was projected to be a first to third round pick in the 1994 draft. But Herring decided against playing in the NFL so that he wouldn't have to work on Sundays and even wrote letters to each NFL team explaining his decision. He was still drafted in the sixth round of the 1995 NFL draft by the Oakland Raiders. Raiders senior assistant Bruce Allen flew to Provo and offered Herring a three-year, $1.5 million contract. Herring rejected it, choosing to teach high school instead. His starting salary as a teacher at Mountain View High School in Orem, Utah was around $22,000 a year (Springer, S. (1995, September 15). Eli's not coming: Former BYU lineman Herring has the ability to play in NFL, but it's never on Sunday for this Mormon. Los Angeles Times).

Religious Celebrations

In 2014, Muslim football player Husain Abdullah "received a 15-yard unsportsmanlike penalty after dropping to his knees and bowing in prayer following a 39-yard interception return for a touchdown [in his] Kansas City Chiefs' 41-14 victory over the New England Patriots on Monday Night" Football (ESPN.com news services. (2014, September 30). NFL: Husain Abdullah penalty wrong). In 2011, while playing for the Denver Broncos, quarterback and outspoken evangelical Christian Tim Tebow would often kneel in prayer after scoring a touchdown or even at the start of a game. The ritual was so common it became known as "tebowing." The ritual never earned Tebow a 15-yard penalty. The apparent double-standard between the rituals of Abdullah and Tebow did not go unnoticed.

Abdullah's penalty was in violation of what was then the NFL's Rule 12, Section 3, Article 1 (d), which states, "Players are prohibited from engaging in any celebrations or demonstrations while on the ground."

The day after Abdullah's penalty, NFL spokesman Michael Signora clarified that "the officiating mechanic in this situation is not to flag a player who goes to the ground as part of religious expression, and as a result, there should have been no penalty on the play."

God Bless America

Before the attacks on September 11, 2001, it was common to have fans stand and sing "Take Me Out to the Ball Game" during the seventh-inning stretch at Major League Baseball games. After September 11, 2001, this song was largely replaced with the song "God Bless America." During a seventh-inning stretch in August, 2009, a Boston Red Socks fan named Bradford Campeau-Laurion decided he wanted to use the restroom while attending a game at Yankee Stadium. (For any non-sports fans, I'll add a note here that the Yankees and Red Socks are rivals. And although I did not confirm this, it would not surprise me if this Red Socks fan was wearing a Red Socks hat and jersey while sitting at Yankee Stadium).

Bradford made his way down an aisle during the playing of "God Bless America" until he was stopped by a police officer who blocked his path and indicated that he could not leave during the song. Bradford explained that he needed to use the restroom and was not concerned about "God Bless America." The police officer grabbed Bradford's right arm and twisted it behind his back. A second officer joined to twist Bradford's left arm behind his back. The two officers then marched Bradford down several ramps to the stadium's exit where one officer told Bradford he should get out of the country if he didn't like it. Bradford sued the Yankees and they reached a settlement which included the Yankees stipulating that the team "has no policy restricting spectators' movement during God Bless America and has no intention of implementing such a policy at the [then] new Yankee Stadium" (*Campeau-Laurion, B. v. Raymond Kelly, The New York Yankees Partnership, et al.* (2009). Challenging forced patriotism at Yankee Stadium. *NYCLU*).

In God We Trust

When discussing whether the police can force someone to listen to "God Bless America," some end up questioning why or how the United States can have a motto that says, "In God we Trust." How does this not violate the Establishment Clause? The motto was adopted in 1956 replacing *E pluribus unum*, which is Latin for "Out of many, one." Courts have held that the phrase "In God we Trust" does not violate the U.S. Constitution because it is a phrase of "patriotic or ceremonial character," that has no "theological or ritualistic impact." As such, courts have determined that it does not constitute governmental sponsorship of a religious exercise and therefore, does not violate the U.S. Constitution (*Aronow v. United States*, 432 F.2d 242, 243 (9th Cir. 1970)).

Title VII of the Civil Rights Act of 1964

Title VII of the Civil Rights Act of 1964 requires employers with at least 15 employees to reasonably accommodate the religious practices of an employee or prospective employee unless doing so would create an undue hardship for the employer. In 1977 the United States Supreme Court decided in *Trans World Airlines v. Hardison* that an "undue hardship" for an employer in the context of Title VII religious accommodations is one that would cause a "*de minimis*" cost to the employer. *De minimis* means something too trivial or minor to merit consideration.

The *de minimis* standard was reversed by a unanimous decision in the 2023 United States Supreme Court case of *Groff v. DeJoy*. Groff was a former United States Postal Services (USPS) employee who sued the "Postal Service for failing to make reasonable accommodations for his Sunday Sabbath practice and instead disciplined him for failing to work as a letter carrier on Sundays" (*Groff v. DeJoy*, 600 U.S. 447, 143 S. Ct. 2279, 216 L. Ed. 2d 1041 (2023)). With Groff unwilling to work on Sundays, the USPS made other arrangements, including having the rest of the staff deliver the mail that would have otherwise been delivered by Groff. The postmaster, whose job ordinarily did not involve delivering the mail, even helped deliver mail that would have been delivered by Groff.

Throughout this time, Groff continued to receive discipline for failing to work on Sundays. He resigned and sued. The appeals court ruled in favor of the USPS because changing schedules was at least a *de minimus* undue burden on the USPS. In *Groff v. DeJoy* the Supreme Court eliminated the *de minimus* standard in favor of defining an "undue hardship" as "a burden [that] is substantial in the overall context of an employer's business" *Groff v. DeJoy*, 600 U.S. 447 (2023). The new standard requires "an employer to show that the burden of granting an accommodation would result in substantial increased costs in relation to the conduct of its particular business." Courts are instructed to test this burden by taking "into account all relevant factors in the case at hand, including the particular accommodations at issue and their practical impact in light of the nature, size, and operating cost of an employer" (*Groff v. DeJoy*, 600 U.S. 447 (2023).

Does this mean that Groff won? Not necessarily. The court's ruling redefined the definition of "undue hardship" and remanded the case back to the lower court for a ruling based on the new definition of "undue hardship." The lower court will now look at the burden on the USPS to determine if granting Groff's accommodation would have resulted in substantial increased costs in light of the operating costs of Groff's former employment at the rural mail delivery service.

Athletes and Ramadan

During the month of Ramadan, devout Muslims only consume food and drink before sunrise and after sunset. This requires elite athletes who observe Ramadan to create nourishment and hydration plans consistent with their fasting. The dates for Ramadan are based on the lunar calendar, causing them to vary with the dates of the Gregorian (January – December) Calendar.

Famous basketball players who have observed Ramadan include Kyrie Irving, Hakeem Olajuwon and Kareem Abdul-Jabbar. According to Dr. Qanta Ahmed, professor at NYU Langone Long Island School of Medicine and co-author of a paper analyzing the impact of Ramadan on Muslim soccer players, these athletes adjust to fasting during Ramadan with an established routine for their sleep, caloric intake, and hydration.

As noted in the discussion on Title VII, employers—including professional sports teams—are required to make reasonable accommodations for individuals observing Ramadan. However, where the law and Ramadan clash most visibly is not in the context of private employers, but in the treatment of federal or state prisoners seeking to observe Ramadan. In 2019, the Alaska Department of Corrections agreed to change its policy to accommodate Muslims seeking to observe Ramadan. In 2018, a jury awarded four Muslim Michigan inmates punitive damages after finding the Michigan Department of Corrections did not give them enough food during Ramadan.

In the words of the court:

> Prisoners do not lose their right to freely exercise their religion by virtue of their incarceration. Freedom of religion being a fundamental right, any regulation which infringes upon it must generally be justified by a "compelling state interest." However, as

a prisoner, Plaintiff's constitutional rights are subject to severe restriction. Rather, the standard by which prison regulations impinging on prisoner constitutional rights is judged is "reasonableness" (*Hardrick v. MacLaren*, No. 2:17-CV-00029, 2018 WL 3624956, at *3 (W.D. Mich. June 18, 2018), report and recommendation adopted, No. 2:17-CV-29, 2018 WL 3619266 (W.D. Mich. July 30, 2018)).

Based on recent settlements and policy changes, it is clear that forcing prisoners to choose between maintaining their sincerely held religious practices or not eating for a month imposes an unreasonable and unconstitutional choice.

Websites and Wedding Cakes

Several recent legal cases at the intersection of law and religion have dealt with same-sex marriage, anti-discrimination laws, and a business owner refusing, on religious grounds, to make a wedding cake or website for a same-sex marriage. The Colorado Anti-Discrimination Act prohibits businesses open to the public from discriminating against their customers on the basis of race, religion, gender, or sexual orientation. In *Masterpiece Cakeshop v. Colorado Civil Rights Commission*, 584 U.S. 617 (2018) a cake shop owner sought review of the decision of the Colorado Civil Rights Commission (CCRC) to issue a cease-and-desist order arising from the shop's refusal to sell a wedding cake to a same-sex couple. In *303 Creative LLC v. Elenis*, 600 U.S. 570 (2023), a website designer brought a pre-enforcement action against the Colorado Civil Rights Commission to enjoin the CCRC from forcing the plaintiffs to make wedding websites inconsistent with the designer's religious belief that marriage should be reserved to unions between one man and one woman. The courts would not allow a business to refuse service to someone based on race. Would the court allow a business to refuse service to someone based on sexual orientation?

I think an analogy is helpful in explaining the Supreme Court's recent decisions on religion. Imagine a Jewish carpenter. He's got long hair and a beard. He wears a robe. His father was also a carpenter. This long-haired, bearded Jewish carpenter is devout—never missing an event at the synagogue. He's even travelled to Jerusalem to celebrate Passover. He memorized the commandments, including the first two: "Thou shalt have no other gods before me" and "Thou shalt not make any carved images."

Although you may be picturing someone born around 2,000 years ago in Bethlehem, the Jewish carpenter in my analogy lives today in New York City—specifically, the Jewish section of Brooklyn. He sells mostly tables and chairs. He has also done some occasional custom work on things like bookshelves, armoires, and chests. One day a devout Hindu man enters our Jewish carpenter's store and asks the carpenter to make him a carving of the Hindu god Vishnu. Vishnu is often depicted with multiple arms and exposed breasts. The law would not allow the Jewish carpenter to prevent the Hindu man from entering the store and purchasing a chair. Would the law require the Jewish carpenter to carve the Hindu god Vishnu in opposition to the carpenter's sincerely held religious beliefs?

The court answered this question in *303 Creative LLC v. Elenis* (2023) with an emphatic "no." The court reasoned that this was not an issue of the free exercise of religion, but of free speech. When an artist is creating an expressive message, the artist is speaking, and the government cannot tell people how to speak.

In the words of the court:

All manner of speech—from "pictures, films, paintings, drawings, and engravings," to "oral utterance and the printed word"—qualify for the First Amendment's protections; no less can hold true when it comes to speech like Ms. Smith's conveyed over the internet.

Colorado does not seek to impose an incidental burden on speech. It seeks to force an individual to "utter what is not in [her] mind" about a question of political and religious significance. Barnette, 319 U. S., at 634, 63 S.Ct. 1178. And that…is something the First Amendment does not tolerate. No government… may affect a "speaker's message" by "forc[ing]" her to "accommodate" other views, 547 U.S. at 63, 126 S.Ct. 1297; no government may "'alter'" the "'expressive content'" of her message…and no government may "interfer[e] with" her "desired message," id., at 64, 126 S.Ct. 1297.

The dissent refuses to acknowledge where its reasoning leads. In a world like that, as Chief Judge Tymkovich highlighted, governments could force "an unwilling Muslim movie director to make a film with a Zionist message," they could compel "an atheist muralist to accept a commission celebrating Evangelical zeal," and they could require a gay website designer to create websites for a group advocating against same-sex marriage, so long as these speakers would accept commissions from the public with different messages. 6 F.4th at 1199 (dissenting opinion). Perhaps the dissent finds these possibilities untroubling because it trusts state governments to coerce only "enlightened" speech. But if that is the calculation, it is a dangerous one indeed.

In this case, Colorado seeks to force an individual to speak in ways that align with its views but defy her conscience about a matter of major significance. In the past, other States in Barnette, Hurley, and Dale have similarly tested the First Amendment's boundaries by seeking to compel speech they thought vital at the time. But, as this Court has long held, the opportunity to think for ourselves and to express those thoughts freely is among our most cherished liberties and part of what keeps our Republic strong. Of course, abiding the Constitution's commitment to the freedom of speech means all of us will encounter ideas we consider "unattractive," (opinion of SOTOMAYOR, J.), "misguided, or even hurtful," Hurley, 515 U. S., at 574, 115 S.Ct. 2338. But tolerance, not coercion, is our Nation's answer. The First Amendment envisions the United States as a rich and complex place where all persons are free to think and speak as they wish, not as the government demands. Because Colorado seeks to deny that promise, the judgment is Reversed.

Chapter 6: Disability Law and Sports

I teach business and sports law courses in a College of Business—not at a law school. I mention this because sometimes our perspective on disability law may vary depending on if we look at a situation as an employee or as an employer. As an employee, you may be thrilled to know that most employers cannot fire you or refuse to hire you because of your disability. As an employer, you may not be thrilled to learn that you are being sued because someone believes your bathroom, pool, or even website is not compliant with the Americans with Disabilities Act. In the context of Sports Law, if you think like a disabled athlete, you may want your own event, an extra few years of high school eligibility, or the ability to ride in a golf cart while other golfers have to walk. If you think like an administrator, you may wonder if it is fair to give a team points at a track meet when a disabled person gets his or her own event, if it is fair or safe to have older high school players playing against younger players, or if riding in a golf cart gives a disabled golfer an advantage over the competitors not allowed to ride in a golf cart. In this chapter, we will look at the history of disability law, how to read a statute, and then how to apply these disability statutes in the world of sports.

Bottom Line up Front

Before I dive into the weeds, I want to give you the bottom-line up front: In most situations, employers must make reasonable accommodations for individuals with disabilities. An unreasonable accommodation would be one that causes an undue burden on the employer. In the area of sports, an undue burden would include an accommodation that would be too difficult or expensive to implement or one that would constitute a fundamental alteration in the nature of the game.

Disability Law in the United States

In 2023, the Pew Research Center reported that Americans with disabilities make up 13% of the civilian noninstitutionalized population and 15% of total enrollment in public schools. The Census Bureau's 2021 American Community Survey found that "46% of Americans ages 75 and older and 24% of those ages 65 to 74 report having a disability" (Pew Research Center. (2023, July 24). 8 facts about Americans with disabilities. Pew Research Center). Since the 1970s, several Acts have been passed to accommodate this large and growing section of our population.

The Rehabilitation Act of 1973

The Rehabilitation Act of 1973 was the United States' first major federal disability rights law. It opened the doors for qualified individuals with disabilities by prohibiting "discrimination on the basis of disability in programs conducted by Federal agencies, in programs receiving Federal financial assistance, in Federal employment, and in the employment practices of Federal contractors."

A key provision of the Rehabilitation Act is Section 504, which states that "'no qualified individual with a disability in the United States shall be excluded from, denied the benefits of, or be subjected to discrimination under' any program or activity that receives Federal financial assistance." This provision was re-emphasized in a "Dear Colleague Letter" from the United States Department of Education Office for Civil Rights dated January 25, 2013. This letter reminded schools that "extracurricular athletics—which include club, intramural, or interscholastic (e.g., freshman, junior varsity, varsity) athletics at all education levels—are an important component of an overall education program, and therefore subject to the Rehabilitation Act of 1973" (U.S. Department of Education, Office for Civil Rights. (2013, January 25). *Dear Colleague Letter on the Inclusion of Students with Disabilities in Extracurricular Athletics*).

An important aspect of the Rehabilitation Act of 1973 is that it has been interpreted to provide a **private right of action** for plaintiffs. A private right of action allows a private individual to sue to enforce their rights. Without a private right of action, someone who is wronged would need to contact a government entity like the justice department or the police department to enforce the rights protected by the law.

The Rehabilitation Act may apply when the following criteria are satisfied:

(1) The plaintiff is a "[disabled] person" under the Act;
(2) The plaintiff is "otherwise qualified" for participation in the program;
(3) The plaintiff is being excluded from participation in, being denied the benefits of, or being subjected to discrimination under the program solely by reason of his [disability]; and
(4) The relevant program or activity is receiving Federal financial assistance (*Sandison v. Michigan High School Athletic Ass'n, Inc.* 64 F.3d 1026, 1030-31)

The Individuals with Disabilities Education Act (IDEA) of 1975

The Individuals with Disabilities Education Act (IDEA) was passed in 1975 under its prior name, the Education for all Handicapped Children Act. The law ensures that students with a disability are provided with Free Appropriate Public Education (FAPE) that is tailored to their individual needs. IDEA mandates that public schools provide free appropriate public education to eligible children with disabilities throughout the nation and ensures special education and related services to those children. The Act provides services to support student learning needs from birth through high school graduation or age 21, whichever comes first.

The Americans with Disability Act (ADA) of 1990

Rebecca Cokley, the Ford Foundation's U.S. Disability Rights Program Officer, shares a story about a single mom applying for a job in 1989. The woman sits across from the tenure committee that will decide her ability to continue in her dream job of running a center for students with disabilities. The chair of the committee leans back in his chair and shares, "Thank you, but we have decided to deny you tenure because you cannot reach more than the bottom six inches of a chalkboard. And what kind of teacher would you be if you couldn't use the top technology in our classroom," meaning, of course, a chalkboard. "Thank you and goodbye." That woman was Rebecca Cokley's mother, Joan Hare. Both Rebecca and her mother were born with achondroplasia, a common cause of dwarfism (Cokley, R. A. (2018, July 25). Reflections from an ADA Generation. TEDx University of Rochester).

This kind of discrimination was not federally illegal prior to the passing of the Americans with Disability Act of 1990 (ADA). The Act was signed by legislators after a group of individuals with physical disabilities shed their wheelchairs and crutches in front of the U.S. Capitol Building and pulled their bodies up the 100 Capitol Building steps to hand deliver their request that politicians make the ADA law.

The ADA is divided into five different sections, called Titles.

Title I	(Employment)
Title II	(Public Services)
Title III	(Public Accommodations)
Title IV	(Telecommunications)
Title V	(Miscellaneous)

We will look at each of these titles.

Title I (Employment)

Title I of the ADA provides that "No covered entity shall discriminate against a qualified individual on the basis of a disability in regard to job application procedures, hiring, advancement, or discharge of employees, employee compensation, job training, and other terms, conditions, and privileges of employment." Instead, these entities must provide a reasonable accommodation to a qualified applicant or employee with a disability unless the employer can show that the accommodation would be an undue hardship—that is, that it would require significant difficulty or expense.

For most practical purposes, it is helpful to translate Title I of the ADA into two simpler sentences:

1) Employers cannot discriminate against the disabled when hiring or firing, and
2) Employers must make reasonable accommodations for the disabled.

However, this translation only works if you are willing to ask more questions. For example, when we read "no covered entity shall discriminate," we need to ask, "What is a **covered entity**?" When we read that "no covered entity shall discriminate against a qualified individual," we need to ask, "What is a **qualified individual**?" When we read that covered entities must make "reasonable accommodations," we need to ask, "What is a **reasonable accommodation?**" Let's dive into these questions now.

Covered Entity

Notice that the Act does not say, "Employers cannot discriminate against the disabled." The Act says, "No covered entity shall discriminate against the disabled." A covered entity is defined as an "employer, employment agency, labor organization, or joint labor management committee." An employer is then defined as "a person engaged in an industry affecting commerce who has 15 or more employees."

These baseline requirements are called **threshold requirements**. These must be established by a plaintiff before a plaintiff can proceed with a case against a defendant. If a defendant does not have the requisite number of employees or is not engaged in an industry affecting commerce, then Title I of the ADA does not apply to them.

Requiring 15 or more employees seems self-explanatory after you ask questions about seasonal and part-time workers. It requires 15 or more employees for each working day in each of 20 or more calendar weeks in the current or preceding calendar year. But what does it mean that the employer must be "engaged in an industry affecting commerce?" You can answer this by asking, what employers are not "engaged in an industry affecting commerce?" One example is religious organizations. Think of the athletic programs at various religious, private high schools and universities. Title I cannot tell these organizations whom to hire. The Act even specifies the following:

(1) In general. - This subchapter shall not prohibit a religious corporation, association, educational institution, or society from giving preference in employment to individuals of a particular religion to perform work connected with the carrying on by such corporation, association, educational institution, or society of its activities.

(2) Religious tenets requirement. - Under this subchapter, a religious organization may require that all applicants and employees conform to the religious tenets of such organization.

The University of Notre Dame in Indiana was established as a Catholic institution. Brigham Young University in Utah is owned and run by the Church of Jesus Christ of Latter-day Saints. The ADA will not require these universities to hire someone with religious convictions contrary to the institution. This is true whether or not the applicant or employee is disabled.

A student once complained that it seemed that these threshold requirements could allow smaller businesses and religious organizations to discriminate against employees and applicants in ways that would be illegal for larger commercial businesses. It violated her sense of justice and her bewildered stare asked me to clarify how this must not be the case. Instead, I shrugged to indicate that it seemed that she understood how threshold requirements work. When we look at employment laws—or really any law—we first look to see if the law applies to a particular defendant. If the law does not apply, the business is not required to comply with the law. Of course, the business could still comply, but if the law does not apply, the business need not comply.

Qualified Individual

Title I states that "No covered entity shall discriminate against a *qualified individual* on the basis of a disability...." We answered, "What is a covered entity." Now we need to ask, "What is a qualified individual."

A qualified individual is an employee or applicant who has:

(A) a physical or mental impairment that substantially limits one or more major life activities of such individual;

(B) a record of such an impairment; or

(C) being regarded as having such an impairment.

This means that a qualified individual could be an athlete with a mental impairment that substantially limits one or more major life activities, someone who once was diagnosed with such an impairment, or someone you suspect has such an impairment, even if the individual does not and never did.

With the definition only applying to those with "physical or mental impairments that substantially limit one or more major life activities," we next need to ask, "What qualifies as a physical or mental impairment?" and "What are major life activities?"

Physical or Mental Impairment

The ADA defines a physical or mental impairment this way:

1) Any physiological disorder or condition, cosmetic disfigurement, or anatomical loss affecting one or more body systems, such as: neurological, musculoskeletal, special sense organs, respiratory (including speech organs), cardiovascular, reproductive, digestive, genitourinary, immune, circulatory, hemic, lymphatic, skin, and endocrine; or

2) Any mental or psychological disorder such as intellectual disability, organic brain syndrome, emotional or mental illness, and specific learning disability.

Examples of mental or psychological impairments in the Psychiatric Enforcement Guidance include major depression, bipolar disorder, anxiety disorders (which include panic disorder, obsessive-compulsive disorder, and post-traumatic stress disorder), schizophrenia, and personality disorders. However, the ADA excludes various sexual conditions (including transvestism, transsexualism, pedophilia, and voyeurism), homosexuality, gender identity disorders, bisexuality, compulsive gambling, kleptomania, pyromania, and psychoactive substance use disorders resulting from current illegal use of drugs (*See* 42 U.S.C. 12211(b) (1994); 29 C.F.R. 1630.3(d) (1999)).

Notice that in the definition it is not enough for an individual to have a physical or mental impairment. The qualified individual must have a physical or mental impairment *that substantially limits a major life activity.*

Major Life Activities

The ADA defines Major Life Activities as including, but not being limited to, the following:

(i) Caring for oneself, performing manual tasks, seeing, hearing, eating, sleeping, walking, standing, sitting, reaching, lifting, bending, speaking, breathing, learning, reading, concentrating, thinking, communicating, interacting with others, and working; and

(ii) The operation of a major bodily function, including functions of the immune system, special sense organs and skin; normal cell growth; and digestive, genitourinary, bowel, bladder, neurological, brain, respiratory, circulatory, cardiovascular, endocrine, hemic, lymphatic, musculoskeletal, and reproductive functions. The operation of a major bodily function includes the operation of an individual organ within a body system.

At this point in reading or hearing definitions, I imagine your eyes are starting to blur or you are starting to daydream. I have seen that blur in my students' eyes, and so I ask the class if anyone wants to admit that they may have a little OCD, short for obsessive-compulsive disorder. I start to give examples of students who may have to have all their pencils lined up and parallel with their notebook and desk. Some smile as I share that OCD is listed as a mental impairment with the ADA. Then I ask if anyone has ever been depressed. The class simultaneously exhales in acknowledgment of a shared humanity that sometimes includes depression. We nod together as I remind them that "major depression" was on the list of mental impairments with the ADA.

But before thinking that everyone can always qualify as being disabled with the ADA, remember that it is not enough to have a physical or mental impairment. The physical or mental impairment must substantially limit a major life activity. Hopefully, our OCD or depression does not cause us to lose control of our bowels or bladder. Hopefully, our depression or other impairments do not prevent us from "caring for ourselves, performing manual tasks, seeing, hearing, eating, sleeping, walking, standing, sitting, reaching, lifting, bending, speaking, breathing, learning, reading, concentrating, thinking, communicating, interacting with others, and working." But if they do, we may be included in the definition of a qualified individual under the ADA.

Reasonable Accommodation in Title I (Employment)

Now that we understand what is a covered entity and who is a qualified individual, we should ask what must the covered entity do for the qualified individual? In a nutshell, employers must give qualified employees with a disability, *reasonable accommodations* that will allow the employees to perform the essential functions of the job. To determine if an accommodation is reasonable, courts will look at the cost and difficulty for an employer to accommodate the applicant's or employee's request.

For example, if an employee can no longer make it up the stairs to her office on the second floor, it may be reasonable for her employer to allow her to work on the first floor. It may be reasonable for her employer to install an elevator, but not necessarily. A court could determine that the cost of installing an elevator to accommodate employees with disabilities is reasonable for an employer with tens of thousands of employees, but unreasonable for an employer with 15 employees.

Notice also that Title I states that "No covered entity shall discriminate against a qualified individual *on the basis of a disability*." It does not say that covered entities cannot discriminate on the basis of something else. Most sports are inherently discriminatory. For example, maybe only the top 10% of track and field athletes in a state advance to the state championship. That seems to discriminate against 90% of track and field athletes. Or maybe a state requires students to be under 19 years old before the beginning of their senior year to be eligible to compete in high school athletics. In these cases, as we will see, courts may determine that individuals with disabilities were not discriminated against because of their disability, but because of their comparative lack of athletic ability or because of their birthdate. Title I only applies when covered entities are discriminating against qualified individuals because of their disability.

Title II (Public Services) and Title III (Public Accommodations)

Both Title II and Title III of the ADA ensure accessibility for individuals with disabilities. Title II applies to public organizations like schools, public transportation, and government buildings. Title III focuses on private businesses that are open to the public like hotels, restaurants, theaters, stores, day-care centers, doctors' offices, etc. These entities are required to give people with disabilities an equal opportunity to benefit from all of the entity's programs, services, and activities. This may require the entities to make "reasonable modifications." However, under both titles, entities are not required to make modifications that would create an undue burden on the entity. An **undue burden** means something that would cause significant difficulty or expense to the entity.

As an example, think of the pools that are open to the public. With respect to individuals with disabilities, have you noticed what they all have in common? You may have noticed that since January 31, 2013, pools that are open to the public contain a fixed lift to help raise and lower individuals with disabilities into and out of the pool. More specifically, these lifts must have a seat height that is between 16 inches and 19 inches high, and the seat must be at least 16 inches wide. The lift must support at least 300 pounds and must submerge to at least 18 inches under the water.

Why did all hotels with pools in the United States decide to install pool lifts before January 31, 2013? Because ADA regulations determined that installing a fixed pool lift was a reasonable modification. As a result, all public entities made the change because they were subject to enforcement under Title II of the ADA. All applicable private places of public accommodation made the change because they were subject to enforcement under Title III of the ADA. For my marketing majors—at least the cynical ones—I note that lobbying can sometimes be a form of marketing. That is, how do you get every hotel in the United States with a pool to buy your pool lift product? You get the government to say it is required.

It is worth noting that disability access includes accessibility to a business's website. In 2023, there were 4,605 web accessibility lawsuits filed—a 42% increase compared to 2022. In 2017, Floridian Deborah Laufer sued Acheson Hotels because its Coast Village Hotel in Maine was not ADA compliant. It did not appear that Laufer had any intention of staying at the Maine hotel, but she accessed the hotel's website and filed her complaint alleging that the website was not ADA compliant. Please note that the plaintiff's complaint was about the website not being ADA compliant, not the hotel itself. The U.S. Supreme Court agreed to hear the complaint, but then dismissed it as moot in December 2023 because Laufer withdrew her complaint and the hotel's website had been updated.

Stadium Facilities and Seating

The largest damages settlement in a case alleging discrimination in public accommodations under ADA Title II and Title III was a $24 million settlement with the San Francisco 49ers's Levi Stadium. The court approved the class action lawsuit that required the stadium to "fix more than 2,600 accessibility barriers and the pedestrian right of way leading to the stadium and pay $24 million to stadium visitors with mobility disabilities" (Cabalo, C. (2020, July 24). Largest damages settlement in Disabilities Case: Levi's Stadium. Peiffer Wolf).

To accommodate fans with disabilities, the ADA requires that one percent (1%) of seating be reserved for disabled fans. This only applies to stadiums built or altered after 1991. Wrigley Field, the famous home of the Chicago Cubs, was built in 1914, but was subject to the 1% rule because of a renovation project that started in 2014. In 2017, wheelchair-bound Cubs fan David Felimon Cerda sued the Cubs, alleging the renovations violated the ADA by removing favorable disability seating to make way for new luxury suites. The Cubs argued that "Wrigley Field had 225 disability-accessible seats evenly distributed across the stadium, 26 more than the 209 such seats the parties agreed were minimally required by the ADA" (Byrnes, D. (2023, June 21). *Judge sides with Chicago Cubs in lawsuit over wheelchair access at Wrigley Field.* Courthouse News Service).

After a trial in 2023, the Honorable Judge Jorge Alonso agreed with the Cubs concluding, "Although Plaintiff's situation is unfortunate, he fails to prove that the Defendant violated the ADA. Specifically, Plaintiff fails to prove by a preponderance of the evidence that Defendant fails to have the required number of accessible seats and that the accessible seats are horizontally dispersed around the stadium. Consequently, the Court enters judgment in favor of Defendant" (*Cerda v. Chicago Cubs Baseball Club, LLC*, No. 1:2017cv09023 - Document 258 (N.D. Ill. 2023).

The University of Michigan's stadium, built in 1927, would have been exempt from the ADA's 1% requirement if it were not for a $226 million renovation approved in 2007. This increased their official capacity to 107,601 seats—the 34th largest sports venue in the world. Unfortunately, the proposed renovation resulted in wheelchair-accessible seats accounting for less than 1% of the total number of seats. In response, the Michigan Paralyzed Veterans of America sued the university in 2007. In 2008 the University of Michigan agreed to a settlement that included expanding their plans to include the required number of permanent wheelchair-accessible seats as required by the ADA.

When Accommodations are Not Reasonable in Sports

In the area of sports, an accommodation's reasonableness is evaluated not only on the difficulty and cost of the accommodation, but also on the impact the accommodation would have on the game. The accommodation will not be reasonable—and therefore not required—if it "alters an essential aspect of the game" or "gives a disabled athlete an advantage over others" (*PGA Tour v. Martin*, 532 U.S. 661(2001). For example, would it change racquetball or give an advantage to the disabled athlete to allow someone in a wheelchair two bounces while those not in wheelchairs only receive one? Would it change golf or give a disabled athlete an advantage to allow disabled athletes to ride in a cart while other athletes must walk? Would it change track and field to allow slower qualifying times or additional events (like wheelchair events) for disabled athletes? We will discuss these cases shortly.

Title IV (Telecommunications)

Title IV of the ADA covers telephone and television access for people with hearing and speech disabilities. It requires telephone and internet companies to provide a nationwide system of telecommunications relay services that allow people with hearing and speech disabilities to communicate over the telephone. Title IV, which is regulated by the Federal Communications Commission (FCC), also requires closed captioning of federally funded public service announcements.

Title V (Miscellaneous)

Title V is a miscellaneous section that addresses current drug and alcohol use, what is not a disability, and attorney fees.

Title V clarifies that although drug and alcohol addiction may make someone disabled—that is, it may cause physical or mental impairments that substantially limit one or more major life activities—current alcohol or drug use is not protected as a disability.

The Act states that a covered entity:

(1) may prohibit the illegal use of drugs and the use of alcohol at the workplace by all employees;

(2) may require that employees shall not be under the influence of alcohol or be engaging in the illegal use of drugs at the workplace;

(3) may require that employees behave in conformance with the requirements established under the Drug Free Workplace Act of 1988 (41 U.S.C. 701 et seq.);

(4) may hold an employee who engages in the illegal use of drugs or who is an alcoholic to the same qualification standards for employment or job performance and behavior that such entity holds other employees, even if any unsatisfactory performance or behavior is related to the drug use or alcoholism of such employee.

As examples, consider the 2020 America Sports Drama "The Way Back" staring Ben Affleck as an alcoholic/former high school basketball phenom who returns to his high school to coach, or the 1976 American Sports Comedy "The Bad News Bears" staring Walter Matthau as the alcoholic ex-baseball pitcher who becomes a youth baseball team coach. In both cases, these coaches would be protected by the ADA if they admitted while applying for the job that they were alcoholics. However, Title V makes it clear that their employers could prohibit the current use of alcohol or the influence of alcohol in the workplace.

Attorney Fees

Title V also provides for the prevailing party in a disability lawsuit to recover reasonable attorney fees. As an attorney, I want to discuss the importance and dangers of this provision.

First, the importance of attorney fees. A student told me a story about a possible ADA situation she encountered at a rustic old restaurant in America's Southwest. (It sounded like a bar, but I'll follow my student's lead and call it a restaurant). The student was heading towards the restroom when she encountered a woman in a wheelchair waiting in the narrow hallway outside of the restroom. The woman apologetically asked if there was any way my student could lift the woman out of her wheelchair and then place her on the toilet and then wait to carry her back to her wheelchair when she was finished. The restroom was too narrow to accommodate a wheelchair, and she needed help. I share the story with my students because they can understand the humiliation of having to ask a stranger this personal question. Then I have my students imagine that I decide that I am going to put on my attorney superhero cape and try to help this woman. We sue under Title III of the ADA and we win. The class cheers.

But what did we win? Students suggest that the restaurant may need to make reasonable modifications to allow individuals with disabilities to use their restroom. Maybe they create a larger space with wider doors, a different sink, and handrails. That's great, but if I was trying to make a living in the practice of law and spent over a year with this case on my desk, what would the win mean for me? If I took the case on a contingency fee, do I get to keep 40% of a bathroom stall door? How would part of a door help me pay my bills?

The attorney fee provision in Title V is crucial for ADA enforcement because it incentivizes attorneys to represent the disabled in their complaints. For example, if an attorney spent $10,000 worth of hours to win a case that results in a restaurant having to install $1,000 worth of handrails at the business, the court could require the restaurant to pay $10,000 for the prevailing party's reasonable attorney fees.

With attorney fees, of course, there is also the possibility of abuse. Between 2009 and 2018, one San Jose, California law firm is believed to have used a single disabled plaintiff to file ADA lawsuits against over 2,000 area businesses. Numerous security cameras from the defendants show footage of the plaintiff walking to the back of his SUV, taking out his wheelchair, and then wheeling it into the business where he encounters an alleged ADA violation. The plaintiff then returns to his SUV, stands up, lifts his heavy wheelchair into the back of his SUV, and presumably drives to the next defendant.

This is not to say that disabled individuals would not be able to lift their wheelchair, but you can imagine that the business owner defendants were incensed. They had to hire attorneys and pay attorney fees. Some allege they were coerced into paying settlements. Some even blamed the lawsuits for forcing them out of business. In response, the law firm that filed these 2,000 ADA claims was sued in 2018, with plaintiff business owners arguing that the law firm was a criminal enterprise in violation of the Racketeer Influenced and Corrupt Organizations (RICO) Act. The law firm settled the case in 2019 (Lopez, P. (2018, March 28). *Civil racketeering case can go forward against two law firms over disability claims*. The Fresno Bee.)

A similar situation happened in New Mexico where a law firm filed 99 ADA lawsuits against businesses using a single plaintiff. The Santa Fe, New Mexico judge dismissed the cases with prejudice, stating, "This type of shotgun litigation undermines both the spirit and purpose of the ADA" (Denver7. (2017, July 7). Judge calls ADA lawsuit machine a 'carnival shell game,' dresses down attorney [https://www.youtube.com/watch?v=x9r3n__EdMY]).

Sports Cases

Now that we have a background in disability law, let us apply it to sports.

Age Limits

Many school districts have an "**Age 19 Rule**" that limits participation in school athletics to students who are under the age of 19 prior to the beginning of the school year (usually in August or September). Some school districts also have an "**Eight-Semester Rule**" that only provides eight consecutive semesters of eligibility in high school athletics following a student's entrance into the 9th grade. These rules are designed "to safeguard other athletes against injuries arising from competing against overage, and thus oversized, athletes; and to prevent overage athletes from gaining an unfair competitive advantage" (*Sandison v. Michigan High School Athletic Ass'n, Inc.* 64 F.3d 1026, 1029).

At times, a student with a learning disability may repeat a grade for academic reasons, and this may result in the student being 19 years old at the start of the final semester of high school. In *Sisson v. Virgina High School League, Inc.*, plaintiff Steven Adam Sisson, missed the birthday deadline by one day. He filed a waiver to play, but the Virginia High School League denied it. In response, Sisson sued alleging that the district violated his Fourteenth Amendment rights to due process and equal protection under the law. The court, although sympathetic to his plight, held that he did not have a constitutionally protected interest in playing high school sports and that the cause of him being held back a grade was not because of his learning disability, but because of his parent's choice.

In *Sandison v. Michigan High School Athletic Ass'n, Inc.,* the Michigan High School Athletic Association determined that cross country runners Ronald Sandison and Craig Stanely were ineligible to compete their senior year of high school because they turned 19 years old prior to the start of their senior year. In response, Sandison and Stanley "alleged that excluding them from playing interscholastic sports amounted to unlawful disability discrimination" and sued their high schools and the Michigan High School Athletic Association for violating the Rehabilitation Act and Titles II and III of the ADA.

The Michigan High School Athletic Association did not dispute that the plaintiffs had learning disabilities. The court concluded that the Rehabilitation Act requires that the "plaintiff is being excluded from participation in, being denied the benefits of, or being subjected to discrimination under the program solely by reason of his disability," and their disability was not the sole reason their participation was denied. Instead, the court held that the plaintiffs were free to participate during their first three years in high school and were now not being discriminated against because of their disability, but "solely by reason of" their dates of birth. (64 F.3d 1026, 1035).

There are cases where courts have granted students over 18 years old a waiver to the Age 19 Rule. For example, in *Dennin v. Connecticut Interscholastic Athletic Conference, Inc.*, 913 F. Supp. 663 (1996), a 19-year-old student with Down Syndrome was allowed to participate on the high school swim team. The court found that Dennis would not provide a competitive advantage, his disability was the sole reason for still being in school at age 19, and allowing his participation would not be an undue burden on the school. Similarly, in *Johnson v. Florida High Sch. Activities Ass'n*, Inc., 899 F.Supp 579 (1997), a 19-year-old football player and wrestler was allowed to compete because he was not "considered a 'star' player," his participation "would not provide any unfair competitive advantage to the respective teams," and his participation "in no way undermines the purposes of safety and fairness."

Here is an excerpt from *Sisson v. Virgina High School League, Inc.* Civil Action No. 7:10CV00530, (W.D. Va. Dec. 14, 2010).

In the words of the Court:

The plaintiff, Steven Adam Sisson, is a senior at Eastern Montgomery High School in Montgomery County, Virginia. Under the eligibility rules promulgated by the defendant, Virginia High School League ("VHSL"), Sisson is one-day too old to participate in League-sponsored athletic activities, because he turned 19 on July 31, 2010. After unsuccessfully attempting to obtain a waiver of the age rule, Sisson filed this action under 42 U.S.C. § 1983, asserting violations of his rights to due process and equal protection. The case is presently before the court on the plaintiff's motion for temporary restraining order and preliminary injunction. For the reasons stated during the hearing on December 10, 2010, and for those that follow, the plaintiff's motion will be denied.

Factual Background and Procedural History

When Sisson was in the third grade, he was identified as having a specific learning disability in reading and writing with an auditory processing deficit. Although his grades were average, Sisson's parents elected for him to repeat the third grade at the recommendation of his private elementary school. After Sisson completed the seventh grade, his parents moved him to a public school in Montgomery County that could better accommodate his particular academic needs.

During his freshman year at Eastern Montgomery High School, Sisson played football, baseball, and basketball at the junior varsity level. He then played the same sports at the varsity level during his sophomore and junior years. As early as his freshman year, Sisson learned that he might not be eligible to play high school sports during his senior year because of his age and date of birth.

The VHSL, of which Eastern Montgomery is a member, has adopted thirteen regulations addressing the eligibility of individual students to participate in League-sponsored activities. One of those regulations, the so-called "age rule," states that a student shall not have reached the age of 19 on or before the first day of August of the school year in which he wishes to compete. Sisson turned 19 on July 31, 2010 and, thus, is one-day too old under the rule.

The VHSL regulations permit students to apply for a waiver of the age rule. According to the rules governing eligibility appeals, a waiver will be considered:

A. For the student who experienced a delayed start or interruption in his/her educational progression due to a significant disability. Disabled persons shall be defined as those, who by reason of one or more of the following conditions, are unable to receive reasonable benefit from ordinary education: long-term physical impairment or illness, significant limited intellectual capacity, significant identifiable emotional disorder, identifiable perceptual or communicative disorder, or speech disorders; or

B. For a non-native language speaking student placed in a lower grade than his/her age would dictate when first enrolling in a new school; or

C. For the foreign student in refugee status.

The rules further provide that a waiver will not be considered "[i]f the student repeats a grade after making grades satisfactory for promotion to the next level."

Sisson applied for a waiver of the age rule in March of 2010. The application was signed by his high school principal, who opined that Sisson experienced an interruption in his educational progression due to a disability and, thus, that he was eligible for a waiver under criterion A, set forth above.

Sisson's application was first reviewed by the local district committee, which recommended granting a waiver. The committee found that Sisson satisfied criterion A and that he would suffer an undue hardship if the age rule was not waived.

The application was subsequently forwarded to Tom Zimorski, the deputy director of the VHSL. Zimorski ultimately declined to follow the district committee's recommendation and denied the waiver request on several grounds. Specifically, Zimorski found that no waiver criterion had been met, that the data provided by Sisson was insufficient to support a waiver, and that no undue hardship had been identified.

Sisson appealed the deputy director's decision to the VHSL's executive committee. The executive committee heard the matter via telephone conference on May 12, 2010, and ultimately voted to deny Sisson's request for a waiver.

Sisson then appealed to an independent hearing officer, the final level of review under the VHSL rules. The hearing officer considered the materials submitted by Sisson and conducted an in-person hearing on May 28, 2010. By letter dated June 1, 2010, the hearing officer denied the request for a waiver. Although the hearing officer found that criterion A may apply as a result of Sisson's documented learning disability, the officer determined that a waiver was not necessary to avoid an inequity or prevent an undue hardship.

Nearly six months later, on November 30, 2010, Sisson filed the instant action against the VHSL, alleging that he was deprived of due process and equal protection as a result of being denied a waiver of the age rule. The following day, Sisson filed a motion for temporary restraining order and preliminary injunction. In the motion, Sisson requests an order requiring the VHSL to permit him to participate in interscholastic athletic programs and competitions.

Discussion

. . . . .

Having carefully reviewed the record in this case and the applicable case law, the court concludes that Sisson has failed to establish that he is entitled to preliminary injunctive relief. First, Sisson has failed to demonstrate that he is likely to succeed on the merits of his claims. As the court explained during the hearing on the instant motion, the facts of this case do not give rise to a viable due process claim. In order to claim the procedural protections of the Due Process Clause of the Fourteenth Amendment, a complainant must establish that he has been deprived of life, liberty, or property. Bd. of Regents v. Roth, 408 U.S. 564, 569 (1972). While Sisson contends that he has a protected property interest in playing interscholastic athletics, he does not cite any legal authority that supports the notion that such interest exists. In the only case cited by Sisson, Goss v. Lopez, 419 U.S. 565 (1975), the United States Supreme Court held that an Ohio law, which mandated free public education and required residents to attend school, gave those students a property interest in public education that could not be taken away without due process. In this case, however, the issue is not whether Sisson has a protected right to public education, but whether he has a legitimate claim of entitlement to play high school football, basketball, and baseball. Because this court and others have rejected the notion that students have a constitutionally protected interest in participating in interscholastic athletics, the court concludes that Sisson's due process claim has little to no likelihood of success on the merits. See Equity in Athletics, Inc. v. Dep't of Educ., 675 F. Supp. 2d 660 (W.D. Va. 2009) (dismissing the plaintiff's claim that students had a protected property interest in playing intercollegiate sports); see also Seamons v. Snow, 84 F.3d 1226, 1235 (10th Cir. 1996) (emphasizing that the Court had interpreted Goss v. Lopez "to speak only in general terms regarding the 'educational process,'" and that "the innumerable separate components of the educational process, such as participation in athletics and membership in school clubs, do not create a property interest subject to constitutional protection"); Davenport v. Randolph County Bd. of Educ., 730 F.2d 1395, 1397 (11th Cir. 1984) ("This court has held that the privilege of participating in interscholastic activities must be deemed to fall . . . outside the protection of due process."); Brindisi v. Regano, 20 F. App'x 508, 510 (6th Cir. 2001) (holding that the plaintiff "has neither a liberty nor a property interest in interscholastic athletics subject to due process protection").

Sisson's equal protection claim is premised on the assertion that students like him, who apply for a waiver of the age rule on the basis of a disability, are treated less favorably than foreign students who apply for waivers. While this claim presents a closer question than Sisson's due process claim, the court nonetheless has serious doubt as to its likelihood of success. To prevail on an equal protection claim, a plaintiff "must first demonstrate that he has been treated differently from others with whom he is similarly situated and that the unequal treatment was the result of intentional or purposeful discrimination." Morrison v. Garraghty, 239 F.3d 648, 654 (4th Cir. 2001). If the plaintiff makes this showing, "the court proceeds to determine whether the disparity in treatment can be justified under the requisite level of scrutiny." Id. In this regard, a decision "that neither proceeds along suspect lines nor infringes fundamental constitutional rights must be upheld against an equal protection challenge if there is any reasonably conceivable state of facts that could provide a rational basis for [it]." FCC v. Beach Communications, Inc., 508 U.S. 307, 313 (1993).

In this case, the court questions whether Sisson will be able to satisfy either of the first required elements — that he was treated differently from others with whom he was similarly situated or that any unequal treatment was the result of intentional discrimination. As the VHSL noted during the hearing on Sisson's motion, eligibility decisions require an examination of facts and circumstances that are often unique to each student who applies for a waiver. In Sisson's case, it is undisputed that he suffers from a learning disability. However, he was not required to repeat a grade as a result of the disability, or otherwise held back at the direction of school officials. Instead, Sisson's parents elected for him to repeat the third grade to improve his chances of academic success, even though his grades would have permitted him to be promoted to the next grade. Given this distinguishing factor, it will be difficult for Sisson to establish that he was similarly situated, in all relevant respects, to students who were granted waivers of the age requirement, or that the denial of his application was the result of purposeful discrimination.

. . . . .

The court is also unable to conclude that Sisson will suffer irreparable harm in the absence of preliminary injunctive relief. As previously stated, Sisson has been aware of his eligibility problems since his freshman year of high school, and his last administrative appeal from the denial of his waiver application concluded on June 1, 2010. Nonetheless, Sisson waited until November 30, 2010 to file the instant action. The court agrees with the VHSL that such delay militates against a finding of irreparable harm. See Quince Orchard Valley Citizens Ass'n, Inc. v. Hodel, 872 F.2d 75, 80 (4th Cir. 1989).

. . . . .

In addition, other courts, when faced with similar circumstances, have rejected the notion that a student suffers "irreparable harm" by not being permitted to participate in interscholastic athletics. See, e.g., Dziewa v. Pa. Interscholastic Athletic Ass'n, 2009 U.S. Dist. LEXIS 3062, at *17 (E.D. Pa. Jan. 16, 2009) ("This court, as well as other federal courts, have previously and consistently held that ineligibility for participation in interscholastic athletic competitions alone does not constitute irreparable harm."). In this case, Sisson had the opportunity to play football, baseball, and basketball for Eastern Montgomery during his first three years of high school, and it appears from the record that he continues to associate with the school's athletic teams. While it is understandable that he would like to actually participate in competitive sporting events sponsored by the VHSL during his final year of high school, it is difficult to conclude that he will be irreparably harmed if he is unable to do so.

Conclusion

In closing, the court is not unsympathetic to Sisson's plight and likely would have granted him a waiver if it had been responsible for making the decision. However, in light of the legal standards governing Sisson's federal claims and the instant motion, the court is unable to conclude that he is entitled to the extraordinary remedy of preliminary injunctive relief. Accordingly, his motion for temporary restraining order and preliminary injunction must be denied.

Discrimination "on the basis of" or "by reason of" Their Disability

In some cases, it may be clear that there is an individual with a disability, but it is unclear if the individual is being discriminated against "on the basis of" or "by reason of" the disability. In the case of A.H. by Holzmueller v. Illinois High Sch. Ass'n, 881 F.3d 587 (7th Cir. 2018), an athlete with spastic quadriplegia related to cerebral palsy requested an accommodation to have the qualifying times for the state championship increased for his events so that he could compete at the state championship. The court agreed that the athlete was disabled, but disagreed that the disability was the cause of the athlete's inability to qualify for the state championship. That is, if only 10% of able-bodied runners qualify for the state championship, how could this athlete argue that *but for his disability*, he would be in the top 10% of all runners.

Fundamental Alterations in the Nature of the Game

Even when a disability is acknowledged as the cause for discrimination, an accommodation may not be granted if it would constitute a fundamental alteration in the nature of the game. For example, the court in *Kuketz v. Petronelli*, 443 Mass. 355, 821 N.E.2d 473 (2005) held that allowing a wheelchair athlete two bounces while his able-bodied opponents received one bounce fundamentally altered the nature of the game of racquetball and was not required under Title III of the Americans with Disabilities Act.

Casey Martin

In *PGA Tour v. Martin* (2001), the United States Supreme Court determined that allowing professional golfer Casey Martin to use a golf cart during tournaments was a reasonable accommodation that would not fundamentally alter the nature of the game. The court held that "the use of carts is not inconsistent with the fundamental character of golf, the essence of which has always been shotmaking." (*PGA Tour, Inc. v. Martin*, 532 U.S. 661, (2001). Having already qualified for professional events, it was also clear that Martin was an athlete who could compete at the highest level and that he requested the accommodation not for an advantage, but to help him compete in spite of his disability. Therefore, Martin was allowed to use a golf cart.

If you are interested in the story beyond the Supreme Court decision, Martin kept full status on the Nike Tour through 2003, but failed to make the Q-School finals in 2003. This relegated him to a limited status in 2004. In 2006, he became the head coach of the University of Oregon's men's golf team in his hometown of Eugene, Oregon. In 2012, he qualified for the U.S. Open by winning a sectional at Emerald Valley Golf Club, again near his hometown of Eugene, Oregon. In 2016, he led the Oregon Ducks to the NCAA Division I National Championship. Discussing the prospect of losing his leg in a 2020 interview with his hometown's Register-Guard newspaper, Martin stated, "I was grateful that I was able to hold it off for a long time. I thought it would happen at 27 not 47." In 2021, Martin successfully underwent surgery to amputate his right leg.

Tatyana McFadden

In January 2021, Women's Running Magazine selected Tatyana McFadden as one of 24 "Power Women of the Year". That may not be surprising when you realize that she is considered one of the fastest women in the world. She has won 20 medals (including eight gold medals), 24 World Major Marathon wins including four consecutive Grand Slams (first place in Boston, Chicago, NYC and London marathons in the same year) and has broken five world records in track and field. What may be surprising is that McFadden was "born with spina bifida and spent the first six years of her life in a Russian orphanage.... Paralyzed from the waist down, and with no other way to move," McFadden developed powerful arms and hands by learning to "walk on her hands to keep up with the other children" (McFadden, T. Retrieved from https://tatyanamcfadden.com/). This helped develop McFadden into the elite wheelchair racer that she is today.

However, as a junior at Maryland's Atholton High School (AHS), the Maryland Public Secondary Schools Athletic Association (MPSSAA) refused to count McFadden's contribution towards her team's score at the state championship. In response, McFadden sued the MPSSAA.

At issue is how track and field team competitions are scored and Maryland's "40% Rule." At state track and field championships, points are awarded to teams based on the individual performances of their athletes. These points are then totaled to determine the overall team scores. The team with the highest score at the end of the competition is declared the winner. The **40% rule** is a policy where team points are only awarded for events where at least 40% of the high schools participated. The defendants pointed out that this rule had also been applied to recent diving and pole-vaulting competitors.

McFadden was the only female wheelchair racer (called "wheelers") in the state. Another high school in the state had "two male wheelers." "Thus, [in the words of the court,] there is the potential that if McFadden is awarded even one point...for her participation in the 2007 tournaments, her school could be named team champion, or otherwise rank higher in team standings, on a basis that is unfair to non-disabled individuals at other schools" (*McFadden v. Grasmick,* 485 F. Supp. 2d

642, 644 (D. Md. 2007)). Similarly, the team with the two male wheelers could gain up to eight points "if each boy participates in the maximum of four events and defendants are ordered to award team points for wheelchair racers." This could result in giving schools with disabled athletes—or a single high-diver or pole vaulter—an unfair advantage over other teams. In response, the court denied McFadden's claim that the defendant's policy of assigning points at state track and field competitions unlawfully discriminated against her in violation of the Rehabilitation Act and the ADA. McFadden was allowed to compete, but her individual points did not contribute to her team's score.

Oscar Pistorius

In 2012, South African Oscar Pistorius made history as the first amputee to compete in an Olympic track event when he competed in the 2012 London Games. Pistorius was born in 1986 without the fibula (a bone between the calf and ankle). At 11 months old, his legs were amputated below the knees. Pistorius began running in 2004 using carbon-fiber-reinforced polymer prosthetic blades. This earned him the nickname "Blade Runner." Pistorius won Paralympic gold in the 200m at the 2004 Athens Games and won another three gold medals in the 2008 Beijing Paralympics. He then set his sights on the 2012 Olympics in London.

Questions arose as to whether his blades gave him an advantage over competitors without disabilities. Using a golf analogy, it would not seem fair for someone to hit a driver off a tee while everyone else could only use a pitching wedge. The driver is a longer club that enables golfers to hit farther than the shorter pitching wedge. Was Pistorius running on artificial drivers for legs against runners born naturally with only pitching wedges?

The answer came from the international governing body of sports for athletes with a disability—the International Paralympic Committee (IPC). "Since 2007, the IPC has used a formula to calculate the permitted length of prostheses for its athletes. For double amputees such as Pistorius…, this is based on measuring each athlete's body and arm span, and using this data to estimate their overall height if they had legs. Athletes are allowed prosthetic limbs and feet that make them up to 3.5% taller than their estimated height including the blade at the end of their prosthesis. Many able-bodied athletes are unusually long-limbed and this margin allows for natural variations in body types as well as the fact that athletes stand taller – on their toes – when they run" (Barkham, P. (2012, September 3). Oscar Pistorius row: what are the rules on blades at the Paralympics? The Guardian).

In the 2012 London Olympic Games, Pistorius finished second out of five runners and advanced to the semifinals where he finished eighth out of eight runners. These accomplishments were overshadowed when, in 2013, he alleges that he mistook his girlfriend for an intruder and shot and killed her through a locked bathroom door. Pistorius was later convicted of murder and sentenced to more than 13 years in prison. He was released from prison and put on parole in January 2024.

Defense of Direct Threat

Under the provisions of the Americans with Disabilities Act and the Rehabilitation Act, a defense against a discrimination claim can be mounted if the requested accommodation would subject the individual with a disability, or others, to what is called a Direct Threat. This is defined as a "significant risk of substantial harm to thei[r] health or safety" (29 CFR § 1630.2(r)). In instances where there is a potential risk to other participants, a waiver could be deemed unreasonable. This has led to debates over whether the inclusion of wheelchairs in certain events might present a hazard to other competitors.

Faking Disabilities

Unfortunately, there have been instances where individuals have faked learning disabilities to gain an unfair advantage. One case involved Florida State University where staff provided "improper academic assistance and arranged for fraudulent academic credit for 61 student-athletes in 10 sports" (Landman, B. (2008, Oct.14). *EX-FSU OFFICIAL: I'M NOT DISHONEST. Tampa Bay Times).* Former Florida State University Learning Specialist, Brenda Monk, told ESPN that "more than a third of the football team, and three-quarters of the basketball team, had learning disabilities. By comparison, experts estimate that 5 to 10 percent of the general adult population has a learning disability" (Farrey, T. (2009, Dec. 12). *Seminoles helped by 'learning disability' diagnosis.* ESPN). By claiming a disability, these students were provided accommodations that included "note-takers and untimed tests" dispensed by the campus disability services, and special private tutoring and readers for athletes with learning disabilities (ibid).

Another scandal occurred during the 2000 Sydney Paralympic Games when the Spanish national basketball team faked intellectual disabilities to win the gold medal. It was later revealed that out of the 12 players in the squad, only two genuinely had a disability. In response, the International Paralympic Committee suspended the intellectual disability category from the 2004 and 2008 Paralympic Games. After establishing stronger guidelines, the International Paralympic Committee voted to include athletes with intellectual impairment ahead of the London 2012 Paralympic Games and beyond (Van de Vliet, P. (2009, Dec. 15). MEMORANDUM: *Re-Inclusion of Athletes with Intellectual Impairment in Paralympic Sports*. International Paralympic Committee).

Chapter 7: Antitrust Law and Sports

When people think about antitrust law in the United States, they often think back to 19th century railroad and oil monopolies controlling their industries to eliminate free competition and consumer choice. What does this have to do with sports? Well, when it comes to consumer choice, how many options do you have for watching or playing competitive, intercollegiate basketball other than the National Collegiate Athletic Association (NCAA)? In this chapter, we will see that antitrust law is not just about oil and railroads, but about anticompetitive behavior that impacts if athletes can change teams or get paid for their name, image, and likeness.

Antitrust Law

United States antitrust laws prohibit commercial anticompetitive behavior. For example, imagine that instead of grocery stores competing over milk prices in the $3 - $6 per gallon range, they all agree to sell milk at $20 per gallon. Grocery stores may appreciate the increased profits, but this would hurt consumers who appreciate the competition that keeps prices in the $3 - $6 per gallon range. The grocery stores agreeing to the inflated price would violate antitrust law as a conspiracy in restraint of trade. It would also violate antitrust laws for the grocery stores to merge into one company to then charge $20 per gallon or for a company to become so dominant—even without merging—that it distorts the free market.

Monopolies and Monopsonies

When a single *seller* controls or dominates the supply of goods and services, the seller has formed a **monopoly.** For example, when John D. Rockefeller's Standard Oil controlled 90% of American oil refineries in the 1880s, they had a monopoly that could control prices on the sale of oil. Some have accused the National Football League (NFL) of being a monopoly because of its control over selling the broadcasts of professional American football.

When a single *buyer* controls or dominates the demand for goods and services, the buyer has formed a **monopsony**. For example, imagine that instead of grocery stores fixing consumer milk prices at $20 per gallon, they tell dairy farmers that they will only buy wholesale milk from them at a price of $1 per gallon. If there are no other buyers, then the dairy farmers have no choice but to sell their milk at $1 per gallon.

In this case, the grocery stores are using their dominance as a buyer to control prices in a way that eliminates free market competition.

In *Nat'l Collegiate Athletic Ass'n v. Alston,* the United States Supreme Court stated that "the NCAA enjoys monopsony control in the relevant market—such that it is capable of depressing wages below competitive levels for student-athletes"(*Nat'l Collegiate Athletic Ass'n v. Alston*, 594 U.S. 69, 86 (2021)).

What is a Trust?

In antitrust law, the term "trust" refers to a combination or consolidation of companies that operate together as a single entity. The new entity could allow the participating companies to pool resources, share profits, fix prices, and otherwise coordinate their activities for their own benefit. These actions could create anti-competitive, monopoly power for the trust.

What is a Cartel?

When reading antitrust case law, you may encounter the term "cartel." A cartel is an association of manufacturers or suppliers that restricts competition and sets prices. An example of a cartel that often makes headlines are the drug cartels that control the supply and prices of illegal drugs. Another example of a cartel is the Organization of the Petroleum Exporting Countries (OPEC). OPEC is a group of 13 of the world's major oil-exporting nations that agree to artificially raise or support oil prices at certain levels by limiting how much oil each country will produce. When these agreements drive oil prices especially high, some U.S. consumers complain that OPEC's actions are or should be illegal. Indeed, in the U.S., these agreements would violate antitrust laws. But the U.S.—even though it is currently the world's number one oil producer—is not a member of OPEC.

The Sherman Antitrust Act

The Sherman Antitrust Act of 1890 was enacted to address the anticompetitive practices of trusts and cartels. It provides the following:

Section 1. Every contract, combination in the form of trust or otherwise, or conspiracy, in restraint of trade or commerce among the several States, or with foreign nations, is hereby declared to be illegal.

Section 2. Every person who shall monopolize, or attempt to monopolize, or combine or conspire with any other person or persons, to monopolize any part of the trade or commerce among the several States, or with foreign nations, shall be deemed guilty of a misdemeanor...."

Enforcement of the Sherman Act falls under the jurisdiction of the U.S. Department of Justice. Individuals can be fined up to $1 million and sentenced to up to 10 years in federal prison for each offense. Corporations can be fined up to $100 million for each offense. The Act also allows for **treble damages**. Treble damages mean "triple" damages. This means that individuals and companies harmed by anticompetitive conduct can seek an award of triple their financial damages. Plaintiffs can also receive an injunction to stop the conduct and recover the costs of the action (including attorney fees) against a party that violates federal antitrust laws.

Per Se and Rule of Reason Analysis

Violations of the Sherman Act are evaluated using either the *per se* rule or a rule of reasons analysis. ***Per se*** violations are considered illegal as a matter of law. These violations include 1) price fixing, 2) bid rigging, and 3) horizontal customer and territorial allocations.

Price fixing is an agreement between competitors to set prices for their products or services at a certain level. This collusion eliminates price competition and harms consumers by keeping prices artificially high. **Bid rigging** occurs when, instead of genuinely competing, competitors conspire to manipulate the bidding process for contracts. This can occur when companies agree to artificially inflate their bids to allow a winner and then rotate which company would win subsequent contracts. For example, imagine that a commercial project should cost $100 million in a competitive bidding process, and there are five companies available to compete on the project. The five companies then decide that four of them will bid over $200 million for the project and leave the fifth company to bid $150 million for the project. This inflates the price by $50 million for their friendly competitor. As you can imagine, they might then agree to rotate who will win subsequent bids. **Horizontal restraints** refer to agreements between competitors operating at the same level of the supply chain. Examples include **market allocation,** where competitors divide markets geographically or by customer type to avoid competing directly, **group boycotts** where competitors jointly refuse to deal with a particular supplier or customer, and **output restrictions**, where competitors agree to limit production to maintain higher prices. These are all considered *per se* violations of antitrust law.

In contrast to the *per se* rule, the **rule of reason** "generally requires a court to 'conduct a fact-specific assessment of market power and market structure' to assess a…restraint's 'actual effect on competition" (*NCAA v. Alston* (2021) quoting *Ohio v. Am. Express Co.,* 585 U.S. 529 (2018)). This may require expert testimony providing evidence that identifies actual anticompetitive effects. Before making it to the U.S. Supreme Court, a district court applied the rule of reason in *NCAA v. Alston* and determined that the "NCAA enjoys 'near complete dominance of, and exercise[s] monopsony power in, the relevant market"—which is defined as the market for "athletic services in men's and women's Division 1 basketball and FBS football…" (*NCAA v. Alston*).

In the cases, you may also see references to a "quick look analysis." The quick look analysis provides a middle ground between the *per se* rule and the full rule of reason analysis. The quick look analysis has fallen out of favor for being unworkable and leading to inconsistent outcomes.

The Clayton Antitrust Act

The Clayton Antitrust Act of 1914 strengthened antitrust laws against anticompetitive practices that were not specifically identified in the Sherman Act. These practices include mergers and acquisitions, interlocking directors, price discrimination, exclusionary practices, and private lawsuits. For example, whereas the Sherman Act outlawed monopolies, the Clayton Antitrust Act went beyond this to prohibit **mergers and acquisitions** that could "lessen competition or tend to create a monopoly" (Section 7). The Clayton Antitrust Act also prevents **interlocking directors** to prevent one individual from serving on the board of directors of two or more competing corporations at the same time (Section 8). The Clayton Antitrust Act also prohibits the anticompetitive practice of **price discrimination** where a seller charges different prices to competing buyers for identical goods or services (Section 2) and the **exclusionary practices** of offering to sell or lease a product only on the condition that the customer will not purchase or lease from a competitor (Section 3). The Clayton Antitrust Act also gives individuals the right to seek compensation through

private lawsuits against violators of the Act (Section 4). This last point is a big deal. Without allowing private lawsuits, plaintiffs would have to depend on the government to file the lawsuit much like private citizens rely on law enforcement to enforce laws against murder or speeding.

The Reserve Clause

The Reserve Clause in baseball was a contractual term that bound players to a single team for their entire career. Even after the contract expired, players remained tied to their teams. Teams could trade, sell, or release players without consulting the players. This limited players' ability to choose where they would work or explore their value in a free market. This was challenged in the 1922 case of *Federal Baseball Club of Baltimore, Inc. v. National League of Prof'l Baseball Clubs*.

Federal Baseball Club of Baltimore, Inc. v. National League of Prof'l Baseball Clubs (1922)

In *Federal Baseball Club of Baltimore, Inc. v. National League of Prof'l Baseball Clubs* (259 U.S. 200 (1922)), a new baseball league called the Federal League sued the team owners of the American and National Leagues. The Federal League claimed that the teams were using the Reserve Clause to buy players and secure their talent forever, thereby monopolizing the business of professional baseball in violation of the Sherman Act. The Supreme Court heard the case and ruled that antitrust laws do not apply to professional baseball because baseball was a form of entertainment—not a business—and therefore did not affect interstate commerce even though players traveled across state lines and were paid. This case provided baseball—and only baseball—with a general exemption from antitrust laws that lasted over a century.

In 2021, the United States Supreme Court recalled the history of this unique precedent and suggested that it may be on shaky ground.

In the words of the court:

> "...this Court once dallied with something that looks a bit like an antitrust exemption for professional baseball. In Federal Baseball Club of Baltimore, Inc. v. National League of Professional Baseball Clubs, 259 U. S. 200 (1922), the Court reasoned that "exhibitions" of "base ball" did not implicate the Sherman Act because they did not involve interstate trade or commerce—even though teams regularly crossed state lines (as they do today) to

make money and enhance their commercial success. Id., at 208–209. But this Court has refused to extend Federal Baseball's reasoning to other sports leagues—and has even acknowledged criticisms of the decision as "'unrealistic'" and "'inconsistent'" and "aberration[al]."

Toolson v. New York Yankees, Inc. (1953)

George Earl Toolson was a pitcher for the New York Yankees farm system. In 1949 he was assigned to the New York Yankee's AAA affiliate, the Newark Bears. Before the 1950 season, the Bears dissolved, and Toolson was assigned to the Yankees' Class-A team, the Binghamton Triplets. Toolson refused to report and instead filed a lawsuit alleging the Reserve Clause violated antitrust law.

In a one paragraph decision, the Supreme Court recalls the precedent in the Federal Baseball Club of Baltimore decision that held that baseball is "not subject to existing antitrust legislation" (Toolson v. New York Yankees, Inc., 346 U.S. 356 (1953)). The court goes on to suggest that if baseball should be subject to antitrust laws, then it would be the job of the legislature to clarify this. Such legislation would not arrive until 45 years later in the Curt Flood Act of 1998.

Radovich v. National Football League (1957)

In *Radovich v. National Football League*, the U.S. Supreme Court made it clear that the 1922 Federal Baseball Club of Baltimore decision only protected baseball from antitrust litigation.

In the words of the court:

[William] Radovich began his professional football career in 1938 when he signed with the Detroit Lions, a National League Club. After four seasons of play he entered the Navy, returning to the Lions for the 1945 season. In 1946 he asked for a transfer to a National League club in Los Angeles because of the illness of his father. The Lions refused the transfer and Radovich broke his player contract by signing with and playing the 1946 and 1947 seasons for the Los Angeles Dons, a member of the All-America Conference. In 1948 the San Francisco Clippers, a member of the Pacific Coast League which was affiliated with but not a competitor of the National League, offered to employ Radovich as a player-coach. However, the National League advised that Radovich was blacklisted and any affiliated club signing him would suffer severe penalties. The Clippers then refused to sign him in any position.

This black-listing effectively prevented his employment in organized professional football in the United States (*Radovich v. Nat'l Football League*, 352 U.S. 445, 448 (1957)).

This sounds like anticompetitive behavior that would violate the Sherman or Clayton Acts, but the NFL argued that if baseball is exempt from antitrust law as held in the cases of *Federal Baseball Club of Baltimore* and *Toolson*, then the NFL should also be exempt. In response, the court noted that the *Toolson* case was "not authority for exempting other businesses" and that the Federal Baseball Club of Baltimore decision "could not be relied upon as a basis of exemption for other segments of the entertainment business, athletic or otherwise" (*Radovich v. Nat'l Football League*, 352 U.S. 445) (1957)). These cases provided a unique antitrust exemption for baseball and baseball only.

Curt Flood

Curtis Charles Flood Sr. (January 18, 1938 – January 20, 1997) was a centerfielder for the St. Louis Cardinals where he was a three-time All-Star, a seven-time Gold Glove winner, and batted over .300 in six seasons. By 1969, he had helped lead the St. Louis Cardinals to three World Series in the previous six years. Then, in 1969, Flood received a phone call informing him that he had been traded from St. Louis to the Philadelphia Phillies. Flood refused to go. Instead, he wrote a letter to Commissioner of Baseball, Bowie Kuhn, asking if any other Major League teams would be interested.

December 24, 1969

Mr. Bowie K. Kuhn
Commissioner of Baseball
680 Fifth Avenue
New York, New York 10019

Dear Mr. Kuhn:

After twelve years in the Major Leagues, I do not feel that I am a piece of property to be bought and sold irrespective of my wishes. I believe that any system which produces that result violates my basic rights as a citizen and is inconsistent with the laws of the United States and of the several States.

It is my desire to play baseball in 1970, and I am capable of playing. I have received a contract offer from the Philadelphia Club, but I believe I have the right to consider offers from other clubs before making any decisions. I, therefore, request that you make known to all the Major League Clubs my feelings in this matter, and advise them of my availability for the 1970 season.

Sincerely yours,

Curt Flood

Team owners were not interested. Flood sat out the 1970 season and sued baseball in a lawsuit that would make its way to the U.S. Supreme Court in *Flood v. Kuhn*, 407 U.S. 258 (1972). Once again, the court concluded that there is a "longstanding exemption of professional baseball's reserve system from federal antitrust laws." It called it "an established aberration, in light of the Court's holding that other interstate professional sports are not similarly exempt," but insisted that it was a "matter for legislative, not judicial, resolution."

After sitting out the 1970 season, Flood joined the Washington Senators in 1971. He played 13 games before sending the team owner a telegram announcing that he was quitting baseball.

Seitz Decision

In 1975, baseball's Reserve Clause was attacked again, this time in arbitration. In arbitration, disputes are resolved by a neutral third-party instead of having the dispute resolved in court. The arbitrator's decision is called an award. In **binding arbitration,** the award is generally final and cannot be appealed to a court absent a showing of fraud or undue influence on behalf of the arbitrator.

This arbitration involved pitchers Andy Messersmith, of the Los Angeles Dodgers, and Dave McNally, of the Montreal Expos. Both played their 1975 seasons without signing their contracts. At the end of the season, they argued that because they were playing without a signed contract, they should be free to sign with other teams for the 1976 season. Team owners disagreed, arguing that the Reserve Clause automatically renewed contracts and bound players to their teams forever.

The parties selected Peter Seitz to be their arbitrator. Seitz was an attorney who had served as an arbitrator in the past for both the owners and the players. Seitz ruled that the Reserve Clause "applied for one year only." Therefore, "Messersmith and McNally were free agents because they had served one year under [the] owner-renewed contracts" (Stetson, D. (1983, October 19). Peter Seitz, 78, *The Arbitrator in Baseball Free-Agent Case*. The New York Times). The owners appealed the decision to the United States District Court for Western Missouri…and fired Seitz. The district court upheld the Seitz decision. The owners then appealed their decision to the Eighth Circuit Court of Appeals.

The Eighth Circuit appeared more sympathetic to the owners, but the court's role was not to apply Supreme Court precedent on how to review the Reserve Clause, but the precedent on how to review arbitration agreements. It ultimately decided to uphold the lower court's ruling because of "the deferential standard it was compelled to follow in reviewing arbitration decisions" (Christopher W. Schmidt, Explaining the Baseball Revolution, 45 Ariz. St. L.J. 1471, 1528 (2013)).

The Curt Flood Act of 1998

It was not until 1998 that Congress passed a law to address the 1922 antitrust ruling in *Federal Baseball Club of Baltimore*. They named it the Curt Flood Act in honor of Curt Flood. The Act amended the Clayton Act to ensure that antitrust laws applied to major league baseball. This provided major league baseball players the same antitrust protections as other professional athletes. However, the Act explicitly did not apply to minor league baseball players. As a result, minor league baseball players lacked union representation and were significantly underpaid when compared to players in the major league. Developments in the 2020s sought to address this. For example, in July 2022, "Major League Baseball agreed to pay $185 million to current and former minor league baseball players to settle a federal class action lawsuit alleging violations of minimum wage laws" (Acevedo, N., & Brogle, C. (2022, July 16). MLB settles minor league players' wage-and-hour class action suit for $185 million. *NBC News*). In August 2022, the Major League Baseball Players Association (MLBPA) announced that "Minor Leaguers have been sent a card to vote on designating the MLBPA as their collective bargaining representative." This resulted in MLB recognizing the minor league union less than three weeks later.

Union representation for minor league players has led to significant salary gains, but some argue they may not be enough. For example, in 2024, MLB sought to exempt minor league players from Arizona's minimum wage law. In 2023, Brad Case, a 27-year-old pitcher in the Pirates' system, recalled, "I mean, $30,000 isn't crazy money, but for us going from $6000 a couple of years ago to $30,000—that change alone is impactful. It's going to make a lot of baseball players' lives better" (Lucas W. Loafman & John T. Holden, <u>Stepping Up to the Plate: Minor Leaguers Attempt to Remedy Their Unconscionable Plight</u>, 60 Am. Bus. L.J. 289, 342 (2023)). For context, the minimum salary for players in baseball's minor league Triple-A system was $35,800 in 2024. Low A had a minimum salary of $26,200. The average salary in Major League Baseball that year was over $4.6 million.

Mackey v. National Football League and the Rozelle Rule

In 1963, National Football League (NFL) commissioner Pete Rozelle instituted what became known as the **Rozelle Rule**. This rule required any team that signed a player who previously belonged to another team to compensate the player's former club with other players and/or draft selections. In response, thirty-six players initiated an antitrust lawsuit against the NFL. The lead plaintiff was Pro Football Hall of Fame tight-end, and the future first president of the National Football League Players Association (NFLPA), John Mackey. Applying the Rule of Reason analysis, the court found "substantial evidence…to support…that there would be increased player movement" and "substantial increase in player salaries" absent the Rozelle Rule (*Mackey v. Nat'l Football League*, 543 F.2d 606, 620 (8th Cir. 1976)).

It concluded, "In sum, we hold that the Rozelle Rule, as enforced, unreasonably restrains trade in violation of Section 1 of the Sherman Act."

For football fans, I will also share that John Mackey was involved in a famous game-changing catch in Super Bowl V where, on January 17, 1971, he caught a record-setting 75-yard touchdown pass from quarterback Johnny Unitas after the ball was deflected twice, once by fellow Baltimore Colts player Eddie Hinton and once by opposing Dallas Cowboys defenseman Mel Renfro. Baltimore won the game 16–13, following a 32-yard field goal with five seconds left.

But Mackey's legacy is in more than his touchdowns and antitrust fights. He was one of the earliest and most visible examples of early dementia linked to head trauma and chronic traumatic encephalopathy, or CTE. At age 60, John's wife Sylvia became a United Airlines flight attendant to pay mounting medical bills. She wrote to then N.F.L. commissioner Paul Tagliabue to describe the "slow, deteriorating, ugly, caregiver-killing, degenerative, brain-destroying tragic horror." In response, Tagliabue and the players union created the 88 Plan which pays up to $88,000 in medical expenses to the families of retired players with dementia. Why $88,000? John Mackey's jersey number was 88. In 2007, Mackey's alma mater, Syracuse University, retired the number 88 in his honor. John Mackey died in 2011 shortly before his 70th birthday.

LA Mem'l Coliseum Comm'n v. NFL

In 1978, Carroll Rosenbloom, then owner of the Los Angeles Rams football team, decided to move the Rams from the Los Angeles Coliseum to the newer "Big A" stadium in Anaheim, California. The "Big A" is where the California Angels baseball team played. The desire to move was partly due to an NFL television blackout policy that existed from 1973 through 2014 that stated that home games would not be televised on local television unless 85 percent of the tickets were sold 72 hours before the start of the game. Whereas the Coliseum had a capacity of nearly 100,000, the "Big A" stadium had a capacity of about 23,000. This made it easier to sell 85 percent of the tickets and be televised in their local market. The Rams' move to Anaheim left the Los Angeles Coliseum empty and looking for a new team.

Conveniently, the lease for the home of the Oakland Raiders—the Oakland Coliseum—was set to expire that same year (1978). Al Davis, then managing general partner of the Oakland Raiders franchise, was unable to persuade Oakland to make substantial improvements to the stadium, and so he looked to the Coliseum in Los Angeles. The parties began negotiating in 1979 and "on March 1, 1980, Al Davis and the Los Angeles Coliseum signed a 'memorandum of agreement' outlining the terms of the Raiders' relocation [to] Los Angeles" (*Los Angeles Mem'l Coliseum Comm'n v. Nat'l Football League*, 726 F.2d 1381, 1385 (9th Cir. 1984)).

But there was a problem with the Raiders moving from Oakland to Los Angeles. It was NFL Rule 4.3. It stated:

> No member club shall have the right to transfer its franchise or playing site to a different city, either within or outside its home territory, without prior approval by the affirmative vote of three-fourths of the existing member clubs of the League.

On March 10, 1980, the NFL teams voted 22-0 against the move. Five teams abstained. The three-quarters approval to move in Rule 4.3 required 21 affirmative votes. Davis got zero. In response, the Los Angeles Memorial Coliseum Commission sued the National Football League, arguing that Rule 4.3 violated federal antitrust law. At trial, a federal district court applied the Rule of Reason analysis to the facts of the case and determined that Rule 4.3 violated Section 1 of the Sherman Act.

The NFL appealed to the Ninth Circuit Court of Appeals, arguing that the NFL was a "single entity" incapable of violating Section 1 of the Sherman Act because Section 1 prevents "contracts, combinations, or conspiracies in restraint on trade," and a single entity would be incapable of contracting, combining, or conspiring with itself. The appeals court rejected the NFL's "single entity" argument. The NFL was 28 separate member clubs that had entered into an agreement in the form of the NFL Constitution and Bylaws. The jury's verdict was affirmed. Rule 4.3 violated antitrust laws and teams were free to move. In response, the Raiders moved from Oakland to Los Angeles in 1982. They then moved back to Oakland in 1995 before moving to Las Vegas, Nevada in 2020. Meanwhile, the Rams moved from Los Angeles to St. Louis, Missouri in 1995 and then back to Los Angeles in 2016 where they now share a stadium with the Los Angeles Chargers who moved to Los Angeles in 2017 after 56 years in San Diego. Teams are clearly now free to move.

So far in the chapter, it may appear that antitrust law is only an issue for professional—not collegiate—sports. That is about to change.

NCAA v. Bd. of Regents of University of Oklahoma

In *NCAA v. Board of Regents of University of Oklahoma,* the United States Supreme Court determined that the National Collegiate Athletic Association's (NCAA) plan to control television contracts violated the Sherman and Clayton Antitrust Acts. The dispute centered around college football broadcasting rights.

In 1977, a group of 63 American colleges with top-level football programs formed the College Football Association (CFA) to counter the NCAA's control of the television market. In 1981, the CFA signed a television broadcasting contract with the National Broadcasting Co. (NBC). Meanwhile, the NCAA already had a 4-year contract with "the American Broadcasting Co. (ABC), Columbia Broadcasting System (CBS), and Turner Broadcasting System (Turner)" (*Nat'l Collegiate Athletic Ass'n v. Bd. of Regents of Univ. of Oklahoma,* 468 U.S. 85)(1984)). The NCAA was not going to let the broadcasting rights to 63 of the best college football programs in the country move without them to NBC without a fight. After the CFA announced its contract with NBC, "the NCAA publicly announced that it would take disciplinary action against any CFA member that complied with the CFA–NBC contract. [Further,] the NCAA made it clear that sanctions would not be limited to the football programs of CFA members, but would apply to other sports as well" (*Nat'l Collegiate Athletic Ass'n v. Bd. of Regents of Univ. of Oklahoma,* 468 U.S. 85 (1984)).

In response, CFA members the University of Oklahoma and the University of Georgia sued the NCAA, alleging the NCAA had "unreasonably restrained trade in the televising of college football games." Let me pause for a second to point out that the CFA's contract with NBC was signed in 1981, and the University of Georgia won the national championship in 1980, and the University of Oklahoma won the championship in 1974, 1975, and 1985. Their television broadcasting contract mattered. The District Court and Court of Appeals agreed with the universities that the NCAA had violated Section 1 of the Sherman Act. The Supreme Court affirmed the decision, noting that the NCAA's output restrictions "blunt[ed] the ability of member institutions to respond to consumer preference…[and] has restricted rather than enhanced the place of intercollegiate athletics in the Nation's life." This decision removed the NCAA's absolute control over college football broadcasting and allowed for the unlimited access to televised games that we see today.

In 2023, one of the lawyers representing Oklahoma in *NCAA v. Oklahoma* admitted that he now regrets the outcome of the *case.* "You feel bad how far it's gone," said the then 88-year-old Andrew Coats, who still taught law at his alma mater, the University of Oklahoma, and who served as the mayor of Oklahoma City from 1983 to 1987. He continued, "But I don't think anyone could have predicted what would happen.... We tried at every stage to negotiate an agreement of some kind, to limit what would happen. But we learned the 'NCAA' stood for 'Never Compromise Anything at Anytime,' and they wouldn't even talk to us" (Bucholtz, Andrew. (2023, August 27). *NCAA v. Oklahoma lawyer: 'I think I screwed up college football.'* Awful Announcing).

Law v. NCAA

In 1991, the NCAA adopted Bylaw 11.02.3, commonly known as the "REC Rule" referring to Restricted-Earnings Coaches. These coaches included part-time assistant, graduate assistant, and volunteer coaches. The REC Rule limited the compensation for these coaches in all Division I sports except football, to a total of $12,000 for the academic year and $4,000 for the summer months. In response, a group of restricted-earnings men's basketball coaches at NCAA Division I institutions sued the NCAA, alleging the REC Rule violated Section 1 of the Sherman Act as an unlawful "contract, combination...or conspiracy, in restraint of trade." The first named plaintiff was a man named Norman Law and that is why the case is referred to as *Law v. NCAA.*

The NCAA argued that the rule was necessary to limit costs. The court found that this was an unconvincing rebuttal to charges of anticompetitive behavior. Instead, they held that the REC Rule's compensation limit was indeed an unlawful restraint of trade.

In the words of the court:

> The NCAA's cost containment justification is illegitimate because the NCAA [i]mproperly assumes that antitrust law should not apply to condemn the creation of market power in an input market. The exercise of market power by a group of buyers virtually always results in lower costs to the buyers—a consequence which arguably is beneficial to the members of the industry and ultimately their consumers. If holding down costs by the exercise of market power over suppliers, rather than just by increased efficiency, is a procompetitive effect justifying joint

conduct, then Section 1 can never apply to input markets or buyer cartels. That is not and cannot be the law.

.....

Cost-cutting by itself is not a valid procompetitive justification. If it were, any group of competing buyers could agree on maximum prices. Lower prices cannot justify a cartel's control of prices charged by suppliers, because the cartel ultimately robs the suppliers of the normal fruits of their enterprises. (*Law v. Nat'l Collegiate Athletic Ass'n*, 134 F.3d 1010, 1023 (10th Cir. 1998)

Using the Rule of Reason analysis, the court determined that the REC Rule's compensation limit was an unlawful restraint of trade. A federal jury awarded plaintiffs $22 million in damages, an amount that was automatically tripled under the Sherman Act to a $67 million judgment. To avoid further litigation, the parties settled for $54.5 million in 2000.

Colon v. NCAA and *Smart v. NCAA*

In 2023, another group of coaches filed a lawsuit against the NCAA alleging antitrust violations. This time, it was volunteer coaches. NCAA bylaws limited the number of paid coaches in each sport, but allowed member schools to hire additional coaches…and pay them nothing. They referred to these coaches as "Volunteer Coaches." The rule was abandoned effective July 1, 2023, but a class of affected "Volunteer Coaches" led by Fresno State wrestling volunteer coach Joseph Colon sued seeking backpay.

In the words of the complaint:

3. The NCAA bylaws, which have been recognized as constituting a binding agreement among all the member schools, refer to these coaches as "Volunteer Coaches." In reality, that means that skilled coaches who are desired by NCAA schools, but not employed as regular (paid) coaches, must provide very valuable services to the schools for free, or not be employed in their profession of choice. Even if one were the most desirable of such coaches, no member school could offer him or her any salary in order to compete for their services. These volunteer coaches frequently work full-time, weekends, early mornings, and late nights and perform many, if not all, of the same job duties as the paid coaches working out of the same set of Athletic Department offices. Yet the volunteer coaches cannot even receive health insurance, housing, or other benefits, much less an actual salary in exchange for work performed.

Advantaging themselves of the career aspirations and love of sport which these coaches bring to their institutions and the student athletes they coach, the NCAA and its member schools abuse their monopsony power by agreeing all will accept the benefits these coaches bring to their respective institutions and student athletes but to pay the coaches nothing for it. The so-called volunteer coach may, indeed, be the only uncompensated employee at the institutions where they work.

4. These agreements among Defendant and its member schools, in antitrust terms, make the member schools a buyer-side cartel: a group of competitors agreeing to abide by naked horizontal pricing restraints to purposefully restrict competition in the labor market for valuable college coaching services so they can collectively reduce their costs. The very purpose and actual effect of this horizontal agreement was to fix and suppress salaries so as to make them unresponsive to a competitive marketplace or even one in which basic wage and hour laws are respected. This amounts to an unlawful restraint under Section 1 of the Sherman Act, 15 U.S.C. § 1.

5. A similar but less draconian NCAA rule regarding a category of so-called "restricted-earnings" coaches was invalidated over 20 years ago in *Law v. N.C.A.A.*, 134 F.3d 1010 (10th Cir. 1998), and was found so plainly unreasonable that it could be condemned as illegal under the Section I Sherman Act "quick look" rule of reason test. The only difference between *Law* and the present action is that restricted-earnings coaches could be paid up to $12,000 per year [and current "volunteer"] coaches may not be paid anything (*Colon et al. v. National Collegiate Athletic Association* - 1:23-cv-00425.

For further reading, you may want to look at *Smart v. Nat'l Collegiate Athletic Ass'n*, No. 1:23-CV-00425 WBS KJN, 2023 WL 4827366 (E.D. Cal. July 27, 2023). This is a similar, but separate class action lawsuit specifically for volunteer baseball coaches.

Tanaka v. University of Southern California

In *Tanaka v. Univ. of S. California*, 252 F.3d 1059, 1061–62 (9th Cir. 2001), soccer player Rhiannon Tanaka alleged that the transfer rules requiring her to sit out a year before playing with a different university violated antitrust laws.

In the words of the court:

A star high school soccer player, Rhiannon Tanaka ("Tanaka") was heavily recruited by the athletic programs of a number of universities, including the University of Southern California ("USC"), which belongs to the Pacific–10 Conference ("Pac–10").... During her senior year of high school, Tanaka met with USC athletic officials, including Michael Garrett and Daryl Gross, who allegedly made certain representations to her regarding the USC women's soccer program. She also inquired about transfer restrictions, and was allegedly told that she would be free to transfer without penalty provided she remained at USC for one year and met minimum academic requirements. Tanaka thereupon signed a letter of intent to enroll at USC and attended USC for the 1994–95 academic year.

Tanaka quickly became dissatisfied with the state of USC's women's soccer program and the quality of her USC education. In particular, she claims that USC was arranging for athletes to receive fraudulent academic credit through sham classes. In the spring of 1995, she received permission from USC to communicate with other schools about transferring to their programs. Because she wished to remain in Los Angeles, and because its women's soccer program was nationally ranked, she decided to transfer to the University of California, Los Angeles ("UCLA"), another Pac–10 member institution.

USC opposed Tanaka's transfer to UCLA...[and] insisted that Tanaka sit out her first year at UCLA and lose one year of athletic eligibility. Tanaka unsuccessfully appealed her sanction.

Tanaka alleges that USC invoked the transfer rule sanctions against her in retaliation for her participation in an investigation into possible academic fraud involving student-athletes at the school. In fact, her complaint expressly alleges that she "is the *only* transferring athlete who had the sanctions imposed on her" (emphasis in original), and further that "[i]n all other instances where student-athletes transferred from USC, Pacific–10 penalties had not been used" (*Tanaka v. Univ. of S. California*, 252 F.3d 1059, 1061–62 (9th Cir. 2001)).

Unfortunately for Tanaka, the fact that she was the only player who faced sanctions hurt her antitrust case.

Again, **in the words of the court:**

> Tanaka depicts USC's invocation of transfer rule sanctions against her as an isolated act of retaliation. While "hundreds of student-athletes transfer each year" without sanction, Tanaka alleges that she was "singled out" in an attempt by USC to "keep her at the school to 'oversee' any testimony that she might give" concerning the alleged incident of academic fraud. In short, Tanaka alleges nothing more than a personal injury to herself, not an injury to a definable market. But the antitrust laws "were enacted for 'the protection of competition, not competitors.'"
>
> .....
>
> By attempting to restrict the relevant market to a single athletic program in Los Angeles based solely on her own preferences, Tanaka has failed to identify a relevant market for antitrust purposes. If the relevant market is national in scope, the Pac–10 transfer rule *could not* have a significant anticompetitive effect, because by its own terms the rule does not apply to interconference transfers. Moreover, even if the relevant market is limited to the Pac–10 itself, Tanaka characterizes the Pac–10's imposition of sanctions against her for her intraconference transfer as an isolated act of retaliation. Tanaka simply has no antitrust cause of action; thus, it is "clear that [her] complaint cannot be saved by further amendment."

Tanaka eventually transferred to UCLA and earned All-American honors at both USC and UCLA. She later played professionally for the San Diego Spirit.

O'Bannon v. NCAA

Imagine that you work at a Las Vegas auto dealership, go to a friend's house, and see a character that looks just like you in a video game your friend's son is playing. The game is EA Sports NCAA Basketball09. In the game, players can select various characters with different heights and skills to play on their team. Your friend's son picked a character that looks just like you. This may seem like a funny coincidence until you realize…the character really is you.

This is what happened to Ed O'Bannon. Unlike most auto dealership employees, O'Bannon is 6 feet 8 inches tall, and he was a member of the 1995 UCLA NCAA Division I championship team where he was named the NCAA Final Four Most Outstanding Player. That year he also won the USBWA College Player of the Year, the PAC-10 co-Player of the Year, and received the John R. Wooden Award which is given annually to "the most outstanding men's and women's college basketball player." In 1995, O'Bannon was selected ninth in the NBA draft. In 1996, UCLA retired his jersey, number 31. This means that no one else will ever play basketball again wearing UCLA's blue and gold jersey number 31. That is, of course, unless they're playing EA Sports NCAA Basketball09, where they can play as a dominant 6'8" forward wearing UCLA's iconic blue and gold jersey number 31.

O'Bannon recalled, "I was at a friend's house and saw my likeness on a video game that his kid was playing. I initially thought it was pretty cool, and was flattered. But then it was brought to my attention that they had paid for that video game, and I didn't get any type of compensation or even, permission to use my likeness on that video game" (The Federalist Society. (2019, January 31). O'Bannon v. NCAA: Intellectual Property, Antitrust, & College Sports. Youtube. https://www.youtube.com/watch?v=iKrlpi9pqBk).

As Michael A. McCann, Professor and Associate Dean for Academic Affairs, Sports and Entertainment Law Institute at the University of New Hampshire School of Law, noted, "It was [O'Bannon's] height, his race, his skillset, his jersey number...everything but his name" (ibid).

How could the NCAA continue to earn revenue off O'Bannon's name, image and likeness without compensating him? It turns out that when he became an NCAA athlete, he signed away his rights to the NCAA. Upon discovering this, O'Bannon sued the NCAA arguing that the NCAA's rules prohibiting student-athletes from receiving compensation for their name, image, and likeness violated Section 1 of the Sherman Act.

The District Court agreed with O'Bannon noting that "The rules prohibiting compensation for the use of student-athletes' NILs are...a price-fixing agreement: recruits pay for the bundles of services provided by colleges with their labor and their NILs, but the 'sellers' of these bundles—the colleges—collectively 'agree to value [NILs] at zero.' Under this theory, colleges and universities behave as a cartel—a group of sellers who have colluded to fix the price of their product" (*O'Bannon v. Nat'l Collegiate Athletic Ass'n*, 802 F.3d 1049, 1057–58 (9th Cir. 2015)).

The NCAA appealed to the Ninth Circuit Court of Appeals arguing, in part, that "preserving 'amateurism" in college sports" served a procompetitive purpose. The court noted that although promoting amateurism could help preserve consumer demand for college sports, the NCAA is not exempt from antitrust laws.

In the words of the court:

> Today, we reaffirm that NCAA regulations are subject to antitrust scrutiny and must be tested in the crucible of the Rule of Reason. When those regulations truly serve procompetitive purposes, courts should not hesitate to uphold them. But the NCAA is not above the antitrust laws, and courts cannot and must not shy away from requiring the NCAA to play by the Sherman Act's rules. In this case, the NCAA's rules have been more restrictive than necessary to maintain its tradition of amateurism in support of the college sports market (*O'Bannon v. Nat'l Collegiate Athletic Ass'n*, 802 F.3d 1049, 1079 (9th Cir. 2015)).

In 2016, EA Sports settled the lawsuit by paying a total of $60 million to 24,819 student-athletes who appeared in EA Sports video games between 2003 and 2014. This amounted to under $1,700 per plaintiff, but it marked the beginning of a significant shift in NCAA student-athlete NIL compensation.

Amateurism

> **NCAA Bylaw 2.9 The Principle of Amateurism.** Student-athletes shall be amateurs in an intercollegiate sport, and their participation should be motivated primarily by education and by the physical, mental, and social benefits to be derived. Student participation in intercollegiate athletics is an avocation, and student-athletes should be protected from exploitation by professional and commercial enterprises (NCAA 2021-22, Division I Manual).

It may help to recall the college athletic landscape as it existed before 2019. At the time, the NCAA still insisted that its athletes be amateurs. This meant that they could not be paid to play their sport. If they did get paid to play, they were ineligible to play in the NCAA. For example, in 2010 the NCAA suspended five Ohio State University football players after the players traded some awards and jerseys for free tattoos because this was viewed as them getting paid in connection with their sport. The University of Colorado had a football player named Jeremy Bloom who was also an Olympic skier. When Bloom received a financial endorsement for a promotion as a skier for the Olympics, the NCAA determined that he was no longer an amateur and was declared permanently ineligible to play NCAA sports. Bloom went on to be a world champion skier, two-time Olympian, and 10-time World Cup gold medalist. He was also drafted by the Philadelphia Eagles football team in 2006.

In 2019, I accepted my dream job of being a College Professor of Business Law at New Mexico State University and started teaching Sports Law. At the time, I wanted to write an article about the one person on the football field who could get compensated for his or her name, image, and likeness—the clarinet player in the marching band. That is right. Band members were paid, and they were paid different amounts at different schools. They could also get paid to play gigs at local restaurants or bars. They could even appear in commercials or on billboards advertising local businesses. Ok, I've never seen a clarinet player on a billboard, but they wouldn't lose their eligibility to play in the band on the football field at halftime if they did.

Student-athletes couldn't believe this because these same activities would get student-athletes kicked off their team as violations of the NCAA's amateurism rules. I thought it would be a fun business marketing exercise for us to pick a band member—like the clarinet player—and see what kind of endorsements and opportunities we could find, all while knowing that everything we were doing would make the collegiate instrumentalist ineligible to be "on the team" if we applied this to sports. The relevance of this clarinet article and exercise ended in 2019 when California passed its Fair Pay to Play Act.

California's Fair Pay to Play Act (2019)

As I keep referencing court decisions about sports law, I realize that I need to address my own bias as an attorney. Attorneys look to court decisions because they interpret the laws. But the courts don't write the laws. Legislators write the laws. The courts only get involved to help answer questions about the laws. For example, "Is the NCAA subject to antitrust law?" is a question for a court to answer. But the courts did not write the Sherman Act. The legislature did.

This same separation of powers is true at the state level and, in October 2019, the California legislature passed the Fair Pay to Play Act. This allowed collegiate athletes to receive compensation for the use of their name, image, or likeness while still maintaining their athletic eligibility.

The California Fair Pay to Play Act states:

(1) A postsecondary educational institution shall not uphold any rule, requirement, standard, or other limitation that prevents a

student of that institution participating in intercollegiate athletics from earning compensation as a result of the use of the student's name, image, or likeness. Earning compensation from the use of a student's name, image, or likeness shall not affect the student's scholarship eligibility.

(2) An athletic association, conference, or other group or organization with authority over intercollegiate athletics, including, but not limited to, the National Collegiate Athletic Association, shall not prevent a student of a postsecondary educational institution participating in intercollegiate athletics from earning compensation as a result of the use of the student's name, image, or likeness.

(3) An athletic association, conference, or other group or organization with authority over intercollegiate athletics, including, but not limited to, the National Collegiate Athletic Association, shall not prevent a postsecondary educational institution from participating in intercollegiate athletics as a result of the compensation of a student athlete for the use of the student's name, image, or likeness.

The Act goes on to clarify that "A postsecondary educational institution, athletic association, conference, or other group or organization with authority over intercollegiate athletics shall not provide a prospective student-athlete with compensation in relation to the athlete's name, image, or likeness."

California's Fair Pay to Play Act opened the flood gates for student-athletes to get paid for their name, image, and likeness by entities other than their schools. Band members would no longer be the only students on the football field able to collect money on the side for their talent on the field.

California's Fair Pay to Play Act was initially scheduled to become effective in 2023, but by 2021, nine states—Arizona, Florida, New Mexico, Mississippi, Alabama, and Georgia—had already followed California's lead and passed laws that would be effective that year.

Trying to stay in the lead, California's state Senate unanimously approved a bill in June 2021 to move up their implementation date to no later than January 1, 2022. By the last day of June 2021, the NCAA changed its stance, announcing that college athletes would now be able to earn compensation through endorsements, sponsorships, and other opportunities while maintaining their amateur status. It may seem that pressure from state legislatures was the key to forcing the NCAA to change, but there was another force in play against the NCAA in June of 2021: The United States Supreme Court.

Before turning to the U.S. Supreme Court, we should note that just because a state passes an NIL law doesn't mean that its law will look like the NIL law of another state. For example, "New Mexico has four pay restrictions compared to forty-five in Illinois. Common restrictions protect a school's intellectual property rights, authorize schools to approve NIL deals, and prohibit certain athlete activities and sponsorships" (Michael H. LeRoy, Do College Athletes Get Nil? Unreasonable Restraints on Player Access to Sports Branding Markets, 2023 U. Ill. L. Rev. 53 (2023)). Athletes, agents, administrators, and businesses navigating the changing landscape of NIL laws need to ensure compliance not only with the NCAA, but also with their own state law.

NCAA v. Alston (2021)

On June 21, 2021, the United States Supreme Court ruled in *NCAA v. Alston* that the NCAA was not exempt from antitrust laws. The case originated with college basketball and football athletes arguing that they should be entitled to both education-related benefits, like internships, graduate school, scholarships, etc., and non-education related benefits, like salaries. The NCAA argued that one of the ways college sports is distinguished from professional sports is that college sports athletes are amateurs. In essence, the NCAA argued that not paying athletes was a feature of the NCAA's product and it would be inappropriate for a court to force a company to redesign its product. The court rejected this argument stating that an entity cannot simply "relabel a restraint as a product feature and declare it 'immune from scrutiny.'"

The NCAA also argued that the "rule of reason analysis" used by District Court Judge Claudia Wilken was "inappropriate because its member schools are not 'commercial enterprises,' but rather institutions that exist to further the societally important noncommercial objective of undergraduate education." The Supreme Court disagreed with the NCAA, noting the millions of dollars the NCAA pays in salaries to administrators and staff and the billions of dollars received in revenues. It also agreed that Judge Wilken's use of the "rule of reason analysis" was the appropriate analysis for the NCAA.

Prior to reaching the Supreme Court, the District Court determined that the NCAA violated antitrust law when it withheld education-related benefits but allowed the NCAA to withhold non-education related benefits. The NCAA appealed to the 9th Circuit Court of Appeals where the District Court's decision was upheld. The NCAA then appealed to the United States Supreme Court. At the Supreme Court, the plaintiffs did not assert their original demand for non-educational benefits. This means that the decision only addresses whether student-athletes are entitled to educational benefits, not salaries. That is, unless you read between the lines or read Justice Kavanaugh's concurrence. The Supreme Court's decision was unanimous, but Justice Kavanaugh added a concurrence that acknowledged that although the case only addressed the educational benefits question that was brought before the court, the NCAA's "remaining [player] compensation rules also raise serious questions under antitrust laws." The decision makes it clear to the NCAA that they are subject to antitrust laws and that any restraints on trade going forward will be evaluated using a factual rule of reason analysis.

What does the Alston decision mean? On the surface, it means that students are entitled to educational benefits, like graduate school. Anecdotally, I can say that this decision has resulted in an increase in the number of student-athletes in my graduate classes. However, more importantly, the decision makes it clear that in future antitrust law cases, the NCAA should not expect a preferential standard, but instead should expect to be subject to the standard fact-based rule of reason analysis.

In the words of the court:

Justice GORSUCH delivered the opinion of the Court.

.....

From the start, American colleges and universities have had a complicated relationship with sports and money. In 1852, students from Harvard and Yale participated in what many regard as the Nation's first intercollegiate competition—a boat race at Lake Winnipesaukee, New Hampshire. But this was no pickup match. A railroad executive sponsored the event to promote train travel to the picturesque lake. T. Mendenhall, The Harvard-Yale Boat Race 1852–1924, pp. 15–16 (1993). He offered the competitors an all-expenses-paid vacation with lavish prizes—along with unlimited alcohol. See A. Zimbalist, Unpaid Professionals 6–7 (1999) (Zimbalist); Rushin, Inside the Moat, Sports Illustrated, Mar. 3, 1997. The event filled the resort with "life and excitement," N.Y. Herald, Aug. 10, 1852, p. 2, *75 col.

2, and one student-athlete described the "'junket'" as an experience "'as unique and irreproducible as the Rhodian colossus,'" Mendenhall, Harvard-Yale Boat Race, at 20.

. . . . .

"By the late 1880s the traditional rivalry between Princeton and Yale was attracting 40,000 spectators and generating in excess of $25,000...in gate revenues." Zimbalist 7. Schools regularly had "graduate students and paid ringers" on their teams. *Ibid.*

Colleges offered all manner of compensation to talented athletes. Yale reportedly lured a tackle named James Hogan with free meals and tuition, a trip to Cuba, the exclusive right to sell scorecards from his games—and a job as a cigarette agent for the American Tobacco Company. *Ibid.*; see also Needham, The College Athlete, McClure's Magazine, June 1905, p. 124. The absence of academic residency requirements gave rise to "'tramp athletes'" who "roamed the country making cameo athletic appearances, moving on whenever and wherever the money was better." F. Dealy, Win at Any Cost 71 (1990). One famous example was a law student at West Virginia University—Fielding H. Yost—"who, in 1896, transferred to Lafayette as a freshman just in time to lead his new teammates to victory against its arch-rival, Penn." *Ibid.* The next week, he "was back at West Virginia's law school." *Ibid.* College sports became such a big business that Woodrow Wilson, then President of Princeton University, quipped to alumni in 1890 that "'Princeton is noted in this wide world for three things: football, baseball, and collegiate instruction.'" Zimbalist 7.

By 1905, though, a crisis emerged. While college football was hugely popular, it was extremely violent. Plays like the flying wedge and the players' light protective gear led to 7 football fatalities in 1893, 12 deaths the next year, and 18 in 1905. *Id.*, at 8. President Theodore Roosevelt responded by convening a meeting between Harvard, Princeton, and Yale to review the rules of the game, a gathering that ultimately led to the creation of what we now know as the NCAA. *Ibid.* Organized primarily as a standard-setting body, the association also expressed a view at its founding about compensating college athletes— admonishing that "[n]o student shall represent a College or University in any intercollegiate game or contest who is paid or receives, directly or indirectly, any money, or financial concession." Intercollegiate Athletic Association of the United States Constitution By-Laws, Art. VII, § 3 (1906); see also Proceedings of the Eleventh Annual Convention of the National **2149 Collegiate Athletic Association, Dec. 28, 1916, p. 34.

Reality did not always match aspiration. More than two decades later, the Carnegie Foundation produced a report on college athletics that found them still "sodden with the commercial and the material and the vested interests that these forces have created." H. Savage, The Carnegie Foundation for the Advancement of Teaching, American College Athletics Bull. 23, p. 310 (1929). Schools across the country sought to leverage sports to bring in revenue, attract attention, boost enrollment, and raise money from alumni. The University of California's athletic revenue was over $480,000, while Harvard's football revenue alone came in at $429,000. *Id.*, at 87. College football was "not a student's game"; it was an "organized commercial enterprise" featuring athletes with "years of training," "professional coaches," and competitions that were "highly profitable." *Id.*, at viii.

The commercialism extended to the market for student-athletes. Seeking the best players, many schools actively participated in a system "under which boys are offered pecuniary and other inducements to enter a particular college." *Id.*, at xiv–xv. One coach estimated that a rival team "spent over $200,000 a year on players." Zimbalist 9. In 1939, freshmen at the University of Pittsburgh went on strike because upperclassmen were reportedly earning more money. Crabb, The Amateurism Myth: A Case for a New Tradition, 28 Stan. L. & Pol'y Rev. 181, 190 (2017). In the 1940s, Hugh McElhenny, a halfback at the University of Washington, "became known as the first college player 'ever to take a cut in salary to play pro football.'" Zimbalist 22–23. He reportedly said: "'[A] wealthy guy puts big bucks under my pillow every time I score a touchdown. Hell, I can't afford to graduate.'" *Id.,* at 211, n. 17. In 1946, a commentator offered this view: "[W]hen it comes to chicanery, double-dealing, and general undercover work behind the scenes, big-time college football is in a class by itself." Woodward, Is College Football on the Level?, Sport, Nov. 1946, Vol. 1, No. 3, p. 35.

In 1948, the NCAA sought to do more than admonish. It adopted the "Sanity Code." Colleges Adopt the 'Sanity Code' To Govern

Sports, N.Y. Times, Jan. 11, 1948, p. 1, col. 1. The code reiterated the NCAA's opposition to "promised pay in any form." Hearings before the Subcommittee on Oversight and Investigations of the House Committee on Interstate and Foreign Commerce, 95th Congress, 2d Sess., pt. 2, p. 1094 (1978). But for the first time the code also authorized colleges and universities to pay athletes' tuition. *Ibid.* And it created a new enforcement mechanism—providing for the "suspension or expulsion" of "proven offenders." Colleges Adopt 'Sanity Code,' N.Y. Times, p. 1, col. 1. To some, these changes sought to substitute a consistent, above-board compensation system for the varying under-the-table schemes that had long proliferated. To others, the code marked "the beginning of the NCAA behaving as an effective cartel," by enabling its member schools to set and enforce "rules that limit the price they have to pay for their inputs (mainly the 'student-athletes')." Zimbalist 10.

The rules regarding student-athlete compensation have evolved ever since. In 1956, the NCAA expanded the scope of allowable payments to include room, board, books, fees, and "cash for incidental expenses such as laundry." *In re National Collegiate Athletic Assn. Athletic Grant-in-Aid Cap Antitrust Litig.*, 375 F.Supp.3d 1058, 1063 (ND Cal. 2019) (hereinafter D. Ct. Op.). In 1974, the NCAA began permitting paid professionals in one sport to compete on an amateur basis in another. Brief for Historians as *Amici Curiae* 10. In 2014, the NCAA "announced it would allow athletic conferences to authorize their member schools to increase scholarships up to the full cost of attendance." *O'Bannon* v. *National Collegiate Athletic Assn.*, 802 F.3d 1049, 1054–1055 (CA9 2015). The 80 member schools of the "Power Five" athletic conferences—the conferences with the highest revenue in Division I—promptly voted to raise their scholarship limits to an amount that is generally several thousand dollars higher than previous limits. D. Ct. Op., at 1064.

. . . . .

Over the decades, the NCAA has become a sprawling enterprise. Its membership comprises about 1,100 colleges and universities, organized into three divisions. *Id.*, at 1063. Division I teams are often the most popular and attract the most money and the most talented athletes. Currently, Division I includes roughly 350 schools divided across 32 conferences. See *ibid.*

At the center of this thicket of associations and rules sits a massive business. The NCAA's current broadcast contract for the March Madness basketball tournament is worth $1.1 billion annually. See *id.,* at 1077, n. 20. Its television deal for the FBS conference's College Football Playoff is worth approximately $470 million per year. See *id.,* at 1063; Bachman, ESPN Strikes Deal for College Football Playoff, Wall Street Journal, Nov. 21, 2012. Beyond these sums, the Division I conferences earn substantial revenue from regular-season games. For example, the Southeastern Conference (SEC) "made more than $409 million in revenues from television contracts alone in 2017, with its total conference revenues exceeding $650 million that year." D. Ct. Op., at 1063. All these amounts have "increased consistently over the years." *Ibid.*

Those who run this enterprise profit in a different way than the student-athletes whose activities they oversee. The president of the NCAA earns nearly $4 million per year. Brief for Players Association of the National Football League et al. as *Amici Curiae* 17. Commissioners of the top conferences take home between $2 to $5 million. *Ibid.* College athletic directors average more than $1 million annually. *Ibid.* And annual salaries for top Division I college football coaches approach $11 million, with some of their assistants making more than $2.5 million. *Id.,* at 17–18.

The plaintiffs are current and former student-athletes in men's Division I FBS football and men's and women's Division I basketball. They filed a class action against the NCAA and 11 Division I conferences (for simplicity's sake, we refer to the defendants collectively as the NCAA). The student-athletes challenged the "current, interconnected set of NCAA rules that limit the compensation they may receive in exchange for their athletic services." D. Ct. Op., at 1062, 1065, n. 5. Specifically, they alleged that the NCAA's rules violate § 1 of the Sherman Act, which prohibits "contract[s], combination[s], or conspirac[ies] in restraint of trade or commerce." 15 U.S.C. § 1.

.....

Before us, as through much of the litigation below, some of the issues most frequently debated in antitrust litigation are uncontested. The parties do not challenge the district court's definition of the relevant market. They do not contest that the NCAA enjoys monopoly (or, as it's called on the buyer side, monopsony) control in that labor market—such that it is capable of depressing wages below competitive levels and restricting the quantity of student-athlete labor. Nor does the NCAA dispute that its member schools compete fiercely for student-athletes but remain subject to NCAA-issued-and-enforced limits on what compensation they can offer. Put simply, this suit involves admitted horizontal price fixing in a market where the defendants exercise monopoly control.

. . . . .

With this much agreed it is unclear exactly what the NCAA seeks. To the extent it means to propose a sort of judicially ordained immunity from the terms of the Sherman Act for its restraints of trade—that we should overlook its restrictions because they happen to fall at the intersection of higher education, sports, and money—we cannot agree. This Court has regularly refused materially identical requests from litigants seeking special dispensation from the Sherman Act on the ground that their restraints of trade serve uniquely important social objectives beyond enhancing competition.

. . . . .

In a related critique, the NCAA contends the district court "impermissibly redefined" its "product" by rejecting its views about what amateurism requires and replacing them with its preferred conception. Brief for Petitioner in No. 20–512, at 35–36.

This argument, however, misapprehends the way a defendant's procompetitive business justification relates to the antitrust laws. Firms deserve substantial latitude to fashion agreements that serve legitimate business interests—agreements that may include efforts aimed at introducing a new product into the marketplace. *Supra.* But none of that means a party can relabel a restraint as a product feature and declare it "immune from § 1 scrutiny." *American Needle*, 560 U.S. at 199, n. 7, 130 S.Ct. 2201. In this suit, as in any, the district court had to determine whether the defendants' agreements harmed competition and whether any procompetitive benefits associated with their restraints could be achieved by "substantially less restrictive alternative" means. D. Ct. Op., at 1104.

Some will think the district court did not go far enough. By permitting colleges and universities to offer enhanced education-related benefits, its decision may encourage scholastic achievement and allow student-athletes a measure of compensation more consistent with the value they bring to their schools. Still, some will see this as a poor substitute for fuller relief. At the same time, others will think the district court went too far by undervaluing the social benefits associated with amateur athletics. For our part, though, we can only agree with the Ninth Circuit: "'The national debate about amateurism in college sports is important. But our task as appellate judges is not to resolve it. Nor could we. Our task is simply to review the district court judgment through the appropriate lens of antitrust law.'" 958 F.3d at 1265. That review persuades us the district court acted within the law's bounds.

The judgment is *Affirmed.*

Justice KAVANAUGH, concurring.

The NCAA has long restricted the compensation and benefits that student athletes may receive. And with surprising success, the NCAA has long shielded its compensation rules from ordinary antitrust scrutiny. Today, however, the Court holds that the NCAA has violated the antitrust laws. The Court's decision marks an important and overdue course correction, and I join the Court's excellent opinion in full.

But this case involves only a narrow subset of the NCAA's compensation rules—namely, the rules restricting the *education-related* benefits that student athletes may receive, such as post-eligibility scholarships at graduate or vocational schools. The rest of the NCAA's compensation rules are not at issue here and therefore remain on the books. Those remaining compensation rules generally restrict student athletes from receiving compensation or benefits from their colleges for playing sports. And those rules have also historically restricted student athletes from receiving money from endorsement deals and the like.

I add this concurring opinion to underscore that the NCAA's remaining compensation rules also raise serious questions under the antitrust laws. Three points warrant emphasis.

First, the Court does not address the legality of the NCAA's remaining compensation rules. As the Court says, "the student-athletes do not renew their across-the-board challenge to the NCAA's compensation restrictions. Accordingly, we do not pass on the rules that remain in place or the district court's judgment upholding them. Our review is confined to those restrictions now enjoined."

Second, although the Court does not weigh in on the ultimate legality of the NCAA's remaining compensation rules, the Court's decision establishes how any such rules should be analyzed going forward. After today's decision, the NCAA's remaining compensation rules should receive ordinary "rule of reason" scrutiny under the antitrust laws. The Court makes clear that the decades-old "stray comments" about college sports and amateurism made in *National Collegiate Athletic Assn. v. Board of Regents of Univ. of* Okla., 468 U.S. 85, 104 S.Ct. 2948, 82 L.Ed.2d 70 (1984), were dicta and have no bearing on whether the NCAA's current compensation rules are lawful. And the Court stresses that the NCAA is not otherwise entitled to an exemption from the antitrust laws. *Ante*; see also *Radovich v. National Football League*, 352 U.S. 445, 449–452, 77 S.Ct. 390, 1 L.Ed.2d 456 (1957). As a result, absent legislation or a negotiated agreement between the NCAA and the student athletes, the NCAA's remaining compensation rules should be subject to ordinary rule of reason scrutiny. See *ante*.

Third, there are serious questions whether the NCAA's remaining compensation rules can pass muster under ordinary rule of reason scrutiny. Under the rule of reason, the NCAA must supply a legally valid procompetitive justification for its remaining compensation rules. As I see it, however, the NCAA may lack such a justification.

The NCAA acknowledges that it controls the market for college athletes. The NCAA concedes that its compensation rules set the price of student athlete labor at a below-market rate. And the NCAA recognizes that student athletes currently have no meaningful ability to negotiate with the NCAA over the compensation rules.

The NCAA nonetheless asserts that its compensation rules are procompetitive because those rules help define the product of college sports. Specifically, the NCAA says that colleges may decline to pay student athletes because the defining feature of college sports, according to the NCAA, is that the student athletes are not paid.

In my view, that argument is circular and unpersuasive. The NCAA couches its arguments for not paying student athletes in innocuous labels. But the labels cannot disguise the reality: The NCAA's business model would be flatly illegal in almost any other industry in America. All of the restaurants in a region cannot come together to cut cooks' wages on the theory that "customers prefer" to eat food from low-paid cooks. Law firms cannot conspire to cabin lawyers' salaries in the name of providing legal services out of a "love of the law." Hospitals cannot agree to cap nurses' income in order to create a "purer" form of helping the sick. News organizations cannot join forces to curtail pay to reporters to preserve a "tradition" of public-minded journalism. Movie studios cannot collude to slash benefits to camera crews to kindle a "spirit of amateurism" in Hollywood.

Price-fixing labor is price-fixing labor. And price-fixing labor is ordinarily a textbook antitrust problem because it extinguishes the free market in which individuals can otherwise obtain fair compensation for their work. See, *e.g.*, *Texaco Inc. v. Dagher*, 547 U.S. 1, 5, 126 S.Ct. 1276, 164 L.Ed.2d 1 (2006). Businesses like the NCAA cannot avoid the consequences of price-fixing labor by incorporating price-fixed labor into the definition of the product. Or to put it in more doctrinal terms, a monopsony cannot launder its price-fixing of labor by calling it product definition.

The bottom line is that the NCAA and its member colleges are suppressing the pay of student athletes who collectively generate **billions** of dollars in revenues for colleges every year. Those enormous sums of money flow to seemingly everyone except the student athletes. College presidents, athletic directors, coaches, conference commissioners, and NCAA executives take in six- and seven-figure salaries. Colleges build lavish new facilities. But the student athletes who generate the revenues, many of whom are African American and from lower-income backgrounds, end up with little or nothing. See Brief for African American Antitrust Lawyers as *Amici Curiae* 13–17.

Everyone agrees that the NCAA can require student athletes to be enrolled students in good standing. But the NCAA's business model of using unpaid student athletes to generate billions of dollars in revenue for the colleges raises serious questions under the antitrust laws. In particular, it is highly questionable whether the NCAA and its member colleges can justify not paying student athletes a fair share of the revenues on the circular theory that the defining characteristic of college sports is that the colleges do not pay student athletes. And if that asserted justification is unavailing, it is not clear how the NCAA can legally defend its remaining compensation rules.

If it turns out that some or all of the NCAA's remaining compensation rules violate the antitrust laws, some difficult policy and practical questions would undoubtedly ensue. Among them: How would paying greater compensation to student athletes affect non-revenue-raising sports? Could student athletes in some sports but not others receive compensation? How would any compensation regime comply with Title IX? If paying student athletes requires something like a salary cap in some sports in order to preserve competitive balance, how would that cap be administered? And given that there are now about 180,000 Division I student athletes, what is a financially sustainable way of fairly compensating some or all of those student athletes?

Of course, those difficult questions could be resolved in ways other than litigation. Legislation would be one option. Or colleges and student athletes could potentially engage in collective bargaining (or seek some other negotiated agreement) to provide student athletes a fairer share of the revenues that they generate for their colleges, akin to how professional football and basketball players have negotiated for a share of league revenues. Cf. *Brown v. Pro Football, Inc.*, 518 U.S. 231, 235–237, 116 S.Ct. 2116, 135 L.Ed.2d 521 (1996); *Wood v. National Basketball Assn.*, 809 F.2d 954, 958–963 (CA2 1987) (R. Winter, J.). Regardless of how those issues ultimately would be resolved, however, the NCAA's current compensation regime raises serious questions under the antitrust laws.

To be sure, the NCAA and its member colleges maintain important traditions that have become part of the fabric of America—game days in Tuscaloosa and South Bend; the packed gyms in Storrs and Durham; the women's and men's lacrosse championships on Memorial Day weekend; track and field meets in Eugene; the spring softball and baseball World Series in Oklahoma City and Omaha; the list goes on. But those traditions alone cannot justify the NCAA's decision to build a massive money-raising enterprise on the backs of student athletes who are not fairly compensated. Nowhere else in America can businesses get away with agreeing not to pay their workers a fair market rate on the theory that their product is defined by not paying their workers a fair market rate. And under ordinary principles of antitrust law, it is not evident why college sports should be any different. The NCAA is not above the law.

(That ends the concurrence of Justice KAVANAUGH in *Nat'l Collegiate Athletic Ass'n v. Alston*, 594 U.S. 69, 72–112, 141 S. Ct. 2141, 2144–69, 210 L. Ed. 2d 314 (2021)).

House v. NCAA

By the time *NCAA v. Alston* was decided by the U.S. Supreme Court, another NCAA antitrust case was before Judge Claudia Wilken at the Northern District of California. The case was *Grant House v. NCAA*. House was a swimmer at Arizona State University (ASU). He was inspired by music students at ASU who could "get paid to play at Carnegie Hall," while as an NCAA athlete, his compensation was capped by the NCAA. He said, it "just didn't sit well with me…that [musicians] can monetize this…[but] I couldn't because I was an athlete." He became the lead plaintiff in a class action lawsuit against the NCAA. Music might not have been House's only inspiration. His teammate's mother, Shelby Smith, was an attorney at the Seattle-based law firm Hagens Berman, which served as co-lead counsel in *NCAA v. Alston*. (Dodd, Dennis. (2023, May 15). *Meet Grant House, the man front and center fighting the NCAA's last gasp to cap athlete compensation.* CBS Sports).

After the Alston decision, any alleged NCAA antitrust violations would be evaluated using a rule of reason analysis. And remember, the Sherman Act allows for treble damages which triples the award plaintiffs may receive. And what are the damages the plaintiffs in House hoped to triple? "The lawsuit focused on the eight-year, $8.8 billion extension the NCAA signed to broadcast coverage of the March Madness basketball tournament, as well as…back-dated damages for payments the suit calls wrongly withheld" (Morse, Ben. (2024, May 23). *College sports could see a dramatic change. Here's what you need to know.* CNN*)*.

On May 23, 2024, the NCAA agreed to settle the lawsuit for nearly $2.8 billion in damages to former college athletes. This includes "an estimated 14,500 Division I athletes who played from June 15, 2016, until the class was established in November 2023 who could have received money for the commercial use of their NIL, video games and broadcasts if the NCAA had permitted it" (Dosh, Kristi. (2024, May 24). 10 Things to Know About the NCAA's House Settlement. Forbes). "The NCAA will pay the damages over the next 10 years ($277M annually) by cutting into its revenue shares with Division I universities" (Clinton, Bryan. (2024, May 24). House v. NCAA Settlement Will Make History on Multiple Fronts. Heartland College Sports).

In January 2025, the U.S. Department of Justice (DOJ) and U.S. Department of Education's Office for Civil Rights (OCR) both expressed their interest in the settlement. The DOJ filed a statement of interest taking issue with the settlement setting a cap on revenue sharing. That is, even if the parties agree to a profit-sharing cap that is greater than the current level of zero, isn't a cap on athlete compensation, by definition, still a potential anticompetitive violation of antitrust law? For its part, the OCR released guidance stating that future revenue distributions from an institution to an athlete for NIL rights would be classified as "athletic financial assistance" that would need to be proportionally divided to avoid violating Title IX.

Yost v. NCAA

In December 2023, Ohio Attorney General Dave Yost filed a lawsuit challenging the NCAA's Transfer Eligibility Rule (NCAA Bylaw 14.5.5) as a violation of Section 1 of the Sherman Act. The lawsuit was joined by Colorado, Illinois, New York, North Carolina, Tennessee, and West Virginia.

As stated in the complaint:

5. The Transfer Eligibility Rule requires a year of academic residency before a transferring Division I college athlete is eligible to participate in NCAA athletic competition. Underscoring its anticompetitive nature, the rule is not universally applied. A college athlete's first transfer is excepted from this process, and there is a discretionary waiver process. But the Rule remains the default for Division I college athletes who transfer a second time.

6. For NCAA college athletes, a one-year waiting period for eligibility can be devastating. This amounts to 20% of the total time allotted by NCAA regulations for the completion of the

college athlete's total seasons of eligibility. Furthermore, only by competing on the field or court can the college athlete receive the full benefits of participation in Division I NCAA athletics.

9. Plaintiff States bring this action to put a stop to Defendant's unjustified overreach into the lives and careers of college athletes, to prevent the unjustified anticompetitive restriction on universities who seek to compete for college athletes, and to restore freedom of economic opportunity.

The Judge in the case, Judge John Preston Bailey of the Northern District of West Virginia, granted the states' request for a preliminary injunction, forbidding the NCAA from enforcing the transfer rule through at least the Spring 2024 sports season.

Following the precedent of *NCAA v. Alston*, the NCAA would be evaluated as a commercial enterprise subject to the fact-based rule of reason analysis. Would it make sense to force laborers in any other commercial enterprise to wait a year before allowing them to work again? I can imagine that hospitals would benefit from lower employee turnover, but it would not make sense to require nurses to sit out and not work for a year when they transfer to work at a different hospital.

On May 30, 2024, Yost and the NCAA reached a settlement to make Judge Bailey's injunction permanent. NCAA student-athletes could now transfer to different schools without sitting out for a season before competing again. The settlement also "prevents retaliation from the NCAA against member institutions and athletes who challenged the rule or supported those" who challenged it and "requires the NCAA to grant an additional year of eligibility to Division I athletes who for any reason were previously deemed ineligible under the transfer eligibility rule since the 2019-2020 academic year" (Office of the Minnesota Attorney General. (2024, May 30). Press release: Minnesota Attorney General Keith Ellison addresses NCAA ruling. *Minnesota Attorney General's Office*).

Closing Thoughts on the NCAA Antitrust Landscape

What do these NCAA antitrust decisions mean for student-athletes? It means they can now get paid for their name, image, and likeness. It means they can transfer schools without having to sit out for a year before playing their sport again at a different school. It means that in 2025, Arch Manning, a highly rated backup quarterback at the

University of Texas, can pocket NIL deals valued at $6.6 million, University of Colorado football player Shedeur Sanders can enjoy NIL deals valued at $6.5 million, and LSU Gymnast Livvy Dunne, with her 7.9 million followers on TikTok, can enjoy NIL deals valued at $4.2 million (On3Nil100 [https://www.on3.com/nil/rankings/player/nil-100/]).

These changes will also affect the competitive landscape of college sports. In late 2021—after the Alston decision—a "new tax-exempt charity...set up by [University of] Texas fans... promised to pay every University of Texas offensive lineman a salary of $50,000 per year" (Fahrenthold, David A. and Witz, Billy. (2023, December 31). *The Best Teams That Money Could Buy*. New York Times). In 2021, the Texas Longhorns finished their season with a conference record of three wins and six losses. By 2024, their conference record improved to eight wins and one loss. This secured them a spot in the College Football Playoff where they lost to the eventual champion, Ohio State University. Not to be outdone, UT rival Texas A&M's recruitment efforts led then Alabama coach Nick Saban to say, "A&M bought every player on their team." Ole Miss coach Lane Kiffin even suggested that "Saudi money has changed [the] transfer market" (Gray, Nick. (2023, July 30). *Lane Kiffin rekindles Texas A&M football beef with tweet about Saudi Arabia, Pep Guardiola*. Mississippi Clarion-Ledger).

This also impacts smaller markets like my employer, New Mexico State University. After a record-breaking season, including beating Auburn at home in a shocking 31-10 victory for which Auburn paid NMSU $1.85 million, NMSU coach Jerry Kill announced his retirement as head coach. Within days, at least 30 NMSU football players entered the transfer portal to play somewhere else because, in a nutshell, they can.

Where did Coach Kill go? He went to Vanderbilt University along with NMSU offensive coordinator Tim Beck, assistant coaches Ghaali Muhammad-Lankford (running backs), Melvin Rice (safeties) and Garrett Altman (quarterbacks). Key players also transferred to Vanderbilt including quarterback Diego Pavia, Tight End Eli Stowers, running backs Jamoni Jones and Makhilyn Young, and quarterback Blaze Berlowitz. They contributed to Vanderbilt's upset victory over #1 ranked Alabama in Week 5 of 2024. It was the first time Vanderbilt had beaten Alabama in 40 years.

Let's zoom in on quarterback Diego Pavia. Pavia excelled at football in high school in Albuquerque, New Mexico, but he did not receive any Division I offers to play football. In response, he played for two years at the junior college level, leading the New Mexico Military Institute to a National Junior College Athletic Association (NJCAA) Championship. He then transferred to NMSU, leading the team to back-to-back winning seasons and a 10-win season for the first time since the 1960s. With antirust precedents paving the way for NIL deals and easy transfers, Pavia then transferred to Vanderbilt where he led the team to wins over historic powerhouses Alabama and Auburn and lost by only a field goal to top 10 ranked Texas and Missouri.

For those who are counting, you may have detected a problem. Two years at junior college plus two years at NMSU plus one year at Vanderbilt adds up to the maximum of five years of NCAA eligibility. And Pavia wanted to play for another year at Vanderbilt. In November 2024, Pavia sued the NCAA, arguing that his years in junior college should not count towards his overall NCAA eligibility years.

In the words of the Court:

> Pavia wants to play football in the 2025-26 season but has no remaining eligibility under the current NCAA Division I Bylaws. This is because his time at New Mexico Military Academy, a junior college that is not a member of any NCAA Division, "counts" as one year of collegiate athletic competition under the challenged rules.

> Pavia seeks relief in time for him to consider his options for next year, commit to a university, and negotiate NIL opportunities.

In December 2024, the NCAA approved a waiver granting an additional year of eligibility for the 2025-26 season for athletes who competed at a non-NCAA school for at least one year and who have exhausted their NCAA eligibility.

Appendix A: An IRAC Illustration: Do Professors Violate Copyright Law When They Copy Articles for Students?

The following is an article that I wrote that originally appeared on the American Bar Association for Law Students' website.

The IRAC method of legal reasoning and writing is fundamental to many entry-level law courses. It represents the acronym for Issue, Rule, Analysis/Application, and Conclusion. The method is helpful once understood, but it can be difficult to learn and teach. This article illustrates how to use the IRAC method by employing it to address a practical legal question facing many professors and students today: Do professors violate copyright law when they copy articles for students?

This legal question arises when professors assign articles for students to read from publications like the Wall Street Journal that provide access to only a limited number of free articles per month. Students who attempt to access more than the limited number of articles in a month are denied access unless they purchase a subscription. Professors and students may wonder if it would violate copyright law for these professors to make copies of the articles and give them to students who would otherwise not read the articles because they are unwilling or unable to pay for a subscription.

IRAC: Issue

The Issue in IRAC is the legal question one is trying to answer. It can be difficult to identify this question in complex or personal situations. For example, imagine that a professor is copying an article for a student that is defamatory, invades an individual's right to privacy, compromises national security, contains trade secrets or child pornography, or involves important constitutional questions about free speech and academic freedom. It is tempting—and natural—to want to explore all, or at least the most sensational of these issues, but answering all of these questions may not be essential to the real legal question that needs to be answered. For example, if you are the person who feels that you were defamed or had your privacy invaded or your speech silenced, it may be difficult to identify that the real issue is about copyright infringement and not legal issues surrounding defamation, invasion of privacy, or free speech.

Multiple IRACs and IRACs within IRACs

Legal questions may contain multiple issues or even issues within issues. The strength of the IRAC method requires boiling down potentially complex legal scenarios into specific, answerable legal questions. For example, if you are a potential plaintiff in the example above, you may have two specific IRACs: 1) Is the defendant liable for defamation? 2) Is the defendant liable for invasion of privacy? These are two distinct legal questions that you would want to address individually using two separate IRACs.

It is also common to have an IRAC within an IRAC. This often occurs after a rule statement. For example, if your issue was, "Is the defendant liable for defamation?" your rule statement may define defamation as a 1) false, 2) defamatory, 3) statement of fact, 4) of or concerning the plaintiff, that is 5) published to a third party. These five elements must be established to prove that someone is liable for defamation. It would then be helpful to analyze these elements in a series of five separate mini-IRACs asking, "Was the statement false, was the statement defamatory, was the statement a statement of fact, was the statement of or concerning the plaintiff, and was the statement published to a third party?" Each question would be its own IRAC with its own rule applied and analyzed to a logical conclusion.

For this article, the legal issue we will explore is provided: Do professors violate copyright law when they copy articles for students? In the process of answering this question, we will also discover the need to answer a mini-IRAC within this IRAC asking, "Does a professor copying articles for students qualify as a 'fair use' under Section 107 of the Copyright Code?"

Helpful Tips:

Phrase your issue statement as a question. Questions end with a question mark. Issue statements that begin with the word "whether" are confusing and lose the power to identify a real question that demands an answer.

IRAC: Rule

The Rule is the law that will provide the authority needed to answer the legal question identified in the issue. If the issue were about defamation, we would cite the applicable state or federal statutes on defamation. In our case, we are asking about copyright infringement, and so we need to look to the U.S. Copyright Code. The U.S. Copyright

Code protects "original works of authorship fixed in any tangible medium of expression" (17 U.S. Code §102). However, Section 107 of the Copyright Code specifically allows copying for what it calls a "fair use...for the purpose of criticism, comment, news reporting, teaching, scholarship, or research" (17 U.S. Code § 107).

In addition to looking at the words in an applicable statute, it is also important to see how prior courts have interpreted and applied the statutes because their interpretations create the precedent rules that future cases will follow. Here are examples of how prior courts have defined fair use:

Not a Fair Use:

Setting up an "off-campus, for profit, copy shop" to copy and sell anthologies to college students is not a fair use. Courts did not like that the protected materials were copied for a commercial purpose and for the "same intrinsic purpose" as the copyrighted material (Princeton Univ. Press v. Mich. Document Servs., 99 F.3d 1381).

Fair Use:

A court determined that copying is a fair use when done by "...nonprofit institutions, devoted solely to the advancement and dissemination of medical knowledge...[that] normally restricted copying on an individual scientist's request to a single copy of an article and to articles of less than fifty pages...[and] medical science would be seriously hurt if such photocopying were stopped...[and] there was no showing of economic injury to [the] publisher" (Williams & Wilkins Co. v. United States, 203 Ct. Cl. 74).

Helpful Tips:

Rules should be narrowly focused on the legal question addressed in the issue yet broad enough to address the intricacies of a complex fact pattern. If you are writing an IRAC essay for a school or state bar exam, your rule statement should state the precise definition of the law that controls your issue. If your rule statement is incomplete, your analysis will fail to address all the nuances your answer should contemplate.

IRAC: Analysis/Application

The Application/Analysis section compares the facts of prior cases to our new situation. In our case, university professors have students who cannot read articles that the professors assign because the students

---

cannot or will not spend money to read an article after they have reached their limit of free articles per month. And the professors do not receive any economic benefit from giving these articles to students. Are these facts more like the unfair "off-campus, for profit, copy shop" or the "fair use" of a nonprofit institution sharing knowledge with no showing of economic injury to the plaintiff?

If a student will not spend money for the article, and the professor and university will not spend money for the student to access the article, then one could argue that copying the article and providing it to the student would not deprive the publisher of any economic benefit because no one in the scenario is going to pay the publisher for the student to access the article. The question is not if the publisher will be paid for the student accessing the article. The publisher will not be paid. The question is only if the student will have access to the article.

Although it is helpful to find a case that appears to apply perfectly to a new situation—especially when it points to an outcome you desire—it is important to analyze precedent cases with different outcomes. Thorough analysis requires distinguishing why prior cases should or should not apply. The purpose of IRAC is to facilitate thoughtful, critical analysis. If the result feels like a thoughtless application of a rule…we're probably not doing it right.

Helpful Tips:

Improve your analysis by using the words "because," "like," and "unlike." Using the word "because" forces you to provide some analysis instead of just a conclusion BECAUSE it requires you to finish the sentence with a clause defending your statement. Using the words "like" and "unlike" help you distinguish the facts in the current case from the facts in prior cases. For example, the facts in the current case are like the facts in the precedent "fair use" case because _____ and unlike the facts in the "unfair use" case because _____.

IRAC: Conclusion

The conclusion should logically follow from the analysis and application of the rules to answer the question presented in the issue. It is a "therefore" statement. For example, imagine your issue is an arithmetic question. Your rule established how to add, your analysis determined that you were adding two plus two, and your conclusion might state, "Therefore, the answer is four."

It is common for professors to say that the conclusion is less important than the process that came up with it. Although true, there are two ways to fail the conclusion section of an IRAC essay: 1) Not providing a conclusion, and 2) Providing a conclusion that does not logically follow the application/analysis of the rules.

Not Providing a Conclusion

The purpose of the IRAC format of legal reasoning and writing is to provide a logical answer to the question identified in the issue statement. In our example, we want to know if professors violate copyright law when they copy articles for students in a specific situation. Any analysis or description of the history of copyright law—however beautifully written—is ultimately useless for IRAC purposes if it fails to answer our legal question.

Providing a Conclusion That Does Not Logically Follow the Application/Analysis of the Rules

Again, the purpose of the IRAC format of legal reasoning and writing is to provide a logical answer to the question identified in the issue statement. If, throughout the analysis, we read that the current case is most like cases where courts have found that the copying is not a "fair use," it would not logically follow to conclude that the copying is somehow fair in this similar case.

The conclusion should naturally flow from the analysis. For example:

Therefore, the limited, noncommercial classroom use of a professor copying articles for students who would not purchase them should qualify as a "fair use" under Section 107 of the U.S. Copyright Code. Based on the facts in our specific situation, we conclude that professors at nonprofit institutions do NOT violate copyright law if they copy articles for students when there is no economic injury to the plaintiff, no economic benefit to the professor, and "science would be seriously hurt if such photocopying were stopped"(Williams & Wilkins Co. v. United States, 203 Ct. Cl. 74).

Helpful Tips: Legal analysis is like math but with ideas instead of numbers. I plus R plus A should equal C. ($I + R + A = C$). The wrong answer is the one that doesn't answer the question or doesn't add up.

Appendix A, An IRAC Illustration

Appendix B: Objection, Relevance: Using the legal rules of evidence to improve your business reasoning and writing

The following is a version of an article that I wrote that originally appeared on Colorado State University's Writing Across the Curriculum's website.

If you have ever watched a courtroom drama, you have probably heard the phrase, "Objection, relevance." What does this mean, and how can it help our thinking, writing, and, as a bonus, maybe make us more informed viewers of our favorite TV shows? In this writing guide, we will use the legal rules of evidence to help writers focus on what is helpful, necessary, and to the point.

Relevance

In order for evidence to be used in a trial, it must be relevant. If it is irrelevant, the evidence is said to be inadmissible and cannot be used. Attorneys can't use it, and juries shouldn't hear it. If one side tries to use information that is not relevant, the other side should protest to the judge, arguing that the information should not be allowed because it is not relevant. Or, as it is commonly stated, "Objection, Relevance." The other side is then given an opportunity to explain to the judge why the evidence is relevant, and should be allowed.

Federal Rule of Evidence 401 tells us that evidence is relevant if:

a) It has any tendency to make a fact more or less probable than it would be without the evidence; and

b) The fact is of consequence in determining the action. (Fed R. Evid. 401)

Rule 401a: Helpful

Evidence that has "any tendency to make a fact more or less probable than it would be without the evidence," must be **helpful** in proving something. For example, imagine you saw someone drink five shots of tequila before getting into a car, and you want to prove that the individual was intoxicated. Is evidence that someone drank five shots of tequila helpful in proving the individual's intoxication? Of course. If the evidence has "any tendency" to make it more or less probable that

---

the individual was intoxicated than it would be without the evidence, the first element of relevance is satisfied.

Rule 401b: Necessary

In addition to being helpful in proving something, what the evidence is trying to prove must also be **necessary**, or "of consequence," in determining the outcome of the action. If the person who consumed the five shots of tequila is being charged with Driving While Intoxicated, then proving the driver's intoxication is necessary in determining the outcome of the DWI action against him. The driver's intoxication is "of consequence in determining the action" because if he was not intoxicated, he can't be convicted of Driving While Intoxicated. But what if the tequila testimony is being offered in a product defect lawsuit against a car manufacturer because when the man stumbled into the car, the airbags immediately detonated, and the man suffered serious bodily harm? If the man drank tequila has nothing to do with if the car manufacturer made a defective car that exploded. In both cases, the tequila consumption is helpful to prove the fact that the man may have been intoxicated. But although intoxication is necessary to charges of DWI, intoxication has nothing to do with if the car manufacturer made a defective product that caused our tequila-drinker harm. Therefore, evidence of the five shots of tequila would be relevant and allowed in the DWI case, and irrelevant—and therefore not allowed—in the product defect lawsuit.

Rule 403: Straight to the Point

I'll leave you with one more rule of evidence to help you with your business reasoning and writing. It's Federal Rule of Evidence 403. It says that even if evidence is relevant, courts may still exclude it if "its probative value is substantially outweighed by a danger of…unfair prejudice, confusing the issues, misleading the jury, undue delay, **wasting time**, or **needlessly presenting cumulative evidence**."

Imagine in our DWI case that the driver had been drinking five shots of tequila every night in the same bar for the past 20 years. There may be 1,000 people lined up who can testify that it is the habit of this individual to consume five shots of tequila every night. Is this evidence relevant to whether or not the individual consumed five shots of tequila, was intoxicated, and should be charged with Driving While Intoxicated? Of course. This evidence is **helpful** in proving the man was probably intoxicated, and proving intoxication is **necessary** to the DWI case. But at some point between the testimony of witness one and witness 1,000, any new value that the testimony could add will be substantially outweighed by the testimony's **waste of time** or its **needless presentation of cumulative evidence**.

Application to Writing: Focus

How can we use these rules of legal relevance to improve our business reasoning and writing?

Focus. Judges and business leaders generally don't pick up memos on a Saturday morning because they're expecting the memos will make them laugh, cry, or feel inspired. Give decision-makers the information that is helpful and necessary to making wise decisions. Sharing extra information—even if expertly researched and beautifully written—doesn't make you look smart or thorough. It suggests that you can't tell the difference between what's important, and what's not.

Appendix C: The Common Law, A Football Story

Sports fans have an advantage when it comes to understanding the U.S. legal system because they understand what it's like to argue about rules and follow case precedent. For example, in football, imagine that it's first down and a quarterback throws a forward pass to a receiver. It looks like the receiver caught the ball, but at nearly the same time, the receiver is hit by a defensive player who knocks the ball loose. The team on defense then jumps on the ball. What is the legal issue facing football fans? They want to know, "Did the receiver catch the ball?" For non-football fans, we should help explain what is at stake. If it was not a catch, then it was an incomplete forward pass and the team on offense maintains possession. It's not a big deal. If the receiver caught the ball, then we have a catch and a fumble that was recovered by the defense. That means the defensive team will now have possession of the ball. That's a big deal. So, how do we know if the receiver really caught the ball or if the ball just bounced off the receiver's hands? We ask a judge. We'll call this judge the referee. The referee will look at the facts and decide if a catch was made.

We expect similar outcomes in similar situations, and so we have a problem when it looks like the same facts were called an incomplete pass in one game and a fumble in another game. To address this, we take the question to a higher court that could issue binding rules that all future games would need to follow. If we are talking about the National Football League, we could call this high court the NFL Competition Committee. This is the committee responsible for establishing the rules for the NFL.

This high court may answer our "was it a catch" question by saying that a catch occurs when a receiver gains control of the ball while in bounds. When asked what "gains control" means, the court could say it means the receiver maintained control long enough to perform a football move. When asked, "What is a football move," the court could say it means the player turned up field, tucked the ball, or took several steps.

The answers to these questions become the rule that future judges, I mean referees, will follow in future cases. Now, would this new NFL rule be binding on NCAA football, flag football, or rugby? No, it would only be binding precedent for the judges under the authority of the NFL. And would these rules apply if the pass was not a forward pass?

No. If it was not a forward pass, then we would call it a lateral or backward pass, and different rules apply. Controlling precedent only applies when a subsequent court is applying the same law as the prior court, and it only applies to courts under the authority of the higher court.

The Common Law Tradition

The football illustration above captures the essence of the U.S. legal system. The U.S. legal system is based on the English Common Law tradition where judicial decisions form a precedent that future courts must follow. This approach is known as *Stare Decisis* which is Latin for "to stand on things decided." In this way, a 15th-century English case about a cow damaging a neighbor's crops could be a distant predecessor to modern cases involving autonomous aerial vehicles causing damage to a neighbor's house. In both scenarios, the law aims to secure financial compensation for the victims harmed by something that escaped the control of the owner.

How *Stare Decisis* Works

Under *Stare Decisis*:

1. A court should uphold its precedents unless there is a compelling reason to overturn them.
2. Decisions made by higher courts are binding on lower courts.

This provides uniformity and predictability while also offering flexibility to address new realities.

For example, imagine a scenario where an individual accidentally burns a field of onions that were about to be harvested. The farmer anticipated earning $200,000 from selling the crop. How much should the farmer be compensated? A judge may consider the anticipated $200,000, subtract any amount saved from the farmer not having to harvest the onions, and then add any other damages to the farm's land, infrastructure, etc. For our purposes, let's assume the judge determined that the person who burned the onion field owes the onion farmer $200,000.

Now imagine that the same fire burned two other fields of identical size. How much should the farmers of those fields receive as compensation? It is tempting to say $200,000, but we need to look at the facts. Maybe the first field was full of onions, the second field was full of tumbleweeds, and the third field was an orchard full of mature pecan trees. Based on these facts, maybe a judge would rule that the onion farmer should receive $200,000, the tumbleweed owner should receive nothing, and the pecan orchard owner should receive $1 million dollars. This illustrates that when we look at prior cases, we consider the reasoning behind the decisions, not just the outcomes.

When Can the Supreme Court Not Follow Precedent?

Of course, the Supreme Court does not always follow precedent. Some of its most significant constitutional decisions have overturned prior rulings. Notable examples include *Brown v. Board of Education* (1954), which reversed the infamous *Plessy v. Ferguson* (1896) segregation decision, and *Dobbs v. Jackson Women's Health Organization* (2022), which reversed *Roe v. Wade* (1973) on abortion. In *Janus v. Am. Fed'n of State, Cnty., & Mun. Emps., Council 31*, 585 U.S. 878 (2018), the Supreme Court identified five factors to consider when deciding whether to overrule a past decision.

1. The quality of the prior decision's reasoning,
2. The workability of the rule the precedent established,
3. The precedent's consistency with other related decisions,
4. Developments since the decision was handed down, and
5. The extent to which individuals or entities have relied on the prior precedent.

After evaluating these factors, the Court may conclude that *stare decisis* does not require retaining a previous decision.

The Civil Law Tradition

Unlike the Common Law tradition, the Civil Law tradition relies on statutes rather than case precedents. For example, a statute might set a fixed fine for burning someone's field. This provides predictability, but it lacks the flexibility of the Common Law tradition. The Civil Law tradition is rooted in Roman law. Its influence continues to this day in countries like France, Spain, and other countries that follow their legal traditions.

Controlling Precedents and Binding Authority

Under *stare decisis*, courts must follow the controlling precedents in their jurisdictions. These controlling precedents are called binding authority because lower courts are bound—that is, required—to follow the precedent. Controlling precedents include constitutions and statutes. Controlling precedent only applies when the subsequent court is applying the same law as the prior court. For example, maybe one fire was caused by accident, and another was started on purpose. A case about a fire caused by arson would not be binding precedent for a fire caused by negligence, just like the precedent on whether a forward pass was a catch was not binding on passes that were not forward passes.

Some cases do not have any binding precedents. These are called cases of first impression. For these cases, courts may look to persuasive authority. For example, recreational marijuana use was legalized in the states of Washington and Colorado in 2012 and in California in 2016. Therefore, Washington and Colorado may have dealt with specific legal issues involving marijuana for four years before California. When California first encountered an issue involving marijuana, it could look to the decisions in Washington and Colorado for guidance. These decisions would not be binding precedent for California, but California could find them persuasive.

The U.S. Constitution and the Role of the U.S. Supreme Court

The U.S. Supreme Court is the highest court in the nation. When it makes a decision, that decision is binding on all lower courts throughout the United States. The supreme law of the United States is the U.S. Constitution. If a state passes a law or a judge issues a ruling that violates the U.S. Constitution, the U.S. Supreme Court has the authority to declare it unconstitutional.

Most cases reach the U.S. Supreme Court through a **writ of certiorari.** This order, issued by the Supreme Court, directs a lower court to send the case to the Supreme Court for review. A writ of certiorari is granted when at least four of the nine justices approve it. This is referred to as the "Rule of Four." If a *writ of certiorari* is denied, it simply means that four justices did not request a review of the case. The denial is not a ruling on the case's merits, it does not indicate agreement with the lower court's opinion, and it does not establish any precedent. The court is just not ordering a review. As a result, the lower court's decision remains binding on the case.

Types of Legal Opinions

The role of the Supreme Court is to answer legal questions. Instead of answering "What is a catch," it may answer "What is due process" or "What process is due?" Notice that the role of the Supreme Court is not to write the rules, but to answer questions about the rules. It is the legislature's job to write the rules.

For example, the legislature passed antitrust laws, but a question arose as to whether these laws applied to baseball. The Supreme Court ruled in *Federal Baseball Club of Baltimore, Inc. v. National League of Prof'l Baseball Clubs* (259 U.S. 200 (1922)), that baseball was not subject to antitrust laws. This became the precedent that the courts followed in subsequent cases. By the 1950s it seemed clear that the precedent was outdated. But in *Toolson v. New York Yankees, Inc.,* 346 U.S. 356 (1953) the court indicated that its role was to follow precedent and if the legislature desired a different outcome, it should pass a new law for the court to apply. This new legislation arrived with the Curt Flood Act of 1998.

Courts answer questions through what are called legal opinions. These opinions not only state a court's decision but also the reasoning behind the decision. There are various types of opinions:

1. **Unanimous Opinion:** Represents the view of all judges who heard the case.
2. **Majority Opinion:** Represents the views of the majority of judges deciding the case. It becomes binding precedent. For the U.S. Supreme Court, a majority opinion requires at least five of the nine justices.
3. **Concurring Opinion:** Written by judges who agree with the majority opinion but have different reasoning or want to emphasize specific points not covered in the majority opinion.
4. **Dissenting Opinion:** Written by judges who disagree with the majority opinion. I often read these opinions first because they tell me what a smart Supreme Court Justice and their smart staff identify as the key contested issue in the case. But it is important not to fall in love with the arguments of the dissent because, well, they lost. It may be influential for future cases,

but it is not part of the majority opinion and, therefore, not binding precedent.

5. **Plurality Opinion:** Supported by the largest number of judges, but not a majority. It reflects a divided court where no single opinion gained a majority.

6. **Per Curiam Opinion:** An unsigned, unanimous opinion of the court. It comes from the Latin meaning, "by the court."

For example, imagine a case where Jack burns Jill's house. The case reaches the U.S. Supreme Court after four justices grant a *writ of certiorari*. Five justices decide that Jill should receive $200,000. That would be the majority opinion. Three justices decide that Jill should not receive $200,000. That would be the dissenting opinion. One justice agrees that Jill should receive $200,000, but for different reasons than the majority. That would be a concurring opinion.

If only four justices agreed on the reason why Jill should get $200,000, three justices disagreed, and two justices had a different opinion, there would be no majority opinion because a majority requires five justices. In this scenario, the four justices would have the plurality opinion because it was supported by the largest number of justices. And, of course, if all justices agreed on an opinion, they could issue an anonymous per curiam opinion.

Case Precedents and Football

To illustrate case precedents, let's get back to football.

Imagine it's first and ten at the quarterback's own 20-yard line. The quarterback drops back to pass but gets sacked by the defense at the 10-yard line. For the second down, the new line of scrimmage would be where the sack occurred. That is, the 10-yard line. However, if the quarterback drops back and throws a pass to an eligible receiver who drops the ball, then there is no loss of yardage, and the line of scrimmage for the second down remains unchanged at the 20-yard line.

Considering this, what if a passer, facing imminent loss of yardage due to defensive pressure, throws a forward pass without a realistic chance of completion to avoid being sacked ten yards behind the line of scrimmage? Treating this as an incomplete pass seems unfair, especially if the quarterback is in his own end zone, where a sack would result in a safety, which would earn the defense two points and possession of the ball.

To address this, football fans know there's a penalty for "intentional grounding." This penalty occurs when a passer, under defensive pressure, throws a forward pass without a realistic chance of completion. The penalty options are:

1. Loss of down and 10 yards from the previous spot,
2. Loss of down at the spot of the foul, or
3. If the passer is in the end zone, it results in a safety.

The Supreme Court's role is like the NFL Rules Committee. Once the Supreme Court answers a legal question, their answer is now the new rule that governs future cases. Some Supreme Court observers sound like old football fans saying things like, "that used to be a sack" or "that used to be an incomplete pass." While historically interesting and maybe insightful for future decisions, the new rule is the binding precedent that all future cases must now follow unless or until it is overruled by a future court.

Even if we do not always agree with the rules, our legal system—and the NFL Rules Committee—gives us predictability and consistency. We saw this in action on a game-deciding play in a Week 16 matchup between the Patriots and Steelers in 2017. Was it a catch and a touchdown and a win for the Steelers, or an incomplete pass and a win for the Patriots? At the time, former New York Giants quarterback Eli Manning shrugged, "I know the rules.... You hate it. When you're watching it live, you don't even think about that not being a catch.... [But] those are the rules." Manning understood precedent. It was an incomplete pass, and the Patriots won. The disappointed Steelers coach Mike Tomlin also understood precedent, but he recognized the need for a higher court to address the workability of the rules. As a member of the NFL Competition Committee—the league's "high court"—Tomlin accepted the loss under the current rules but added, "We all can acknowledge that all of this needs to be revisited," and, "As a member of the committee, I acknowledge we got our work cut out for us this offseason." Tomlin understood both the obligation to follow precedent and the responsibility to review it. Football and the Common Law tradition remind us that although we may not always agree with the rules, our system allows us to enjoy the predictability of precedent while preserving the flexibility to ask a higher court if there is now a compelling reason to overturn an old rule.

www.ingramcontent.com/pod-product-compliance
Lightning Source LLC
Chambersburg PA
CBHW021555210326
41599CB00010B/449